"Dr. Maltz's discovery of Psycho-Cybernetics is an important and valuable contribution to man's knowledge of himself and to his ability to improve himself."

Lewis Gruber
Chairman of the Board
P. LORILLARD & CO.

THE AUTHOR

Dr. Maxwell Maltz, M.D., F.I.C.S., received his baccalaureate in science from Columbia University and his doctorate in medicine at its College of Physicians and Surgeons. One of the world's most widely known and highly regarded plastic surgeons, he has lectured before the University of Amsterdam, the University of Paris, and the University of Rome. He has been Professor of Plastic Surgery at the University of Nicaragua and the University of El Salvador. He is the author of eight previous books, including ADVENTURES IN STAYING YOUNG, the best seller DR. PYGMALION, and his latest book CREATIVE LIVING FOR TODAY which incorporates the Psycho-Cybernetics theory.

PSYCHO-CYBERNETICS
was originally published by Prentice-Hall, Inc.

PSYCHO-CYBERNETICS

by

Maxwell Maltz

M.D., F.I.C.S.

 A POCKET BOOK EDITION published by
Simon & Schuster of Canada, Ltd. • Richmond Hill, Ontario, Canada
Registered User of the Trademark

PSYCHO-CYBERNETICS

Prentice-Hall edition published October, 1960

A *Pocket Book* edition
1st printing..........March, 1969
3rd printing...........May, 1969

Standard Book Number: 671-77075-6.
Copyright, ©, 1960, by Prentice-Hall, Inc. All rights reserved.
This *Pocket Book* edition is published by arrangement with Prentice-Hall, Inc.
Printed in Canada

Preface:
The Secret of Using This Book
To Change Your Life

DISCOVERY of the "self-image" represents a break-through in psychology and the field of creative personality.

The significance of the self-image has been recognized for more than a decade. Yet there has been little written about it. Curiously enough, this is not because "self-image psychology" has not worked, but because it has worked so amazingly well. As one of my colleagues expressed it, "I am reluctant to publish my findings, especially for the lay public, because if I presented some of my case histories and described the rather amazing and spectacular improvements in personality, I would be accused of exaggerating, or trying to start a cult, or both."

I, too, felt the same sort of reluctance. Any book I might write on the subject would be sure to be regarded as somewhat unorthodox by some of my colleagues for several reasons. In the first place, it is somewhat unorthodox for a plastic surgeon to write a book on psychology. In the second place, it will probably be regarded in some quarters as even more unorthodox to go outside the tight little dogma—the "closed system" of the "science of psychology"—and seek answers concerning human behavior in the fields of physics, anatomy and the new science of Cybernetics.

My answer is that any good plastic surgeon *is* and *must* be a psychologist, whether he would have it so or not. When you change a man's face you almost invariably change his future. Change his physical image and nearly

always you change the man—his personality, his behavior
—and sometimes even his basic talents and abilities.

BEAUTY IS MORE THAN SKIN DEEP

A plastic surgeon does not simply alter a man's face. He
alters the man's inner self. The incisions he makes are
more than skin deep. They frequently cut deep into the
psyche as well. I decided a long time ago that this is an
awesome responsibility and that I owe it to my patients
and to myself to know something about what I am doing.
No responsible M.D. would attempt to perform extensive
plastic surgery without specialized knowledge and training. Just so, I feel that if changing a man's face is going
to change the inner man as well, I have a responsibility to
acquire specialized knowledge in that field, also.

FAILURES THAT LED TO SUCCESS

In a previous book, written some 20 years ago *(New
Faces—New Futures)* I published a more or less collec-
tion of case histories where plastic surgery, and particularly facial plastic surgery, had opened the door to a new
life for many people. That book told of the amazing
changes that often occur quite suddenly and dramatically
in a person's personality when you change his face. I was
elated at my successes in this respect. But, like Sir Humphry Davy, I learned more from my failures than from
my successes.

Some patients showed *no* change in personality after
surgery. In *most cases* a person who had a conspicuously
ugly face, or some "freakish" feature corrected by surgery, experienced an almost immediate (usually within 21
days) rise in self-esteem, self-confidence. But in *some
cases,* the patient continued to feel inadequate and experienced feelings of inferiority. In short, these "failures" continued to feel, act and behave *just as if* they still had an
ugly face.

This indicated to me that reconstruction of the physical image itself was not "the" real key to changes in personality. There was something else which was *usually* influenced by facial surgery, but sometimes not. When this "something else" was reconstructed, the person himself changed. When this "something else" was not reconstructed the person himself remained the same, although his physical features might be radically different.

THE FACE OF PERSONALITY

It was as if personality itself had a "face." This nonphysical "face of personality" seemed to be the real key to personality change. If it remained scarred, distorted, "ugly," or inferior, the person himself acted out this role in his behavior regardless of the changes in physical appearance. If this "face of personality" could be reconstructed, if old emotional scars could be removed; then the person himself changed, even without facial plastic surgery. Once I began to explore this area, I found more and more phenomena which confirmed the fact that the "self-image," the individual's mental and spiritual concept or "picture" of himself, was the real key to personality and behavior. More about this in the first chapter.

TRUTH IS WHERE YOU FIND IT

I have always believed in going wherever it may be necessary to find truth, even if international boundaries must be crossed. When I decided to become a plastic surgeon years ago, German doctors were far ahead of the rest of the world in this field. So I went to Germany.

In my search for the "self-image" I also had to cross boundaries, although invisible ones. Although the science of psychology acknowledged the self-image and its key role in human behavior, psychology's answer to the questions of how the self-image exerts its influence, how it *creates* a new personality, what happens inside the human nervous system when the self-image is changed, was "somehow."

I found most of my answers in the new science of Cybernetics, which restored teleology as a respectable concept in science. It is rather strange that the new science of Cybernetics grew out of the work of physicists and mathematicians rather than that of psychologists, especially when it is understood that Cybernetics has to do with teleology—goal-striving, goal-oriented behavior of mechanical systems. Cybernetics explains "what happens" and "what is necessary" in the purposeful behavior of machines. Psychology, with all its vaunted knowledge of the human psyche, had no satisfactory answer for such a simple goal-oriented, purposeful situation as, for example, how it is possible for a human being to pick up a cigarette from a coffee table and place it in his mouth. But the physicist had an answer. The proponents of many psychological theories were somewhat comparable men who speculated as to what was in outer space and on other planets, but could not tell what was in their own backyards.

The new science of Cybernetics made possible an important breakthrough in psychology. I myself take no credit for the breakthrough, other than the recognition of it.

The fact that this breakthrough came from the work of physicists and mathematicians should not surprise us. Any breakthrough in science is likely to come from outside the system. "Experts" are the most thoroughly familiar with the developed knowledge inside the prescribed boundaries of a given science. Any *new* knowledge must usually come from the outside—not from "experts," but from what someone has defined as an "inpert."

Pasteur was not an M.D. The Wright brothers were not aeronautical engineers but bicycle mechanics. Einstein, properly speaking, was not a physicist but a mathematician. Yet his findings in mathematics completely turned upside down all the pet theories in physics. Madame Curie was not an M.D. but a physicist, yet she made important contributions to medical science.

How You Can Use This New Knowledge

In this book I have attempted not only to inform you of this new knowledge from the field of Cybernetics but also to demonstrate how you can use it in your own life to achieve goals that are important to you.

GENERAL PRINCIPLES

The "self-image" is the key to human personality and human behavior. Change the self-image and you change the personality and the behavior.

But more than this. The "self-image" sets the boundaries of individual accomplishment. It defines what you can and cannot do. Expand the self-image and you expand the "area of the possible." The development of an adequate, realistic self-image will seem to imbue the individual with new capabilities, new talents and literally turn failure into success.

Self-image psychology has not only been proved on its own merits, but it explains many phenomena which have long been known but not properly understood in the past. For example, there is today irrefutable clinical evidence in the fields of individual psychology, psychosomatic medicine and industrial psychology that there are "success-type personalities" and "failure-type personalities," "happiness-prone personalities" and "unhappiness-prone personalities," and "health-prone personalities" and "disease-prone personalities." Self-image psychology throws new light on these and many other observable facts of life. It throws new light on "the power of positive thinking," and more importantly, explains why it "works" with some individuals and not with others. ("Positive thinking" does indeed "work" when it is consistent with the individual's self-image. It literally *cannot* "work" when it is

inconsistent with the self-image—until the self-image itself has been changed.)

In order to understand self-image psychology, and use
it in your own life, you need to know something of the
mechanism it employs to accomplish its goal. There is an
abundance of scientific evidence which shows that the
human brain and nervous system operate purposefully in
accordance with the known principles of Cybernetics to
accomplish goals of the individual. Insofar as function is
concerned, the brain and nervous system constitute a marvelous and complex "goal-striving mechanism," a sort of
built-in automatic guidance system which works *for* you
as a "success mechanism," or *against* you as a "failure
mechanism," depending on how "YOU," the operator,
operate it and the goals you set for it.

It is also rather ironic that Cybernetics, which began as
a study of machines and mechanical principles, goes far
to restore the dignity of man as a unique, creative being.
Psychology, which began with the study of man's psyche,
or soul, almost ended by depriving man of his soul. The
behaviorist, who understood neither the "man" nor his
machine, and thereby confused the one with the other,
told us that thought is merely the movement of electrons
and consciousness merely a chemical action. "Will" and
"purpose" were myths. Cybernetics, which began with the
study of physical machines, makes no such mistake. The
science of Cybernetics does not tell us that "man" is a
machine but that man *has* and *uses* a machine. Moreover,
it tells us how that machine functions and how it can be
used.

EXPERIENCING IS THE SECRET

The self-image is changed, for better or worse, not by
intellect alone, nor by intellectual knowledge alone, but
by "experiencing." Wittingly or unwittingly you developed your self-image by your creative experiencing in the
past. You can change it by the same method.

It is not the child who is taught *about* love but the child who has experienced love that grows into a healthy, happy, well-adjusted adult. Our present state of self-confidence and poise is the result of what we have "experienced" rather than what we have learned intellectually.

Self-image psychology also bridges the gap and resolves apparent conflicts between the various therapeutic methods used today. It furnishes a common denominator for direct and indirect counselling, clinical psychology, psychoanalysis, and even auto-suggestion. All in one way or another use creative experiencing to build a better self-image. Regardless of theories, this is what *really happens,* for example, in the "therapeutic situation" employed by the psychoanalytical school: The analyst never criticizes, disapproves, or moralizes, is never shocked, as the patient pours out his fears, his shames, his guilt-feelings and his "bad thoughts." For perhaps the first time in his life the patient *experiences* acceptance as a human being; he "feels" that his self has some worth and dignity, and he comes to accept himself, and to conceive of his "self" in new terms.

SCIENCE DISCOVERS "SYNTHETIC" EXPERIENCE

Another discovery, this time in the field of experimental and clinical psychology, enables us to use "experiencing" as a direct and controlled method of changing the self-image. Actual, real-life experience can be a hard and ruthless teacher. Throw a man in water over his head and the experience may teach him to swim. The same experience may cause another man to drown. The Army "makes a man" out of many young boys. But there is no doubting that Army experience also makes many psycho-neurotics. For centuries it has been recognized that "Nothing succeeds like success." We learn to function successfully by experiencing success. Memories of past successes act as built-in "stored information" which gives us self-confidence for the present task. But how can a person draw upon memories of past successful experiences when he has experienced only failure? His plight is somewhat comparable to the young man who cannot secure a job because he has no experience, and cannot acquire experience because he cannot get a job.

This dilemma was solved by another important discovery which, for all practical purposes, allows us to synthesize "experience," to literally create experience, and control it, in the laboratory of our minds Experimental and clinical psychologists have proved beyond a shadow of a doubt that the human nervous system cannot tell the difference between an "actual" experience and an experience *imagined vividly and in detail*. Although this may appear to be a rather extravagant statement in this book we will examine some controlled laboratory experiments where this type of "synthetic" experience has been used in very practical ways to improve skill in dart throwing and shooting basketball goals. We will see it at work in the lives of individuals who have used it to improve their skill in public speaking, overcome fear of the dentist, develop social poise, develop self-confidence, sell more goods, become more proficient in chess—and in practically every other conceivable type of situation where "experience" is recognized to bring success. We will take a look at an amazing experiment in which two prominent doctors arranged things so that neurotics could experience "normally," and thereby cured them!

Perhaps most important of all, we will learn how chronically unhappy people have learned to enjoy life by "experiencing" happiness!

THE SECRET OF USING THIS BOOK TO CHANGE YOUR LIFE

This book has been designed not merely to be read but to be *experienced*.

You can acquire information from reading a book. But

to "experience" you must creatively respond to information. Acquiring information itself is passive. Experiencing is active. When you "experience," something happens inside your nervous system and your midbrain. New "engrams" and "neural" patterns are recorded in the gray matter of your brain.

This book has been designed to force you literally to "experience." Tailor-made, prefabricated "case histories" have been kept intentionally to a minimum. Instead, you are asked to furnish your own "case histories" by exercising imagination and memory.

I have not supplied "summaries" at the end of each chapter. Instead, you are asked to jot down the most important points which appeal to you as key points which should be remembered. You will digest the information in this book better if you do your own analysis and summation of the chapters.

Finally, you will find throughout the book certain things to do and certain practice exercises which you are asked to perform. These exercises are simple and easy to perform, but they must be done regularly if you are to derive maximum benefit from them.

RESERVE JUDGMENT FOR 21 DAYS

Do not allow yourself to become discouraged if nothing seems to happen when you set about practicing the various techniques outlined in this book for changing your self-image. Instead reserve judgment—and go on practicing—for a minimum period of 21 days.

It usually requires a minimum of about 21 days to effect any perceptible change in a mental image. Following plastic surgery it takes about 21 days for the average patient to get used to his new face. When an arm or leg is amputated the "phantom limb" persists for about 21 days. People must live in a new house for about three weeks before it begins to "seem like home." These, and may other commonly observed phenomena tend to show that it requires a minimum of about 21 days for an old mental image to dissolve and a new one to jell.

Therefore you will derive more benefit from this book if you will secure your own consent to reserve critical judgment for at least three weeks. During this time do not be continually looking over your shoulder, so to speak, or trying to measure your progress. During these 21 days do not argue intellectually with the ideas presented, do not debate with yourself as to whether they will work or not. Perform the exercises, even if they seem impractical to you. Persist in playing your new role, in thinking of yourself in new terms, even if you seem to yourself to be somewhat hypocritical in doing so, and even if the new self-image feels a little uncomfortable or "unnatural."

You can neither prove nor disprove with intellectual argument the ideas and concepts described in this book, or simply by talking about them. You *can* prove them to yourself by *doing* them and judging results for yourself. I am only asking that you reserve critical judgment and analytical argument for 21 days so that you will give yourself a fair chance to prove or disprove their validity in your own life.

The building of an adequate self image is something that should continue throughout a lifetime. Admittedly you cannot accomplish a lifetime of growth in three weeks' time. But, you can experience improvement within three weeks' time—and sometimes the improvement is quite dramatic.

WHAT IS SUCCESS?

Since I use the words "success" and "successful" throughout this book, I think it is important at the outset that I define those terms.

As I use it, "success" has nothing to do with prestige symbols, but with creative accomplishment. Rightly speaking no man should attempt to be "a success," but every man can and should attempt to be "successful."

Trying to be "a success" in terms of acquiring prestige symbols and wearing certain badges leads to neuroticism, and frustration and unhappiness. Striving to be "successful" brings not only material success, but satisfaction, fulfillment and happiness.

Noah Webster defined success as "the satisfactory accomplishment of a goal sought for." Creative striving for a goal that is important to *you* as a result of your own deep-felt needs, aspirations and talents (and not the symbols which the "Joneses" expect you to display) brings happiness as well as success because you will be functioning as you were meant to function. Man is by nature a goal-striving being. And because man is "built that way" he is not happy unless he is functioning as he was made to function—as a goal-striver. Thus true success and true happiness not only go together but each enhances the other.

Table of Contents

PSYCHO-CYBERNETICS

CHAPTER ONE

The Self Image:
Your Key to a Better Life

DURING the past decade a revolution has been quietly going on in the fields of psychology, psychiatry, and medicine.

New theories and concepts concerning the "self" have grown out of the work and findings of clinical psychologists, practicing psychiatrists and cosmetic or so-called "plastic surgeons." New methods growing out of these findings have resulted in rather dramatic changes in personality, health, and apparently even in basic abilities and talents. Chronic failures have become successful. "F" students have changed into "straight A" pupils within a matter of days and with no extra tutoring. Shy, retiring, inhibited personalities have become happy and outgoing.

Writing in the January, 1959 issue of *Cosmopolitan* magazine, T. F. James summarizes the results obtained by various psychologists and M.D.'s as follows:

"Understanding the psychology of the self can mean the difference between success and failure, love and hate, bitterness and happiness. The discovery of the real self can rescue a crumbling marriage, recreate a faltering career, transform victims of 'personality failure.' On another plane, discovering your real self means the difference between freedom and the compulsions of conformity."

1

Your Key to a Better Life

The most important psychologic discovery of this century is the discovery of the "self-image." Whether we realize it or not, each of us carries about with us a mental blueprint or picture of ourselves. It may be vague and ill-defined to our conscious gaze. In fact, it may not be consciously recognizable at all. But it is there, complete down to the last detail. This self-image is our own conception of the "sort of person I am." It has been built up from our own *beliefs* about ourselves. But most of these beliefs about ourselves have unconsciously been formed from our past experiences, our successes and failures, our humiliations, our triumphs, and the way other people have reacted to us, especially in early childhood. From all these we mentally construct a "self" (or a picture of a self). Once an idea or belief about ourselves goes into this picture it becomes "true," as far as we personally are concerned. We do not question its validity, but proceed to act upon it *just as if it were true*.

This self-image becomes a golden key to living a better life because of two important discoveries:

(1) All your actions, feelings, behavior—even your abilities—are always consistent with this self-image.

In short, you will "act like" the sort of person you conceive yourself to be. Not only this, but you literally cannot act otherwise, in spite of all your conscious efforts or will power. The man who conceives himself to be a "failure-type person" will find some way to fail, in spite of all his good intentions, or his will power, even if opportunity is literally dumped in his lap. The person who conceives himself to be a victim of injustice, one "who was meant to suffer," will invariably find circumstances to verify his opinions.

The self-image is a "premise," a base, or a foundation upon which your entire personality, your behavior, and even your circumstances are built. Because of this our experiences seem to verify, and thereby strengthen our self images, and a vicious or a beneficent cycle, as the case may be, is set up.

For example, a schoolboy who sees himself as an "F" type student, or one who is "dumb in mathematics," will invariably find that his report card bears him out. He then has "proof." A young girl who has an image of herself as the sort of person nobody likes will find indeed that she is avoided at the school dance. She literally invites rejection. Her woe-begone expression, her hang-dog manner, her over-anxiousness to please, or perhaps her unconscious hostility towards those she anticipates will affront her—all act to drive away those whom she would attract. In the same manner, a salesman or a businessman will also find that his actual experiences tend to "prove" his self-image is correct.

Because of this objective "proof" it very seldom occurs to a person that his trouble lies in his self-image or his own evaluation of himself. Tell the schoolboy that he only "thinks" he cannot master algebra, and he will doubt your sanity. He has tried and tried, and still his report card tells the story. Tell the salesman that it is only an idea that he cannot earn more than a certain figure, and he can prove you wrong by his order book. He knows only too well how hard he has tried and failed. Yet, as we shall see later, almost miraculous changes have occurred both in grades of students, and in the earning capacity of salesmen—when they were prevailed upon to change their self-images.

(2) The self-image can be changed. Numerous case histories have shown that one is never too young nor too old to change his self-image and thereby start to live a new life.

One of the reasons it has seemed so difficult for a person to change his habits, his personality, or his way of life, has been that heretofore nearly all efforts at change have been directed to the circumference of the self, so to speak, rather than to the center. Numerous patients have said to me something like the following:"If you are talking about 'positive thinking,' I've tried that before, and it just doesn't work for me." However, a little questioning invariably brings out that these individuals have employed "positive thinking," or attempted to employ it, either upon particular external circumstances, or upon some particular habit or character defect ("I will get that job." "I will be more calm and relaxed in the future." "This business venture will turn out right for me," etc.) But they had never thought to change their thinking of the "self" which was to accomplish these things.

Jesus warned us about the folly of putting a patch of new material upon an old garment, or of putting new wine into old bottles. "Positive thinking" cannot be used effectively as a patch or a crutch to the same self image. In fact, it is literally impossible to really think about a particular situation, as long as you hold a negative concept of self. And, numerous experiments have shown that once the concept of self is changed, other things *consistent with* the new concept of self, are accomplished easily and without strain.

One of the earliest and most convincing experiments along this line was conducted by the late Prescott Lecky, one of the pioneers in self-image psychology. Lecky conceived of the personality as a "system of ideas," all of which *must seem* to be consistent with each other. Ideas which are inconsistent with the system are rejected, "not believed," and not acted upon. Ideas which *seem* to be consistent with the system are accepted. At the very center of this system of ideas—the keystone—the base upon which all else is built, is the individual's "ego ideal," his "self-image," or his conception of himself. Lecky was a school teacher and had an opportunity to test his theory upon thousands of students.

Lecky theorized that if a student had trouble learning a certain subject, it could be because (from the student's point of view) it would be inconsistent for him to learn it. Lecky believed, however, that if you could change the student's self-conception, which underlies this viewpoint, his attitude toward the subject would change accordingly. If the student could be induced to change his self-definition, his learning ability should also change. This proved to be the case. One student who misspelled 55 words out of a hundred and flunked so many subjects that he lost credit for a year, made a general average of 91 the next year and became one of the best spellers in school. A boy who was dropped from one college because of poor grades, entered Columbia and became a straight "A" student. A girl who had flunked Latin four times, after three talks with the school counselor, finished with a grade of 84. A boy who was told by a testing bureau that he had no aptitude for English, won honorable mention the next year for a literary prize.

The trouble with these students was not that they were dumb, or lacking in basic aptitudes. The trouble was an inadequate self-image ("I don't have a mathematical mind"; "I'm just naturally a poor speller"). They "identified" with their mistakes and failures. Instead of saying "I failed that test" (factual and descriptive) they concluded "I am a failure." Instead of saying "I flunked that subject" they said "I am a flunk-out." For those who are interested in learning more of Lecky's work, I recommend securing a copy of his book: *Self Consistency, a Theory of Personality,* The Island Press, New York, N.Y.

Lecky also used the same method to cure students of such habits as nail biting and stuttering.

My own files contain case histories just as convincing: the man who was so afraid of strangers that he seldom ventured out of the house, and who now makes his living as a public speaker. The salesman who had already prepared a letter of resignation because he "just wasn't cut out for selling," and six months later was number one man on a force of 100 salesmen. The minister who was considering retirement because "nerves" and the pressure of preparing a sermon a week were getting him down, and now delivers an average of three "outside talks" a week in addition to his weekly sermons and doesn't know he has a nerve in his body.

How a Plastic Surgeon Became Interested in Self-Image Psychology

Offhand, there would seem to be little or no connection between surgery and psychology. Yet, it was the work of the plastic surgeon which first hinted at the existence of the "self image" and raised certain questions which led to important psychologic knowledge.

When I first began the practice of plastic surgery many years ago, I was amazed by the dramatic and sudden changes in character and personality which often resulted when a facial defect was corrected. Changing the physical image in many instances appeared to create *an entirely new person*. In case after case the scalpel that I held in my hand became a magic wand that not only transformed the patient's appearance, but transformed his whole life. The shy and retiring became bold and courageous. A "moronic," "stupid" boy changed into an alert, bright youngster who went on to become an executive with a prominent firm. A salesman who had lost his touch and his faith in himself became a model of self confidence. And perhaps the most startling of all was the habitual "hardened" criminal who changed almost overnight from an incorrigible who had never showed any desire to change, into a model prisoner who won a parole and went on to assume a responsible role in society.

Some twenty years ago I reported many such case histories in my book *New Faces—New Futures*. Following its publication, and similar articles in leading magazines, I was besieged with questions by criminologists, sociologists and psychiatrists.

They asked questions that I could not answer. But they did start me upon a search. Strangely enough, I learned as much if not more from my failures as from my successes.

It was easy to explain the successes. The boy with the too-big ears, who had been told that he looked like a taxi-cab with both doors open. He had been ridiculed all his life—often cruelly. Association with playmates meant humiliation and pain. Why shouldn't he avoid social contacts? Why shouldn't he become afraid of people and retire into himself? Terribly afraid to express himself in any way it was no wonder he became known as a moron. When his ears were corrected, it would seem only natural that the cause of his embarrassment and humiliation had been removed and that he should assume a normal role in life—which he did.

Or consider the salesman who suffered a facial disfigurement as the result of an automobile accident. Each morning when he shaved he could see the horrible disfiguring scar on his cheek and the grotesque twist to his mouth. For the first time in his life he became painfully self-conscious. He was ashamed of himself and felt that his appearance must be repulsive to others. The scar became an obsession with him. He was "different" from other people. He began to "wonder" what others were thinking of him. Soon his ego was even more mutilated than his face. He began to lose confidence in himself. He became bitter and hostile. Soon almost all his attention was directed toward himself—and his primary goal became the protection of his ego and the avoidance of situations which might bring humiliation. It is easy to understand how the correction of his facial disfigurement and the restoration of a "normal" face would overnight change this man's entire attitude and outlook, his feelings about himself, and result in greater success in his work.

But what about the exceptions who didn't change? The Duchess who all her life had been terribly shy and self-conscious because of a tremendous hump in her nose? Although surgery gave her a classic nose and a face that was truly beautiful, she still continued to act the part of the ugly duckling, the unwanted sister who could never bring herself to look another human being in the eye. If the scalpel itself was magic, why did it not work on the Duchess?

Or what about all the others who acquired new faces but went right on wearing the same old personality? Or how explain the reaction of those people who insist that the surgery has made *no difference whatsoever* in their appearance? Every plastic surgeon has had this experience and has probably been as baffled by it as I was. No matter how drastic the change in appearance may be, there are certain patients who will insist that "I look just the same as before—you didn't do a thing." Friends, even family, may scarcely recognize them, may become enthusiastic over their newly acquired "beauty," yet the patient herself insists that she can see only slight or no improvement, or in fact deny that any change at all has been made. Comparison of "before" and "after" photographs does little good, except possibly to arouse hostility. By some strange mental alchemy the patient will rationalize, "Of course, I can see that the hump is no longer in my nose —but my nose still *looks* just the same," or, "The scar may not show any more, but it's *still there.*"

Scars That Bring Pride Instead of Shame

Still another clue in search of the elusive self image was the fact that not all scars or disfigurements bring shame and humiliation. When I was a young medical student in Germany, I saw many another student proudly wearing his "saber scar" much as an American might wear the Medal of Honor. The duelists were the elite of college society and a facial scar was the badge that proved you a member in good standing. To these boys, the *acquisition* of a horrible scar on the cheek had the same psychologic effect as the eradication of the scar from the cheek of my salesman patient. In old New Orleans a Creole wore an eye patch in much the same way. I began to see that a knife itself held no magical powers. It could be used on one person to inflict a scar and on another to erase a scar, with the same psychological results.

The Mystery of Imaginary Ugliness

To a person handicapped by a genuine congenital defect, or suffering from an actual facial disfigurement as a result of an accident, plastic surgery can indeed seemingly perform magic. From such cases it would be easy to theorize that the cure-all for all neuroses, unhappiness, failure, fear, anxiety and lack of self-confidence would be wholesale plastic surgery to remove all bodily defects. However, according to this theory, persons with normal or acceptable faces should be singularly free from all psychological handicaps. They should be cheerful, happy, self-confident, free from anxiety and worry. We know only too well this is not true.

Nor can such a theory explain the people who visit the office of a plastic surgeon and demand a "face lift" to cure a purely imaginary ugliness. There are the 35- or 45-year-old women who are convinced that they look "old" even though their appearance is perfectly "normal" and in many cases unusually attractive.

There are the young girls who are convinced that they are "ugly" merely because their mouth, nose or bust measurement does not exactly match that of the currently reigning movie queen. There are men who *believe* that their ears are too big or their noses too long. No ethical plastic surgeon would even consider operating upon these people, but unfortunately the quacks, or so-called "beauty doctors" whom no medical association will admit to membership, have no such qualms.

Such "imaginary ugliness" is not at all uncommon. A recent survey of college co-eds showed that 90 per cent were dissatisfied in some way with their appearance. If the words "normal" or "average" mean anything at all, it is obvious that 90 per cent of our population cannot be "abnormal" or "different" or "defective" in appearance.

Yet, similar surveys have shown that approximately the same percentage of our general population find some reason to be ashamed of their body-image.

These people react *just as if* they suffered an actual disfigurement. They feel the same shame. They develop the same fears and anxieties. Their capacity to really "live" fully is blocked and choked by the same sort of psychologic roadblocks. Their "scars," though mental and emotional rather than physical, are just as debilitating.

The Self-Image—the Real Secret

Discovery of the self-image explains all the apparent discrepancies we have been discussing. It is the common denominator—the *determining factor* in all our case histories, the failures as well as the successes.

The secret is this: To really "live," that is to find life reasonably satisfying, you must have an adequate and realistic self image that you can live with. You must find your self acceptable to "you." You must have a wholesome self-esteem. You must have a self that you can trust and believe in. You must have a self that you are not ashamed to "be," and one that you can feel free to express creatively, rather than to hide or cover up. You must have a self that corresponds to reality so that you can function effectively in a real world. You must know yourself—both your strengths and your weaknesses and be honest with yourself concerning both. Your self-image must be a reasonable approximation of "you," being neither more than you are, nor less than you are.

When this self-image is intact and secure, you feel "good." When it is threatened, you feel anxious and insecure. When it is adequate and one that you can be wholesomely proud of, you feel self-confident. You feel free to "be yourself" and to express yourself. You function at your optimum. When it is an object of shame, you attempt to hide it rather than express it. Creative expression is blocked. You become hostile and hard to get along with.

If a scar on the face enhances the self-image (as in the case of the German duelist), self-esteem and self-confidence are increased. If a scar on the face detracts from the self-image (as in the case of the salesman), loss of self-esteem and self-confidence results.

When a facial disfigurement is corrected by plastic surgery, dramatic psychologic changes result *only* if there is a corresponding correction of the mutilated self-image. Sometimes the image of a disfigured self persists even after successful surgery, much the same as the "phantom limb" may continue to feel pain years after the physical arm or leg has been amputated.

I Begin a New Career

These observations led me into a new career. Some 15 years ago I became convinced that the people who consult a plastic surgeon need more than surgery and that some of them do not need surgery at all. If I were to treat these people as patients, as a whole person rather than as merely a nose, ear, mouth, arm or leg, I needed to be in a position to give them something more. I needed to be able to show them how to obtain a spiritual face lift, how to remove emotional scars, how to change their attitudes and thoughts as well as their physical appearance.

This study has been most rewarding. Today, I am more convinced than ever that what each of us really wants, deep down, is more LIFE. Happiness, success, peace of mind, or whatever your own conception of supreme good may be, is experienced in its essence as more life. When we experience expansive emotions of happiness, self-confidence, and success, we enjoy more life. And to the degree that we inhibit our abilities, frustrate our God-given talents, and allow ourselves to suffer anxiety, fear, self-condemnation and self-hate, we literally choke off the life force available to us and turn our back upon the gift which our Creator has made. To the degree that we deny the gift of life, we embrace death.

YOUR PROGRAM FOR BETTER LIVING

In my opinion, psychology during the past 30 years has become far too pessimistic regarding man and his potentiality for both change and greatness. Since psychologists and psychiatrists deal with so-called "abnormal" people, the literature is almost exclusively taken up with man's various abnormalities, his tendencies toward self-destruction. Many people, I am afraid, have read so much of this type of thing that they have come to regard such things as hatred, the "destructive instinct," guilt, self-condemnation, and all the other negatives as "normal human behavior." The average person feels awfully weak and impotent when he thinks of the prospect of pitting his puny will against these negative forces in human nature, in order to gain health and happiness. If this were a true picture of human nature and the human condition, "self-improvement" would indeed be a rather futile thing.

However, I believe, and the experiences of my many patients have confirmed the fact, that you do not have to do the job alone. There is within each one of us a "life instinct," which is forever working toward health, happiness, and all that makes for more life for the individual. This "life instinct" works *for you* through what I call the Creative Mechanism, or when used correctly the "Success Mechanism" built into each human being.

New Scientific Insights into "Subconscious Mind"

The new science of "Cybernetics" has furnished us with convincing proof that the so-called "subconscious mind" is not a "mind" at all, but a mechanism—a goal-striving "servo-mechanism" consisting of the brain and nervous system, which is *used by,* and *directed by* mind. The latest, and most usable concept is that man does not have two "minds," but a mind, or consciousness, which "operates" an automatic, goal-striving machine. This automatic, goal-striving machine functions very similarly to the way that electronic servo-mechanisms function, as far as basic principles are concerned, but it is much more marvelous, much more complex, than any electronic brain or guided missile ever conceived by man.

This Creative Mechanism within you is impersonal. It will work automatically and impersonally to achieve goals of success and happiness, or unhappiness and failure, depending upon the goals which you yourself set for it. Present it with "success goals" and it functions as a "Success Mechanism." Present it with negative goals, and it operates just as impersonally, and just as faithfully as a "Failure Mechanism."

Like any other servo-mechanism, it must have a clear-cut goal, objective, or "problem" to work upon.

The goals that our own Creative Mechanism seeks to achieve are MENTAL IMAGES, or mental pictures, which we create by the use of IMAGINATION.

The key goal-image is our Self-Image.

Our Self-Image prescribes the limits for the accomplishment of any particular goals. It prescribes the "area of the possible."

Like any other servo-mechanism, our Creative Mechanism works upon information and data which we feed into it (our thoughts, beliefs, interpretations). Through our attitudes and interpretations of situations, we "describe" the problem to be worked upon.

If we feed information and data into our Creative Mechanism to the effect that we ourselves are unworthy, inferior, undeserving, incapable (a negative self-image) this data is processed and acted upon as any other data in giving us the "answer" in the form of objective experience.

Like any other servo-mechanism, our Creative Mechanism makes use of stored information, or "memory," in solving current problems and responding to current situations.

Your program for getting more living out of life consists in first of all, learning something about this Creative Mechanism, or automatic guidance system within you and how to use it as a Success Mechanism, rather than as a Failure Mechanism.

The method itself consists in learning, *practicing,* and *experiencing,* new habits of thinking, imagining, remembering, and *acting* in order to (1) develop an adequate and realistic Self-Image, and (2) use your Creative Mechanism to bring success and happiness in achieving particular goals.

If you can remember, worry, or tie your shoe, you can succeed.

As you will see later, the method to be used consists of creative mental picturing, creatively experiencing through your imagination, and the formation of new automatic reaction patterns by "acting out" and "acting as if."

I often tell my patients that "If you can remember, worry, or tie your shoe, you will have no trouble applying this method." The things you are called upon to do are simple, but you must practice and "experience." Visualizing, creative mental picturing, is no more difficult than what you do when you remember some scene out of the past, or worry about the future. Acting out new action patterns is no more difficult than "deciding," then following through on tying your shoes in a new and different manner each morning, instead of continuing to tie them in your old "habitual way," without thought or decision.

CHAPTER TWO

Discovering the Success Mechanism Within You

IT may seem strange, but it is nevertheless true that up until ten years ago scientists had no idea of just how the human brain and nervous system worked "purposely" or to achieve a goal. They knew *what* happened from having made long and meticulous observations. But no single theory of underlying principles tied all these phenomena together into a concept that made sense. R. W. Gerard, writing in *Scientific Monthly* in June, 1946, on the brain and imagination, stated that it was sad but true that most of our understanding of the mind would remain as valid and useful if, for all we knew, the cranium were stuffed with cotton wadding.

However, when man himself set out to build an "electronic brain," and to construct goal-striving mechanisms of his own, he *had* to discover and utilize certain basic principles. Having discovered them, these scientists began to ask themselves: Could this be the way that the human brain works also? Could it be that in making man, our Creator provided us with a servo-mechanism more marvelous and wonderful than any electronic brain or guidance system ever dreamed of by man, *but operating according to the same basic principles?* In the opinion of famous Cybernetic scientists like Dr. Norbert Wiener, Dr. John von Newmann, and others, the answer was an unqualified "yes."

Your Built-in Guidance System

Every living thing has a built-in guidance system or goal-striving device, put there by its Creator to help it achieve its goal—which is, in broad terms—to "live." In the simpler forms of life the goal "to live" simply means physical survival for both the individual and the species. The built-in mechanism in animals is limited to finding food and shelter, avoiding or overcoming enemies and hazards, and procreation to insure the survival of the species.

In man, the goal "to live" means more than mere survival. For an animal to "live" simply means that certain physical needs must be met. Man has certain emotional and spiritual needs which animals do not have. Consequently for man to "live" encompasses more than physical survival and procreation of the species. It requires certain emotional and spiritual satisfactions as well. Man's built-in "Success Mechanism" also is much broader in scope than an animal's. In addition to helping man avoid or overcome danger, and the "sexual instinct" which helps keep the race alive, the Success Mechanism in man can help him get answers to problems, invent, write poetry, run a business, sell merchandise, explore new horizons in science, attain more peace of mind, develop a better personality, or achieve success in any other activity which is intimately tied in to his "living" or makes for a fuller life.

The Success "Instinct"

A squirrel does not have to be taught how to gather nuts. Nor does it need to learn that it should store them for winter. A squirrel born in the spring has never experienced winter. Yet in the fall of the year it can be observed busily storing nuts to be eaten during the winter months when there will be no food to be gathered. A bird does not need to take lessons in nest-building. Nor does it need to take courses in navigation. Yet birds do navigate thousands of miles, sometimes over open sea. They have no newspapers or TV to give them weather reports, no books written by explorer or pioneer birds to map out for them the warm areas of the earth. Nonetheless the bird "knows" when cold weather is imminent and the exact location of a warm climate even though it may be thousands of miles away.

In attempting to explain such things we usually say that animals have certain "instincts" which guide them. Analyze all such instincts and you will find they assist the animal to successfully cope with its environment. In short, animals have a "success instinct."

We often overlook the fact that man too has a success instinct, much more marvelous and much more complex than that of any animal. Our Creator did not short-change man. On the other hand, man was exceptionally blessed in this regard.

Animals cannot select their goals. Their goals (self-preservation and procreation) are pre-set, so to speak. And their success mechanism is limited to these built-in goal-images, which we call "instincts."

Man, on the other hand, has something animals haven't —Creative Imagination. Thus man of all creatures is more than a creature, he is also a creator. With his imagination he can formulate a variety of goals. Man alone can direct his Success Mechanism by the use of imagination, or imaging ability.

We often think of "Creative Imagination" as applying only to poets, inventors, and the like. But imagination *is* creative in everything we do. Although they did not understand why, or how imagination sets our creative mechanism into action, serious thinkers of all ages, as well as hard-headed "practical" men, have recognized the fact and made use of it. "Imagination rules the world," said Napoleon. "Imagination of all man's faculties is the most

God-like," said Glenn Clark. "The faculty of imagination is the great spring of human activity, and the principal source of human improvement . . . Destroy this faculty, and the condition of man will become as stationary as that of the brutes," said Dugold Stewart, the famous Scottish philosopher. "You can imagine your future," says Henry J. Kaiser, who attributes much of his success in business to the constructive, positive use of creative imagination.

HOW YOUR SUCCESS MECHANISM WORKS

"You" are not a machine.

But new discoveries in the science of Cybernetics all point to the conclusion that your physical brain and nervous system make up a servo-mechanism which "You" use, and which operates very much like an electronic computer, and a mechanical goal-seeking device. Your brain and nervous system constitute a goal-striving mechanism which operates automatically to achieve a certain goal, very much as a self-aiming torpedo or missile seeks out its target and steers its way to it. Your built-in servo-mechanism functions both as a "guidance system" to automatically steer you in the right direction to achieve certain goals, or make correct responses to environment, and also as an "electronic brain" which can function automatically to solve problems, give you needed answers, and provide new ideas or "inspirations." In his book *The Computer and the Brain,* Dr. John von Newmann says that the human brain possesses the attributes of both the analogue and the digital computer.

The word "Cybernetics" comes from a Greek word which means literally, "the steersman."

Servo-mechanisms are so constructed that they automatically "steer" their way to a goal, target, or "answer."

"PSYCHO-CYBERNETICS"—A NEW CONCEPT OF HOW YOUR BRAIN WORKS

When we conceive of the human brain and nervous system as a form of servo-mechanism, operating in accordance with Cybernetic principles, we gain a new insight into the why and wherefore of human behavior.

I choose to call this new concept "Psycho-Cybernetics": the principles of Cybernetics as applied to the human brain.

I must repeat. Psycho-Cybernetics does not say that man *is* a machine. Rather, it says that man *has* a machine which he uses. Let us examine some of the similarities between mechanical servo-mechanisms and the human brain:

THE TWO GENERAL TYPES OF SERVO-MECHANISMS

Servo-mechanisms are divided into two general types: (1) where the target, goal, or "answer" is *known*, and the objective is to reach it or accomplish it, and (2) where the target or "answer" is not known and the objective is to discover or locate it. The human brain and nervous system operates in both ways.

An example of the first type is the self-guided torpedo, or the interceptor missile. The target or goal is known—an enemy ship or plane. The objective is to reach it. Such machines must "know" the target they are shooting for. They must have some sort of propulsion system which propels them forward in the general direction of the target. They must be equipped with "sense organs" (radar, sonar, heat perceptors, etc.) which bring information from the target. These "sense organs" keep the machine informed when it is on the correct course (positive feedback) and when it commits an error and gets off course (negative feedback). The machine does not react or respond to positive feedback. It is doing the correct thing already and "just keeps on doing what it is doing." There must be a corrective device, however, which will respond to negative feedback. When negative feedback informs the mechanism that it is "off the beam" too far to the right, the corrective mechanism automatically causes the rudder to move so that it will steer the machine back to the left. If it "overcorrects" and heads too far to the left, this mistake is made known through negative feedback, and the corrective device moves the rudder so it will steer the machine back to the right. The torpedo accomplishes its goal by *going forward, making errors,* and continually correcting them. By a series of zigzags it literally "gropes" its way to the goal.

Dr. Norbert Wiener, who pioneered in the development of goal-seeking mechanisms in World War II, believes that something very similar to the foregoing happens in the human nervous system whenever you perform any purposeful activity—even in such a simple goal-seeking situation as picking up a package of cigarettes from a table.

We are able to accomplish the goal of picking up the cigarettes because of an automatic mechanism, and not by "will" and forebrain thinking alone. All that the forebrain does is to select the goal, trigger it into action by desire, and feed information to the automatic mechanism so that your hand continually corrects its course.

In the first place, said Dr. Wiener, only an anatomist would know all the muscles involved in picking up the cigarettes. And if you knew, you would not consciously say to yourself, "I must contract my shoulder muscles to elevate my arm, now I must contract my triceps to extend my arm, etc." You just go ahead and pick up the cigarettes, and are not conscious of issuing orders to individual muscles, nor of computing just how much contraction is needed.

When "YOU" select the goal and trigger it into action, an automatic mechanism takes over. First of all, you have

picked up cigarettes, or performed similar movements before. Your automatic mechanism has "learned" something
of the correct response needed. Next, your automatic
mechanism uses feedback data furnished to the brain by
your eyes, which tells it "the degree to which the cigarettes are not picked up." This feedback data enables the
automatic mechanism to continually correct the motion
of your hand, until it is steered to the cigarettes.

In a baby, just learning to use its muscles, the correction of the hand in reaching for a rattle is very obvious.
The baby has little "stored information" to draw upon.
Its hand zigzags back and forth and gropes obviously as
it reaches. It is characteristic of all learning that as learning takes place, correction becomes more and more re-
fined. We see this in a person just learning to drive a car,
who "over-corrects" and zigzags back and forth across
the street.

*Once, however, a correct or "successful response" has
been accomplished—it is "remembered" for future use.
The automatic mechanism then duplicates this successful
response* on future trials. It has "learned" how to respond
successfully. It *"remembers" its successes, forgets its
failures,* and repeats the successful action without any further conscious "thought"—or as a habit.

How Your Brain Finds Answers to Problems

Now let us suppose that the room is dark so that you
cannot see the cigarettes. You know, or hope, there is a
package of cigarettes on the table, along with a variety of
other objects. Instinctively, your hand will begin to
"grope" back and forth, performing zigzag motions (or
"scanning") rejecting one object after another, until the
cigarettes are found and "recognized." This is an example of the second type of servo-mechanism. Recalling a
name temporarily forgotten is another example. A "Scanner" in your brain scans back through your stored memories until the correct name is "recognized." An electron-

ic brain solves problems in much the same way. First of all, a great deal of data must be fed into the machine. This stored, or recorded information is the machine's "memory." A problem is posed to the machine. It scans back through its memory until it locates the only "answer" which is consistent with and meets all the conditions of the problem. Problem and answer together constitute a "whole" situation or structure. When part of the situation or structure (the problem) is given to the machine, it locates the only "missing parts," or the right size brick, so to speak, to complete the structure.

The more that is learned about the human brain, the more closely it resembles—insofar as function is concerned —a servo-mechanism. For example, Dr. Wilder Penfield, director of the Montreal Neurological Institute, recently reported at a meeting of the National Academy of Sciences, that he had discovered a recording mechanism in a small area of the brain, which apparently records everything that a person has ever experienced, observed or learned. During a brain operation in which the patient was fully awake, Dr. Penfield happened to touch a small area of the cortex with a surgical instrument. At once the patient exclaimed that she was "reliving" an incident from her childhood, which she had consciously forgotten. Further experiments along this line brought the same results. When certain areas of the cortex were touched, patients did not merely "remember" past experiences, they "relived" them, experiencing as very *real* all the sights, sounds and sensations of the original experience. It was just as if past experiences had been recorded on a tape recorder and played back. Just how a mechanism as small as the human brain can store such a vast amount of information is still a mystery.

British neurophysicist W. Grey Walter has said that at least ten billion electronic cells would be needed to build a facsimile of man's brain. These cells would occupy about a million and a half cubic feet, and several additional millions of cubic feet would be needed for the "nerves" or wiring. Power required to operate it would be one billion watts.

A Look at the Automatic Mechanism in Action

We marvel at the awesomeness of interceptor missiles which can compute in a flash the point of interception of another missile and "be there" at the correct instant to make contact.

Yet, are we not witnessing something just as wonderful each time we see a center fielder catch a fly ball? In order to compute where the ball will fall, or where the "point of interception" will be, he must take into account the speed of the ball, its curvature of fall, its direction, windage, initial velocity and the rate of progressive decrease in velocity. He must make these computations so fast that he will be able to "take off" at the crack of the bat. Next, he must compute just how fast he must run, and in what direction in order to arrive at the point of interception at the same time the ball does. The center fielder doesn't even think about this. His built-in goal-striving mechanism computes it for him from data which he feeds it through his eyes and ears. The computer in his brain takes this information, compares it with stored data (memories of other successes and failures in catching fly balls). All necessary computations are made in a flash and orders are issued to his leg muscles—and he "just runs."

Science Can Build the Computer but Not the Operator

Dr. Wiener has said that at no time in the foreseeable future will scientists be able to construct an electronic brain anywhere near comparable to the human brain. "I think that our gadget-conscious public has shown an unawareness of the special advantages and special disadvantages of electronic machinery, as compared with the human brain," he says. "The number of switching devices in the human brain vastly exceeds the number in any computing machine yet developed, or even thought of for design in the near future."

But even should such a machine be built, it would lack an "operator." A computer does not have a forebrain, nor an "I." It cannot pose problems to itself. It has no imagination and cannot set goals for itself. It cannot determine which goals are worthwhile and which are not. It has no emotions. It cannot "feel." It works only on new data fed to it by an operator, by feedback data it secures from its own "sense organs" and from information previously stored.

Is There an Infinite Storehouse of Ideas, Knowledge, and Power?

Many great thinkers of all ages have believed that man's "stored information" is not limited to his own memories of past experiences, and learned facts. "There is one mind common to all individual men," said Emerson, who compared our individual minds to the inlets in an ocean of universal mind.

Edison believed that he got some of his ideas from a source outside himself. Once, when complimented for a creative idea, he disclaimed credit, saying that "ideas are in the air," and if he had not discovered it, someone else would have.

Dr. J. B. Rhine, head of Duke University's Parapsychology Laboratory, has proved experimentally that man has access to knowledge, facts, and ideas, other than his own individual memory or stored information from learning or experience. Telepathy, clairvoyance, precognition have been established by scientific laboratory experiments. His findings, that man possesses some "extra sensory factor," which he calls "Psi," are no longer doubted by scientists who have seriously reviewed his work. As Professor R. H. Thouless of Cambridge University says, "The reality of the phenomena must be regarded as proved as certainly as anything in scientific research can be proved."

"We have found," says Dr. Rhine, "that there is a capacity for acquiring knowledge that transcends the sensory functions. This extra sensory capacity can give us knowledge certainly of objective and very likely of subjective states, knowledge of matter and most probably of minds."

Schubert is said to have told a friend that his own creative process consisted in "remembering a melody" that neither he nor anyone else had ever thought of before.

Many creative artists, as well as psychologists who have made a study of the creative process, have been impressed by the similarity of creative inspiration, sudden revelation, intuition, etc., and ordinary human memory.

Searching for a new idea, or an answer to a problem, is in fact, very similar to searching memory for a name you have forgotten. You know that the name is "there," or else you would not search. The scanner in your brain scans back over stored memories until the desired name is "recognized" or "discovered."

The Answer Exists Now

In much the same way, when we set out to find a new idea, or the answer to a problem, *we must assume that the answer exists already—somewhere,* and set out to find it. Dr. Norbert Wiener has said, "Once a scientist attacks a problem which he knows to have an answer, his entire attitude is changed. He is already some fifty per cent of his way toward that answer." (Norbert Wiener, *The Human Use of Human Beings,* Houghton Mifflin, New York.)

When you set out to do creative work—whether in the field of selling, managing a business, writing a sonnet, improving human relations, or whatever, you begin with a goal in mind, an end to be achieved, a "target" answer, which, although perhaps somewhat vague, will be "recognized" when achieved. If you really mean business, have an intense desire, and begin to think intensely about all angles of the problem—your creative mechanism goes to work—and the "scanner" we spoke of earlier begins to scan back through stored information, or "grope" its way to an answer. It selects an idea here, a fact there, a series of former experiences, and relates them—or "ties them together" into a meaningful whole which will "fill out" the incompleted portion of your situation, complete your equation, or "solve" your problem. When this solution is served up to your consciousness—often at an unguarded moment when you are thinking of something else—or perhaps even as a dream while your consciousness is asleep —something "clicks" and you at once "recognize" this as the answer you have been searching for.

In this process, does your creative mechanism also have access to stored information in a universal mind? Numerous experiences of creative workers would seem to indicate that it does. How else, for example, explain the experience of Louis Agassiz, told by his wife:

"He had been striving to decipher the somewhat obscure impression of a fossil fish on the stone slab in which it was preserved. Weary and perplexed, he put his work aside at last and tried to dismiss it from his mind. Shortly after, he waked one night persuaded that while asleep he had seen his fish with all the missing features perfectly restored.

"He went early to the Jardin des Plantes, thinking that on looking anew at the impression he would see something to put him on the track of his vision. In vain—the blurred record was as blank as ever. The next night he saw the fish again, but when he waked it disappeared from his memory as before. Hoping the same experience might be repeated, on the third night he placed a pencil and paper beside his bed before going to sleep.

"Towards morning the fish reappeared in his dream, confusedly at first, but at last with such distinctness that he no longer had any doubt as to its zoological characters.

Still half dreaming, in perfect darkness, he traced these characters on the sheet of paper at the bedside.

"In the morning he was surprised to see in his nocturnal sketch features which he thought it impossible the fossil itself would reveal. He hastened to the Jardin des Plantes and, with his drawing as a guide, succeeded in chiseling away the surface of the stone under which portions of the fish proved to be hidden. When wholly exposed, the fossil corresponded with his dream and his drawing, and he succeeded in classifying it with ease."

PRACTICE EXERCISE NO. 1

Get a New Mental Picture of Yourself

The unhappy, failure-type personality cannot develop a new self-image by pure will power, or by arbitrarily deciding to. There must be some grounds, some justification, some reason for deciding that the old picture of self is in error, and that a new picture is appropriate. You cannot merely imagine a new self-image; unless you feel that it is based upon *truth*. Experience has shown that when a person does change his self-image, he has the feeling that for one reason or another, he "sees," or realizes the truth about himself.

The truth in this chapter can set you free of an old inadequate self-image, if you read it often, think intently about the implications, and "hammer home" its truths to yourself.

Science has now confirmed what philosophers, mystics, and other intuitive people have long declared: every human being has been literally "engineered for success" by his Creator. Every human being has access to a power greater than himself.

This means "YOU."

As Emerson has said, "There are no great and no small."

If you were engineered for success and happiness, then the old picture of yourself as unworthy of happiness, of a person who was "meant" to fail, must be in error.

Read this chapter through at least three times per week for the first 21 days. Study it and digest it. Look for examples in your experiences, and the experiences of your friends, which illustrate the creative mechanism in action.

Memorize the following basic principles by which your success mechanism operates. You do not need to be an electronic engineer, or a physicist, to operate your own servo-mechanism, any more than you have to be able to engineer an automobile in order to drive one, or become an electrical engineer in order to turn on the light in your room. You do need to be familiar with the following, however, because having memorized them, they will throw "new light" on what is to follow:

1. Your built-in success mechanism must have a goal or "target." This goal, or target, must be conceived of as "already in existence—now" either in actual or potential form. It operates by either (1) steering you to a goal already in existence or by (2) "discovering" something already in existence.

2. The automatic mechanism is teleological, that is, operates, or must be oriented to "end results," goals. Do not be discouraged because the "means whereby" may not be apparent. It is the function of the automatic mechanism to supply the "means whereby" when you supply the goal. Think in terms of the end result, and the means whereby will often take care of themselves.

3. Do not be afraid of making mistakes, or of temporary failures. All servo-mechanisms achieve a goal by negative feedback, or by going forward, making mistakes, and immediately correcting course.

4. Skill learning of any kind is accomplished by trial and error, mentally correcting aim after an error, until a "successful" motion, movement or performance has been achieved. *After that,* further learning, and continued success, is accomplished by *forgetting the past*

errors, and *remembering the successful response,* so that it can be "imitated."

5. You must learn to trust your creative mechanism to do its work and not "jam it" by becoming too concerned or too anxious as to whether it will work or not, or by attempting to force it by too much conscious effort. You must "let it" work, rather than "make it" work. This trust is necessary because your creative mechanism operates below the level of consciousness, and you cannot "know" what is going on beneath the surface. Moreover, its nature is to operate *spontaneously* according to *present need.* Therefore, you have no guarantees in advance. It comes into operation *as you act* and as you place a demand upon it by your actions. You must not wait to act until you have proof—you must act as if it is there, and it will come through. "Do the thing and you will have the power," said Emerson.

CHAPTER THREE

Imagination—The First Key
to Your Success Mechanism

IMAGINATION plays a far more important role in our lives than most of us realize.

I have seen this demonstrated many times in my practice. A particularly memorable instance of this fact concerned a patient who was literally forced to visit my office by his family. He was a man of about 40, unmarried, who held down a routine job during the day and kept himself in his room when the work day was over, never going anywhere, never doing anything. He had had many jobs and never seemed able to stay with any of them for any great length of time. His problem was that he had a rather large nose and ears that protruded a little more than is normal. He considered himself "ugly" and "funny looking." He imagined that the people he came into contact with during the day were laughing at him and talking about him behind his back because he was so "odd." His imaginings grew so strong that he actually feared going out into the business world and moving among people. He hardly felt "safe" even in his own home. The poor man even imagined that his family was "ashamed" of him because he was "peculiar looking," not like "other people."

Actually, his facial deficiencies were not serious. His nose was of the "classical Roman" type, and his ears, though somewhat large, attracted no more attention than those of thousands of people with similar ears. In desperation, his family brought him to me to see if I could help him. I saw that he did not need surgery . . . only an understanding of the fact that his imagination had wrought such havoc with his self-image that he had lost sight of the truth. He was not really ugly. People did not consider him odd and laugh at him because of his appearance. His imagination alone was responsible for his misery. His imagination had set up an automatic, negative, failure mechanism within him and it was operating full blast, to his extreme misfortune. Fortunately, after several sessions with him, and with the help of his family, he was able gradually to realize that the power of his own imagination was responsible for his plight, and he succeeded in building up a true self-image and achieving the confidence he needed by applying creative imagination rather than destructive imagination.

"Creative imagination" is not something reserved for the poets, the philosophers, the inventors. It enters into our every act. For imagination sets the goal "picture" which our automatic mechanism works on. We act, or fail to act, not because of "will," as is so commonly believed, but because of imagination.

A human being always acts and feels and performs in accordance with what he *imagines* to be *true* about himself and his environment.

This is a basic and fundamental law of mind. It is the way we are built.

When we see this law of mind graphically and dramatically demonstrated in a hypnotized subject, we are prone to think that there is something occult or supra-normal at work. Actually, what we are witnessing is the normal operating processes of the human brain and nervous system.

For example, if a good hypnotic subject is told that he is at the North Pole he will not only shiver and *appear* to be cold, his body will react just as if he were cold and goose pimples will develop. The same phenomenon has been demonstrated on wide awake college students by asking them to *imagine* that one hand is immersed in ice water. Thermometer readings show that the temperature does drop in the "treated" hand. Tell a hypnotized subject that your finger is a red hot poker and he will not only grimace with pain at your touch, but his cardiovascular and lymphatic systems will react just as if your finger were a red hot poker and produce inflammation and perhaps a blister on the skin. When college students, wide awake, have been told to *imagine* that a spot on their foreheads was hot, temperature readings have shown an actual increase in skin temperature.

Your nervous system cannot tell the difference between an *imagined experience* and a "real" experience. In either case, it reacts automatically to information which you give to it from your forebrain.

Your nervous system reacts appropriately to what "you" *think* or *imagine* to be *true*.

The Secret of "Hypnotic Power"

Dr. Theodore Xenophon Barber has conducted extensive research into the phenomena of hypnosis, both when he was associated with the psychology department of American University in Washington, D. C., and also after becoming associated with the Laboratory of Social Relations at Harvard. Writing in *Science Digest* recently he said:

"We found that hypnotic subjects are able to do surprising things only when *convinced* that the hypnotist's words are true statements . . . When the hypnotist has guided the subject to the point where he is convinced that the hypnotist's words are *true statements,* the subject then behaves differently because he *thinks* and *believes* differently.

"The phenomena of hypnosis have always seemed mysterious because it has always been difficult to understand how belief can bring about such unusual behavior.

It always seemed as if there must be something more, some unfathomable force or power, at work.

"However, the plain truth is that when a subject is convinced that he is deaf, he behaves as if he is deaf; when he is convinced that he is insensitive to pain, he can undergo surgery without anesthesia. The mysterious force or power does not exist." ("Could You Be Hypnotized?", *Science Digest,* January, 1958).

A little reflection will show why it is a very good thing for us that we do feel and act according to what we believe or imagine to be true.

Truth Determines Action and Behavior

The human brain and nervous system are engineered to react automatically and appropriately to the problems and challenges in the environment. For example, a man does not need to stop and think that self-survival requires that he run if he meets a grizzly bear on a trail. He does not need to decide to become afraid. The fear response is both automatic and appropriate. First, it makes him want to flee. The fear then triggers bodily mechanisms which "soup up" his muscles so that he can run faster than he has ever run before. His heart beat is quickened. Adrenalin, a powerful muscle stimulant, is poured into the bloodstream. All bodily functions not necessary to running are shut down. The stomach stops working and all available blood is sent to the muscles. Breathing is much faster and the oxygen supply to the muscles is increased manifold.

All this, of course, is nothing new. Most of us learned it in high school. What we have not been so quick to realize, however, is that the brain and nervous system which reacts automatically to environment is the same brain and nervous system which tells us what the environment *is.* The reactions of the man meeting the bear are commonly thought of as due to "emotion" rather than to ideas. Yet, it was an idea—*information* received from the outside world, and evaluated by the forebrain—which sparked the so-called "emotional reactions." Thus, it was basically *idea* or *belief* which was the true causative agent, rather than emotion—which came as a result. In short, the man on the trail reacted to what he *thought,* or *believed* or *imagined* the environment to be. The "messages" brought to us from the environment consist of nerve impulses from the various sense organs. These nerve impulses are decoded, interpreted and evaluated in the brain and made known to us in the form of ideas or mental images. In the final analysis it is these mental images that we react to.

You act, and feel, not according to what things are really like, but according to the image your mind holds of what they are like. You have certain mental images of yourself, your world, and the people around you, and you behave as though these images were the truth, the reality, rather than the things they represent.

Let us suppose, for example, that the man on the trail had not met a real bear, but a movie actor dressed in a bear costume. If he *thought* and *imagined* the actor to be a bear, his emotional and nervous reactions would have been exactly the same. Or let us suppose he met a large shaggy dog, which his fear-ridden imagination mistook for a bear. Again, he would react *automatically* to what he *believed* to be true concerning himself and his environment.

It follows that if our ideas and mental images concerning ourselves are distorted or unrealistic, then our reaction to our environment will likewise be inappropriate.

Why Not Imagine Yourself Successful?

Realizing that our actions, feelings and behavior are the result of our own images and beliefs gives us the lever that psychology has always needed for changing personality.

It opens a new psychologic door to gaining skill, success, and happiness.

Mental pictures offer us an opportunity to "practice" new traits and attitudes, which otherwise we could not do. This is possible because again—your nervous system cannot tell the difference between an actual experience and one that is vividly imagined.

If we picture ourselves performing in a certain manner, it is nearly the same as the actual performance. Mental practice helps to make perfect.

In a controlled experiment, psychologist R. A. Vandell proved that mental practice in throwing darts at a target, wherein the person sits for a period each day in front of the target, and imagines throwing darts at it, improves aim as much as actually throwing darts.

Research Quarterly reports an experiment on the effects of mental practice on improving skill in sinking basketball free throws. One group of students actually practiced throwing the ball every day for 20 days, and were scored on the first and last days.

A second group was scored on the first and last days, and engaged in no sort of practice in between.

A third group was scored on the first day, then spent 20 minutes a day, imagining that they were throwing the ball at the goal. When they missed they would imagine that they corrected their aim accordingly.

The first group, which actually practiced 20 minutes every day, improved in scoring 24 per cent.

The second group, which had no sort of practice, showed no improvement.

The third group, which practiced in their imagination, improved in scoring 23 per cent!

How Imagination Practice Won a Chess Championship..

The April, 1955 issue of *Reader's Digest* contained an article from *The Rotarian* by Joseph Phillips, called: "Chess: They Call It a Game."

In this article Phillips tells how the great chess champion, Capablanca, was so superior to all competition that it was believed by experts that he would never be beaten in match play. Yet, he lost the championship to a rather obscure player, Alekhine, who had given no hint that he even posed a serious threat to the great Capablanca.

The chess world was stunned by the upset, which today would be comparable to a Golden Gloves finalist defeating the heavyweight champion of the world.

Phillips tells us that Alekhine had trained for the match very much like a boxer conditioning himself for a fight. He retired to the country, cut out smoking and drinking and did calisthenics. "For three months, *he played chess only in his mind,* building up steam for the moment when he would meet the champion."

Mental Pictures Can Help You Sell More Goods

In his book, *How to Make $25,000 a Year Selling,* Charles B. Roth tells how a group of salesmen in Detroit who tried a new idea increased their sales 100 per cent. Another group in New York increased their sales by 150 per cent. And individual salesmen, using the same idea, have increased their sales up to 400 per cent. (Charles B. Roth, *How to Make $25,000 a Year Selling,* Englewood Cliffs, N.J., Prentice-Hall, Inc.)

"And what is this magic that accomplishes so much for salesmen?

"It is something called role-playing, and you should know about it, because if you will let it, it may help you to double your sales.

"What is role-playing?

"Well, it is simply *imagining* yourself in various sales situations, then solving them *in your mind,* until you know what to say and what to do whenever the situation comes up in real life.

"It is what is called on the football field 'skull practice.'

"The reason why it accomplishes so much is that selling is simply a matter of situations.

"One is created every time you talk to a customer. He says something or asks a question or raises an objection. If you always know how to counter what he says or answer his question or handle the objection, you make sales. . . .

"A role-playing salesman, at night when he is alone, will create these situations. He will imagine the prospect throwing the widest kind of curves at him. Then he will work out the best answer to them . . .

"No matter what the situation is, you can prepare for it beforehand by means of imagining yourself and your prospect face to face while he is raising objections and creating problems and you are handling them properly."

Use Mental Pictures to Get a Better Job

The late William Moulton Marston, well-known psychologist, recommended what he called "rehearsal practice" to men and women who came to him for help in job advancement. If you have an important interview coming up, such as making an application for a job, his advice was: plan for the interview in advance. Go over in your mind, all the various questions that you are likely to be asked. Think about the answers you are going to give. Then "rehearse" the interview in your mind. Even if none of the questions you have rehearsed come up, the rehearsal practice will still work wonders. It gives you confidence. And even though real life has not set lines to be recited like a stage play, rehearsal practice will help you to ad lib and react spontaneously to whatever situation you find yourself in, *because you have practiced* reacting spontaneously.

"Don't be a ham actor," Dr. Marston would say, explaining that we are always acting out *some* role in life. Why not select the right role, the role of a successful person—and rehearse it?

Writing in *Your Life* magazine, Dr. Marston said, "Frequently the next step in your career cannot be taken without first gaining some experience in the work you will be called upon to perform. Bluff may open the door to a job you know nothing about but in nine cases out of ten it won't keep you from being fired when your inexperience becomes evident. There's only one way I know to project your practical knowledge beyond your present occupation and that is rehearsal planning."

A Concert Pianist Practices "In His Head"

Artur Schnabel, the world famous concert pianist, took lessons for only seven years. He hated practice and seldom does practice for any length of time at the actual piano keyboard. When questioned about his small amount of practice, as compared with other concert pianists, he said, "I practice in my head."

C. G. Kop, of Holland, a recognized authority on teaching piano, recommends that *all* pianists "practice in their heads." A new composition, he says, should be first gone over in the mind. It should be memorized, and played in the mind, before ever touching fingers to the keyboard.

Imagination Practice Can Lower Your Golf Score

Time magazine reported that when Ben Hogan is playing in a tournament, he mentally rehearses each shot, just before making it. He makes the shot perfectly in his imagination—"feels" the clubhead strike the ball just as it should, "feels" himself performing the perfect follow-through—and then steps up to the ball, and depends upon what he calls "muscle memory" to carry out the shot just as he has imagined it.

Alex Morrison, perhaps the most well-known golf teacher in the world, has actually worked out a system of mental practice. It enables you to improve your golf score by sitting in an easy chair, and practicing mentally what he calls the "Seven Morrison Keys." The mental side of golf represents 90 per cent of the game, he says, the physical side 8 per cent, and the mechanical side 2 per cent. In his book, *Better Golf Without Practice* (New York, Simon and Schuster), Morrison tells how he taught Lew Lehr to break 90 for the first time, with no actual practice whatsoever.

Morrison had Lehr sit in an easy chair in his living room and relax while he demonstrated for him the correct swing and gave a brief lecture on the "Morrison Keys." Lehr was instructed to engage in no actual practice on the links, but instead spend five minutes each day, relaxing in his easy chair, visualizing himself attending to the "Keys" correctly.

Morrison goes on to tell how several days later, with no physical preparation whatever, Lehr joined his regular foursome, and amazed them by shooting 9 holes in an even par, 36.

The core of the Morrison system is "You must have a clear mental picture of the correct thing before you can do it successfully." Morrison, by this method, enabled Paul Whiteman, and many other celebrities, to chop as much as ten to twelve strokes off their scores.

Johnny Bulla, the well-known professional golfer, wrote an article several years ago in which he said that having a clear mental image of just where you wanted the ball to go and what you wanted it to do was more important than "form" in golf. Most of the pros, said Bulla, have one or more serious flaws in their "form." Yet they manage to shoot good golf. It was Bulla's theory that if you would picture the end result—"see" the ball going where you wanted it to go, and have the confidence to "know" that it was going to do what you wanted, your subconscious would take over and direct your muscles correctly. If your grip was wrong, and your stance not in the best form, your subconscious would still take care of that by directing your muscles to do whatever was necessary to compensate for the error in form.

The Real Secret of Mental Picturing

Successful men and women have, since the beginning of time, used "mental pictures," and "rehearsal practice," to achieve success. Napoleon, for example, "practiced" soldiering, in his imagination, for many years before he ever went on an actual battlefield. Webb and Morgan in their book *Making the Most of Your Life,* tell us that "the notes Napoleon made from his readings during these years of study filled, when printed, four hundred pages. He imagined himself as a commander, and drew maps of the island of Corsica showing where he would place various defenses, making all his calculations with mathematical precision."*

Conrad Hilton imagined himself operating a hotel long before he ever bought one. When a boy he used to "play" that he was a hotel operator.

Henry J. Kaiser has said that each of his business accomplishments was realized in his imagination before it appeared in actuality.

It is no wonder that the art of "mental picturing" has in the past sometimes been associated with "magic."

However, the new science of Cybernetics gives us an insight into why mental picturing produces such amazing results, and shows that these results are not due to "magic," but the natural, normal functioning of our minds and brains.

Cybernetics regards the human brain, nervous system, and muscular system, as a highly complex "servo-mechanism." (An automatic goal-seeking machine which "steers"

* *Making the Most of Your Life* by John J. B. Morgan and Ewing T. Webb. Copyright, 1932 by John J. B. Morgan and Ewing T. Webb. Reprinted by permission of Doubleday and Company, Inc.

its way to a target or goal by use of feedback data and stored information, automatically correcting course when necessary.)

As stated earlier, this new concept does not mean that "YOU" are a machine, but that your physical brain and body functions as a machine which "YOU" operate.

This automatic creative mechanism within you can operate in only one way. It must have a target to shoot at. As Alex Morrison says, you must first clearly see a thing in your mind before you can do it. When you do see a thing clearly in your mind, your creative "success mechanism" within you takes over and does the job much better than you could do it by conscious effort, or "will power."

Instead of trying hard by conscious effort to do the thing by iron-jawed will power, and all the while worrying and picturing to yourself all the things that are likely to go wrong, you simply relax the strain, stop trying to "do it" by strain and effort, picture to yourself the target you really want to hit, and "let" your creative success mechanism take over. Thus, mental-picturing the desired end result, literally forces you to use "positive thinking." You are not relieved thereafter from effort and work, but your efforts are used to carry you forward toward your goal, rather than in futile mental conflict which results when you "want" and "try" to do one thing, but picture to yourself something else.

Finding Your Best Self

This same creative mechanism within you can help you achieve your best possible "self" if you will form a picture in your imagination of the self you wanted to be and "see yourself" in the new role. This is a necessary condition to personality transformation, regardless of the method of therapy used. Somehow, before a person can change, he must "see" himself in a new role.

Edward McGoldrick uses this technique in helping alcoholics cross the "bridge" from the old self to the new self. Each day, he has his "students" close their eyes, relax the body as much as possible, and create a "mental motion picture" of themselves as they would like to be. In this mental motion picture they see themselves as sober, responsible persons. They see themselves actually *enjoying* life without liquor. This is not the only technique used by McGoldrick, but it is one of the basic methods used at "Bridge House" which has a higher record of cure for alcoholics than any other organization in the country.

I myself have witnessed veritable miracles in personality transformation when an individual changes his self image. However, today we are only beginning to glimpse the potential creative power which stems from the human imagination, and particularly our images concerning ourselves. Consider the implications, for example, in the following news release, which appeared a couple of years ago under an Associated Press dateline:

Just Imagine You're Sane

"*San Francisco.* Some mental patients can improve their lot and perhaps shorten their stay in hospitals just by imagining they are normal, two psychologists with the Veterans Administration at Los Angeles reported.

"Dr. Harry M. Grayson and Dr. Leonard B. Olinger told the American Psychological Assn. they tried the idea on 45 men hospitalized as neuropsychiatrics.

"The patients first were given the usual personality test. Then they were asked flatly to take the test a second time and answer the questions as they would if they were 'a typical, well-adjusted person on the outside.'

"Three-fourths of them turned in improved test performances and some of the changes for the better were dramatic, the psychologists reported."

In order for these patients to answer the questions "as a typical, well-adjusted person" would answer, they had to imagine how a typical well-adjusted person would act. They had to imagine themselves in the role of a well-adjusted person. And this in itself was enough to cause them to begin "acting like" and "feeling like" a well-adjusted person.

We can begin to see why the late Dr. Albert Edward Wiggam called your mental picture of yourself "the strongest force within you."

Know the Truth About Yourself

The aim of self-image psychology is not to create a fictitious self which is all-powerful, arrogant, egoistic, all-important. Such an image is as inappropriate and unrealistic as the inferior image of self. Our aim is to find the "real self," and to bring our mental images of ourselves more in line with "the objects they represent." However, it is common knowledge among psychologists that most of us under-rate ourselves; short change ourselves and sell ourselves short. Actually, there is no such thing as a "superiority complex." People who seem to have one are actually suffering from feelings of inferiority—their "superior self" is a fiction, a cover-up, to hide from themselves and others their deep-down feelings of inferiority and insecurity.

How can you know the truth about yourself? How can you make a true evaluation? It seems to me that here psychology must turn to religion. The Scriptures tell us that God created man "a little lower than the angels" and "gave him dominion"; that God created man in his own Man. In the first place such an all-wise and all-powerful all-loving Creator, then we are in a position to draw some logical conclusions about that which He has created— Man. In the first place such an all-wise and all-powerful Creator would not turn out inferior products, any more than a master painter would paint inferior canvases. Such a Creator would not deliberately engineer his product to fail, any more than a manufacturer would deliberately build failure into an automobile. The Fundamentalists tell us that man's chief purpose and reason for living is to "glorify God," and the Humanists tell us that man's primary purpose is to "express himself fully."

However, if we take the premise that God is a loving Creator and has the same interest in his Creation that an earthly father has in his children, then it seems to me that the Fundamentalists and the Humanists are saying the same thing. What brings more glory, pride, and satisfaction to a father than seeing his offspring do well, succeed and express to the full their abilities and talents? Have you ever sat by the father of a football star during a game? Jesus expressed the same thought when he told us not to hide our light under a bushel, but to let *our* light shine —"so that your Father may be glorified." I cannot believe that it brings any "glory" to God when his children go around with hang-dog expressions, being miserable, afraid to lift up their heads and "be somebody."

As Dr. Leslie D. Weatherhead has said, "If . . . we have in our minds a picture of ourselves as fear-haunted and defeated nobodies, we must get rid of that picture at once and hold up our heads. That is a false picture and the false must go. God sees us as men and women in whom and through whom He can do a great work. He sees us as already serene, confident, and cheerful. He sees us not as pathetic victims of life, but masters of the art of living; not wanting sympathy, but imparting help to others, and therefore thinking less and less of ourselves, and full, not of self-concern, but of love and laughter and a desire to serve. . . . Let us look at the real selves which are in the making the moment we believe in their existence. We must recognize the possibility of change and believe in the self we are now in the process of becoming. That old sense of unworthiness and failure must go. It is false and we are not to believe in what is false." (Leslie D. Weatherhead, *Prescription for Anxiety,* New York, Abingdon Press.)

PRACTICE EXERCISE:

"Hold a picture of yourself long and steadily enough in your mind's eye and you will be drawn toward it," said Dr. Harry Emerson Fosdick. "Picture yourself vividly as defeated and that alone will make victory impossible. Picture yourself vividly as winning and that alone will contribute immeasurably to success. Great living starts with a picture, held in your imagination, of what you would like to do or be."

Your present self-image was built upon your own imagination pictures of yourself in the past which grew out of interpretations and evaluations which you placed upon *experience.* Now you are to use the same method to build an adequate self-image that you previously used to build an inadequate one.

Set aside a period of 30 minutes each day where you can be alone and undisturbed. Relax and make yourself as comfortable as possible. Now close your eyes and exercise your imagination.

Many people find they get better results if they imagine themselves sitting before a large motion picture screen—and imagine that they are seeing a motion picture of themselves. The important thing is to make these pictures as *vivid* and as *detailed* as possible. You want your mental pictures to approximate actual experience as much as possible. The way to do this is pay attention to small details, sights, sounds, objects, in your imagined environment. One of my patients was using this exercise to overcome her fear of the dentist. She was unsuccessful, until she began to notice small details in her imagined picture—the smell of the antiseptic in the office, the feel of the leather on the chair arms, the sight of the dentist's well-manicured nails as his hands approached her mouth, etc. *Details* of the imagined environment are all-important in this exercise, because for all practical purposes, you are creating a *practice experience*. And if the imagination is vivid enough and detailed enough, your imagination practice is equivalent to an actual experience, insofar as your nervous system is concerned.

The next important thing to remember is that during this 30 minutes you see yourself acting and reacting appropriately, successfully, ideally. It doesn't matter how you acted yesterday. You do not need to try to have faith you will act in the ideal way tomorrow. Your nervous system will take care of that in time—if you continue to practice. See yourself acting, feeling, "being," as you want to be. Do not say to yourself, "I am going to act this way tomorrow." Just say to yourself—"I am going to imagine myself acting in this way now—for 30 minutes—today." Imagine how you would feel if you were already the sort of personality you want to be. If you have been shy and timid, see yourself moving among people with ease and poise—and *feeling good* because of it. If you have been fearful and anxious in certain situations—see yourself acting calmly and deliberately, acting with confidence and courage—and feeling expansive and confident because you are.

This exercise builds new "memories" or stored data into your mid-brain and central nervous system. It builds a new image of self. After practicing it for a time, you will be surprised to find yourself "acting differently," more or less automatically and spontaneously—"without trying." This is as it should be. You do not need to "take thought" or "try" or make an effort now in order to feel ineffective and act inadequately. Your present inadequate feeling and doing is automatic and spontaneous, because of the memories, real and imagined, you have built into your automatic mechanism. You will find it will work just as automatically upon positive thoughts and experiences as upon negative ones.

Key Points to Remember
(You fill in here.)

1.
2.
3.
4.
5.

CASE HISTORY: List here some experience out of your past that is explained by the principles given in this chapter:

CHAPTER FOUR

Dehypnotize Yourself
From False Beliefs

MY friend Dr. Alfred Adler had an experience when a young boy which illustrates just how powerful belief can be upon behavior and ability. He got off to a bad start in arithmetic and his teacher *became convinced* that he was "dumb in mathematics." The teacher then advised the parents of this "fact" and told them not to expect too much of him. They too were convinced. Adler passively accepted the evaluation they had placed upon him. And his grades in arithmetic proved they had been correct. One day, however, he had a sudden flash of insight and thought he saw how to work a problem the teacher had put on the board, and which none of the other pupils could work. He announced as much to the teacher. She and the whole class laughed. Whereupon, he became indignant, strode to the blackboard, and worked the problem much to their amazement. In doing so, he realized that he could understand arithmetic. He felt a new confidence in his ability, and went on to become a good math student.

Dr. Adler's experience was very much like that of a patient of mine some years back, a businessman who wanted to excel in public speaking because he had a vital message to impart about his outstanding success in a difficult field. He had a good voice and an important topic, but he was unable to get up in front of strangers and put his message over. What held him back was his belief that he could not make a good talk, and that he would fail to impress his audience, simply because he did not have an imposing appearance . . . he did not "look like a successful executive." This belief had burrowed so deeply into him that it threw up a road block every time he stood up before a group of people and began to talk. He mistakenly concluded that, if he could have an operation to improve his appearance, he would then gain the confidence he needed. An operation might have done the trick and it might not . . . my experience with other patients had shown that physical change did not always guarantee personality change. The solution in this man's case was found when he became convinced that his negative belief was preventing him from delivering the vital information he had. He succeeded in replacing the negative belief with a positive belief that he had a message of extreme importance that he alone could deliver, no matter what he looked like. In due time, he was one of the most sought after speakers in the business world. The only change was in his belief and in his self-image.

Now the point I want to make is this: Adler had been *hypnotized* by a false belief about himself. Not figuratively, but literally and actually hypnotized. Remember that we said in the last chapter that the power of hypnosis is the power of belief. Let me repeat here Dr. Barber's explanation of the "power" of hypnosis: "We found that hypnotic subjects are able to do surprising things only when *convinced* that the hypnotist's words are true statements. . . . When the hypnotist has guided the subject to the point where he is convinced that the hypnotist's words are true statements, the subject then behaves differently because he *thinks* and *believes* differently."

The important thing for you to remember is that it does not matter in the least *how* you got the idea or *where* it came from. You may never have met a professional hypnotist. You may have never been formally hypnotized. But if you have accepted an idea—from yourself, your teachers, your parents, friends, advertisements—or from any other source, and further, if you are firmly *convinced* that idea is *true*, it has the same power over you as the hypnotist's words have over the hypnotized subject.

Scientific research has shown that Dr. Adler's experience was not "one in a million," but typical of practically all students who make poor grades. In Chapter One we told of how Prescott Lecky had brought about almost miraculous improvement in the grades of school children by showing them how to change their self-image. After thousands of experiments and many years of research Lecky concluded that poor grades in school are, *in almost every case,* due in some degree to the student's "self-conception" and "self-definition." These students had been literally hypnotized by such ideas as "I am dumb," "I have a weak personality," "I am poor in arithmetic," "I am a naturally poor speller," "I am ugly," "I do not have a mechanical type mind," etc. With such self-definitions, the student had to make poor grades in order to be true to himself. Unconsciously, making poor grades became a "moral issue" with him. It would be as "wrong," from his own viewpoint, for him to make good grades, as it would be to steal if he defines himself as an honest person.

The Case of the Hypnotized Salesman

In the book, *Secrets of Successful Selling,* John D. Murphy tells how Elmer Wheeler used Lecky's theory to increase the earnings of a certain salesman:

"Elmer Wheeler had been called in as a sales consultant to a certain firm. The sales manager called his attention to a very remarkable case. A certain salesman always managed to make almost exactly $5,000 per year, regardless of the territory they assigned to him or the commission he was paid.

"Because this salesman had done well in a rather small territory, he had been given a larger and much better one. But the next year his commission amounted to almost the same amount as that he had made in the smaller one—$5,000. The following year the company increased the commission paid to all salesmen, but this salesman still managed to make only $5,000. He was then assigned one of the company's poorest territories—and again made the usual $5,000.

"Wheeler had a talk with this salesman and found that the trouble was not in the territory but in the salesman's own valuation of himself. He thought of himself as a $5,000-per-year man and as long as he held that concept of himself, outside conditions didn't seem to matter much.

"When he was assigned a poor territory, he worked hard to make that $5,000. When he was assigned a good territory, he found all sorts of excuses to coast when the $5,000 was in sight. Once, when the goal had been reached, he got sick and was unable to work any more that year, although doctors could find nothing wrong with him and he miraculously recovered by the first of the next year."

How a False Belief Aged a Man 20 Years

In a previous book (Maxwell Maltz, *Adventures in Staying Young,* New York, Thomas Y. Crowell Co.) I gave a detailed case history of how "Mr. Russell" aged 20 years almost overnight because of a false idea, then regained his youth almost as quickly when he accepted the truth. Briefly, the story is this: I performed a cosmetic operation on "Mr. Russell's" lower lip for a very modest fee, under the condition that he must tell his girl friend that the operation had cost him his entire savings of a lifetime. His girl friend had no objection to his spending money on her, and she insisted that she loved him, but explained she could never marry him because of his too-large lower lip. However, when he told her this and proudly exhibited his new lower lip, her reaction was just as I had expected, but not as Mr. Russell had anticipated. She became hysterically angry, called him a fool for hav-

ing spent all his money, and advised him in no uncertain
terms that she had never loved him and never would, and
that she had merely played him for a sucker as long as he
had money to spend on her. However, she went further
than I had counted on. In her anger and disgust she also
announced that she was placing a "Voodoo curse" upon
him. Both Mr. Russell and his girl friend had been born
on an island in the West Indies where Voodoo was practiced by the ignorant and superstitious. His family had
been rather well-to-do. His background was one of culture
and he was a college graduate.

Yet, when in the heat of anger, his girl friend "cursed"
him, he felt vaguely uncomfortable but did not think too
much about it.

However, he remembered and wondered when a short
time later he felt a strange small hard "bump" on the inside of his lip. A "friend" who knew of the Voodoo curse,
insisted that he see a "Dr. Smith," who promptly assured
him that the bump inside his mouth was the feared "African Bug," which would slowly eat away all his vitality
and strength. "Mr. Russell" began to worry and look for
signs of waning strength. He was not long in finding them.
He lost his appetite and his ability to sleep.

I learned all this from "Mr. Russell" when he returned
to my office several weeks after I had dismissed him. My
nurse didn't recognize him, and no wonder. The "Mr.
Russell" who had first called upon me had been a very
impressive individual, slightly too-large lip and all. He
stood about six feet four, a large man with the physique
of an athlete and the bearing and manner that bespoke of
an inner dignity and gave him a magnetic personality.
The very pores of his skin seemed to exude an animal-
like vitality.

The Mr. Russell who now sat across the desk from me
had aged at least 20 years. His hands shook with the
tremor of age. His eyes and cheeks were sunken. He had
lost perhaps 30 pounds. The changes in his appearance

were all characteristic of the process which medical science, for want of a better name, calls "aging."

After a quick examination of his mouth I assured Mr. Russell I could get rid of the African Bug in less than 30 minutes, which I did. The bump which had caused all the trouble was merely a small bit of scar tissue from his operation. I removed it, held it in my hand, and showed it to him. The important thing is he saw the truth and believed it. He gave a sigh of relief, and it seemed as if there was an almost immediate change in his posture and expression.

Several weeks later, I received a nice letter from Mr. Russell, together with a photograph of him with his new bride. He had gone back to his home and married his childhood sweetheart. The man in the picture was the *first* Mr. Russell. Mr. Russell had grown young again—overnight. A false belief aged him 20 years. The truth had not only set him free of fear and restored his confidence—but had actually reversed the "aging process."

If you could have seen Mr. Russell as I did, both "before" and "after," you would never again entertain any doubts about the power of belief, or that an idea accepted as true from any source, can be every bit as powerful as hypnosis.

Is Everyone Hypnotized?

It is no exaggeration to say that every human being is hypnotized to some extent, either by ideas he has uncritically accepted from others, or ideas he has repeated to himself or convinced himself are true. These negative ideas have exactly the same effect upon our behavior as the negative ideas implanted into the mind of a hypnotized subject by a professional hypnotist. Have you ever seen a demonstration of honest-to-goodness hypnosis? If not, let me describe to you just a few of the more simple phenomena which result from the hypnotist's suggestion.

The hypnotist tells a football player that his hand is

stuck to the table and that he *cannot* lift it. It is not a question of the football player "not trying." He simply *cannot*. He strains and struggles until the muscles of his arm and shoulder stand out like cords. But his hand remains fully rooted to the table.

He tells a championship weight-lifter that he *cannot* lift a pencil from the desk. And although normally he can hoist a 400 pound weight overhead, he now actually *cannot* lift the pencil.

Strangely enough, in the above instances, hypnosis does not weaken the athletes. They are potentially as strong as ever. But *without realizing it consciously* they are working against themselves. On the one hand they "try" to lift their hand, or the pencil, by voluntary effort and actually contract the proper lifting muscles. But on the other hand, the idea "you cannot do it" causes contrary muscles to contract quite apart from their will. The negative idea causes them to defeat themselves—they cannot express, or bring into play their actual available strength.

The gripping strength of a third athlete has been tested on a dynometer and has been found to be 100 pounds. All his effort and straining cannot budge the needle beyond the 100 pound mark. Now he is hypnotized and told, "You are very, very strong. Stronger than you have ever been in your life. Much, much stronger. You are surprised at how strong you are." Again the gripping strength of his hand is tested. This time he easily pulls the needle to the 125 pound mark.

Again, strangely enough, hypnosis has not added anything to his actual strength. What the hypnotic suggestion did do was to overcome a negative idea which had previously prevented him from expressing his full strength. In other words, the athlete in his normal waking state had imposed a limitation upon his strength by the negative belief that he could only grip 100 pounds. The hypnotist merely removed this mental block, and allowed him to express his true strength. The hypnosis literally "dehypnotized" him temporarily from his own self-limiting beliefs about himself.

As Dr. Barber has said, it is awfully easy to assume that the hypnotist himself must have some magical power when you see rather miraculous things happen during a hypnotic session. The stutterer talks fluently. The timid, shy, retiring Caspar Milquetoast becomes outgoing, poised, and makes a stirring speech. Another individual who is not especially good in adding figures with a pencil and paper when awake, multiplies two three-digit figures in his head. All this happens apparently merely because the hypnotist tells them that they *can* and instructs them to go ahead and do it. To on-lookers, the hypnotist's "word" has a magical power. Such, however, is not the case. The power, the basic ability, to do these things was inherent in the subjects all the time—even before they met the hypnotist. The subjects, however, were unable to *use* this power because they themselves did not know it was there. They had bottled it up, and choked it off, *because of their own* negative beliefs. Without realizing it, they had hypnotized themselves into believing they could not do these things. And it would be truer to say that the hypnotist had "dehypnotized" them than to say he had hypnotized them.

Within you, whoever you may be, regardless of how big a failure you may think yourself to be, is the ability and the power to do whatever you need to do to be happy and successful. Within you right now is the power to do things you never dreamed possible. This power becomes available to you just as soon as you can change your beliefs. Just as quickly as you can dehypnotize yourself from the ideas of "I can't," "I'm not worthy," "I don't deserve it" and other self-limiting ideas.

You Can Cure Your Inferiority Complex

At least 95 per cent of the people have their lives blighted by feelings of inferiority to some extent, and to millions this same feeling of inferiority is a serious handicap to success and happiness.

In one sense of the word every person on the face of the earth is inferior to some other person or persons. I *know* that I cannot lift as much weight as Paul Anderson, throw a 16 pound shot as far as Parry O'Brien, or dance as well as Arthur Murray. I *know* this, but it does not *induce feelings* of inferiority within me and blight my life —simply because I do not compare myself unfavorably with them and feel that I am no good merely because I cannot do certain things as skillfully or as well as they. I also *know* that in certain areas, every person I meet, from the newsboy on the corner to the president of the bank, is superior to me in certain respects. But neither can any of these people repair a scarred face, or do any number of other things as well as I. And I am sure they do not feel inferior because of it.

Feelings of inferiority originate not so much from "facts" or experiences, but our conclusions regarding facts, and our evaluation of experiences. For example, the fact is that I am an *inferior weight-lifter* and an *inferior dancer*. This does not, however, make me an "inferior person." Paul Anderson's and Arthur Murray's inability to perform surgery makes them "inferior surgeons," but not "inferior persons." It all depends upon "what" and "whose" norms we measure ourselves by.

It is not *knowledge* of actual inferiority in skill or knowledge which gives us an inferiority complex and interferes with our living. It is the *feeling* of inferiority that does this.

And this *feeling of inferiority* comes about for just one reason: We judge ourselves, and measure ourselves, not against our own "norm" or "par" but against some other individual's "norm." When we do this, we always, without exception, come out second best. But because we *think,* and *believe* and *assume* that we *should* measure up to some other person's "norm," we *feel* miserable, and second-rate, and conclude that there is something wrong with us. The next logical conclusion in this cockeyed reasoning process is to conclude that we are not "worthy"; that we do not deserve success and happiness, and that it would be out of place for us to fully express our own abilities and talents, whatever they might be, without apology, or without feeling guilty about it.

All this comes about because we have allowed ourselves to be hypnotized by the entirely erroneous idea that "I should be like so-and-so" or "I should be like everybody else." The fallacy of the second idea can be readily seen through, if analyzed, for in truth there are no fixed standards common to "everybody else." "Everybody else" is composed of individuals, no two of whom are alike.

The person with an inferiority complex invariably compounds the error by striving for superiority. His feelings spring from the false premise that he is inferior. From this false premise, a whole structure of "logical thought" and feeling is built. If he feels bad because he is inferior, the cure is to make himself as good as everybody else, and the way to feel really good is to make himself superior. This striving for superiority gets him into more trouble, causes more frustration, and sometimes brings about a neurosis where none existed before. He becomes more miserable than ever, and "the harder he tries," the more miserable he becomes.

Inferiority and Superiority are reverse sides of the same coin. The cure lies in realizing that the coin itself is spurious.

The *truth* about you is this:

You are not "inferior."

You are not "superior."

You are simply "You."

"You" as a personality are not in competition with any other personality simply because there is not another person on the face of the earth like you, or in your particular class. You are an individual. You are unique. You are not "like" any other person and can never become "like" any other person. You are not "supposed" to be like any other person and no other person is "supposed" to be like you.

God did not create a standard person and in some way label that person by saying "this is it." He made every human being individual and unique just as He made every snowflake individual and unique.

God created short people and tall people, large people and small people, skinny people and fat people, black, yellow, red and white people. He has never indicated any preference for any one size, shape or color. Abraham Lincoln once said, "God must have loved the common people for he made so many of them." He was wrong. There is no "common man"—no standardized, common pattern. He would have been nearer the truth had he said, "God must have loved uncommon people for he made so many of them."

An "inferiority complex," and its accompanying deterioration in performance, can be made to order in the psychological laboratory. All you need to do is to set up a "norm" or "average," then convince your subject he does not measure up. A psychologist wanted to find out how feelings of inferiority affected ability to solve problems. He gave his students a set of routine tests. "But then he solemnly announced that the *average person* could complete the test in about one-fifth the time it would really take. When in the course of the test a bell would ring, indicating that the 'average man's time' was up, some of the brightest subjects became very jittery and incompetent indeed, thinking themselves to be morons." ("What's On Your Mind?", *Science Digest,* Feb. 1952.)

Stop measuring yourself against "their" standards. You are not "them" and can never measure up. Neither can "they" measure up to yours—nor should they. Once you see this simple, rather self-evident truth, accept it and believe it, your inferior feelings will vanish.

Dr. Norton L. Williams, psychiatrist, addressing a medical convention, said recently that modern man's anxiety and insecurity stemmed from a lack of "self-realization," and that inner security can only be found "in finding in oneself an individuality, uniqueness and distinctiveness that is akin to the idea of being created in the image of God." He also said that self-realization is gained by "a simple belief in one's own uniqueness as a human being, a sense of deep and wide awareness of all people and all things and a feeling of constructive influencing of others through one's own personality."

HOW TO USE RELAXATION TO DEHYPNOTIZE YOURSELF

Physical relaxation plays a key role in the dehypnotization process. Our currently held beliefs, whether good or bad, true or false, were formed *without effort,* with no sense of strain, and without the exercise of "will power." Our habits, whether good or bad, were formed in the same way. It follows that we must employ the same process in forming new beliefs, or new habits, that is, in a relaxed condition.

It has been amply demonstrated that attempting to use effort or will power to change beliefs or to cure bad habits has an adverse, rather than a beneficial effect. Emile Coué, the little French pharmacist who astonished the world around 1920 with the results he obtained with "the power of suggestion," insisted that effort was the one big reason most people failed to utilize their inner powers. "Your suggestions (ideal goals) must be made without effort if they are to be effective," he said. Another famous Coué saying was his "Law of Reversed Effort": "When the will and the imagination are in conflict, the imagination invariably wins the day."

The late Dr. Knight Dunlap made a lifelong study of habits and learning processes and perhaps performed more experiments along this line than any other psychologist. His methods succeeded in curing such habits as nail-biting, thumb-sucking, facial tics, and more serious habits where other methods had failed. The very heart of his system was his finding that effort was the one big deterrent to either breaking a bad habit, or learning a new one. Making an effort to refrain from the habit, actually reinforced the habit, he found. His experiments proved that the best way to break a habit is to form a clear mental image of the desired end result, and to practice without effort toward reaching that goal. Dunlap found that either "positive practice" (refraining from the habit) or "negative practice" (performing the habit consciously and voluntarily), would have beneficial effect provided the desired end result was kept constantly in mind.

"If a response habit is to be learned, or if a response pattern is to be made habitual," he said, "it is essential that the learner *shall have an idea* of the response that *is to be achieved* or *shall have an idea* of the change in the environment that the response will produce . . . The important factor in learning, in short, is the thought of an objective to be attained, either as a specific behavior pattern or as the result of the behavior, together with a desire for the attainment of the object." (Knight Dunlap, *Personal Adjustment,* McGraw-Hill Book Company, New York.)

In many cases, the mere relaxation of effort, or too much conscious straining, is in itself enough to eradicate the negative behavior pattern. Dr. James S. Greene, founder of the National Hospital for Speech Disorders, New York City, had a motto: "When they can relax, they can talk." Dr. Matthew N. Chappell has pointed out that often the effort or "will power" used to fight against or resist worry, is the very thing that perpetuates worry and keeps it going. (Matthew N. Chappell, *How to Control Worry,* New York, Permabooks.)

Physical relaxation, when practiced daily, brings about an accompanying "mental relaxation," and a "relaxed attitude" which enables us to better consciously control our automatic mechanism. Physical relaxation also, in itself, has a powerful influence in "dehypnotizing" us from negative attitudes and reaction patterns.

How to Use Mental Pictures to Relax

PRACTICE EXERCISE: (To be practiced for at least
30 minutes daily)

Seat yourself comfortably in an easy chair or lie down
on your back. Consciously "let go" the various muscle
groups as much as possible without making too much of
an effort of it. Just consciously pay attention to the various
parts of your body and let go a little. You will find that
you can always voluntarily relax to a certain degree. You
can stop frowning and let your forehead relax. You can
ease up a little on the tension in your jaws. You can let
your hands, your arms, your shoulders, legs, become a
little more relaxed than they are. Spend about five minutes
on this and then stop paying any attention to your muscles.
This is as far as you are going to try to go by conscious
control. From here on you will relax more and more by
using your creative mechanism to automatically bring
about a relaxed condition. In short, you are going to use
"goal pictures," held in imagination and let your automatic mechanism realize those goals for you.

Mental Picture No. 1

In your mind's eye see yourself lying stretched out upon
the bed. Form a picture of your legs as they would look
if made of concrete. See yourself lying there with two
very heavy concrete legs. See these very heavy concrete
legs sinking far down into the mattress from their sheer
weight. Now picture your arms and hands as made of
concrete. They also are very heavy and are sinking down
into the bed and exerting tremendous pressure against the
bed. In your mind's eye see a friend come into the room
and attempt to lift your heavy concrete legs. He takes
hold of your feet and attempts to lift them. But they are

too heavy for him. He cannot do it. Repeat with arms, neck, etc.

Mental Picture No. 2

Your body is a big marionette doll. Your hands are tied loosely to your wrists by strings. Your forearm is connected loosely by a string to your upper arm. Your upper arm is connected very loosely by a string to your shoulder. Your feet, calves, thighs, are also connected together with a single string. Your neck consists of one very limp string. The strings which control your jaw and hold your lips together have slackened and stretched to such an extent that your chin has dropped down loosely against your chest. All the various strings which connect the various parts of your body are loose and limp and your body is just sprawled loosely across the bed.

Mental Picture No. 3

Your body consists of a series of inflated rubber balloons. Two valves open in your feet, and the air begins to escape from your legs. Your legs begin to collapse and continue until they consist only of deflated rubber tubes, lying flat against the bed. Next a valve is opened in your chest and as the air begins to escape, your entire trunk begins to collapse limply against the bed. Continue with arms, head, and neck.

Mental Picture No. 4

Many people will find this the most relaxing of all. Just go back in memory to some relaxing and pleasant scene from your past. There is always some time in everyone's life when he felt relaxed, at ease, and at peace with the world. Pick out your own relaxing picture from your past and call up detailed memory images. Yours may be a peaceful scene at a mountain lake where you went fishing.

If so, pay particular attention to the little incidental things in the environment. Remember the quiet ripples on the water. What sounds were present? Did you hear the quiet rustling of the leaves? Maybe you remember sitting perfectly relaxed, and somewhat drowsy before an open fireplace long ago. Did the logs crackle and spark? What other sights and sounds were present? Maybe you choose to remember relaxing in the sun on a beach. How did the sand feel against your body? Could you feel the warm relaxing sun, touching your body, almost as a physical thing? Was there a breeze blowing? Were there gulls on the beach? The more of these incidental details you can remember and picture to yourself, the more successful you will be.

Daily practice will bring these mental pictures, or memories, clearer and clearer. The effect of learning will also be cumulative. Practice will strengthen the tie-in between mental image and physical sensation. You will become more and more proficient in relaxation, and this in itself will be "remembered" in future practice sessions.

Points to Remember in This Chapter
(Fill in)

1.

2.

3.

4.

5.

CASE HISTORY:

CHAPTER FIVE

How to Utilize
The Power of Rational Thinking

MANY of my patients are plainly disappointed when I. prescribe something as simple as using their God-given power of reason as a method of changing negative beliefs and behavior. To some, it seems incredibly naïve and unscientific. Yet, it does have one advantage—it works. And as we shall see later, it is based upon sound scientific findings.

There is a widely accepted fallacy that rational, logical, conscious thinking has no power over unconscious processes or mechanisms, and that to change negative beliefs, feelings or behavior, it is necessary to dig down and dredge up material from the "unconscious."

Your automatic mechanism, or what the Freudians call the "unconscious," is absolutely impersonal. It operates as a machine and has no "will" of its own. It always tries to react appropriately to your current beliefs and interpretations concerning environment. It always seeks to give you appropriate feelings, and to accomplish the goals which you consciously determine upon. It works only upon the data which you feed it in the form of ideas, beliefs, interpretations, opinions.

It is *conscious thinking* which is the "control knob" of your unconscious machine. It was by conscious thought, though perhaps irrational and unrealistic, that the unconscious machine developed its negative and inappropriate reaction patterns, and it is by conscious rational thought that the automatic reaction patterns can be changed.

The late Dr. John A. Schindler, of the famous Monroe Clinic, Monroe, Wisconsin, won nation-wide fame for his outstanding success in helping unhappy, neurotic people regain the joy of living and return to productive, happy lives. His percentage of cures far exceeded that of psycho-analysis. One of the keys to his method of treatment was what he called "conscious thought control." ". . . Regardless of the omissions and commissions of the past," he said, "a person has to start in the present to acquire some maturity so that the future may be better than the past. The present and the future depend on learning new habits and new ways of looking at old problems. There simply isn't any future in digging continually into the past . . . the underlying emotional problem has the same common denominator in every patient. This common denominator is that the patient has forgotten how, or probably never learned how, to control his *present thinking* to produce enjoyment." (John A. Schindler, *How To Live 365 Days a Year,* Englewood Cliffs, N.J., Prentice-Hall, Inc.)

Let Sleeping Dogs Lie

The fact that there are "buried" in the unconscious, memories of past failures, unpleasant and painful experiences, does not mean that these must be "dug out," exposed or examined, in order to effect personality changes. As we have pointed out earlier, all skill learning is accomplished by trial and *error,* by making a trial, missing the mark, consciously remembering the degree of error, and making correction on the next trial—until finally a "hit," or successful attempt is accomplished. The successful reaction pattern is then remembered, or recalled, and "imitated" on future trials. This is true for a man learning to pitch horseshoes, throw darts, sing, drive a car, play golf, get along socially with other human beings, or any other skill. It is also true of a "mechanical rat," learning its way through a maze. Thus, all servo-mechanisms, by their very nature contain "memories" of past errors, failures, painful and negative experiences. These negative experiences do not inhibit, but *contribute to* the learning process, as long as they are used properly as "negative feedback data," and are seen as deviations from the positive goal which is desired.

However, as soon as the error has been recognized as such, and correction of course made, it is equally important that the *error be consciously forgotten,* and the successful attempt remembered and "dwelt upon."

These memories of past failures do no harm as long as our conscious thought and attention is focused upon the positive goal to be accomplished. Therefore, it is best to let these sleeping dogs lie.

Our errors, mistakes, failures, and sometimes even our humiliations, were necessary steps in the learning process. However, they were meant to be means to an end—and not an end in themselves. When they have served their purpose, they *should be forgotten.* If we consciously dwell upon the error, or consciously feel guilty about the error, and keep berating ourselves because of it, then—unwittingly—the error or failure itself becomes the "goal" which is consciously held in imagination and memory. The unhappiest of mortals is that man who insists upon reliving the past, over and over in imagination—continually criticising himself for past mistakes—continually condemning himself for past sins.

I shall never forget one of my women patients who tortured herself with her unhappy past, so much so that she destroyed any chance for happiness in the present. She had lived for years in bitterness and resentment, as a direct result of a serious harelip that caused her to shun people, and to develop over the years a personality that was stunted, crabby, and completely turned against the world and everything in it. She had no friends because she imagined that no one would be friendly with a person who looked so "awful." She deliberately avoided people, or, what was worse. consistently alienated people with her sour, defensive attitude. Surgery cured her physical problem. She tried to make the adjustment and to begin living with people in harmony and friendliness. but found that her past experiences kept getting in the way. She felt that, despite her new appearance, she could not make friends and be happy because no one would forgive her for what she had been before the operation. She wound up making the same mistakes she had made before and was as unhappy as ever. She did not really begin to live until she learned to stop condemning herself for what she had been in the past and to stop reliving in her imagination all the unhappy events that had brought her to my office for surgery.

Continually criticising yourself for past mistakes and errors does not help matters, but on the other hand tends to perpetuate the very behavior you would change. Memories of past failures *can* adversely affect present performance. if we dwell upon them and foolishly conclude —"I failed yesterday—therefore it follows that I will fail again today." However, this does not "prove" that unconscious reaction patterns have any power in themselves to repeat and perpetuate themselves, or that all buried memories of failure must be "eradicated" before behavior can be changed. If we are victimized. it is by our conscious, thinking mind and not by the "unconscious." For it is with the thinking part of our personality that we draw conclusions. and select the "goal images" that we shall concentrate upon. The minute that we *change our minds,* and stop giving power to the past, the past with its mistakes loses power over us.

Ignore Past Failures and Forge Ahead

Here again. hypnosis furnishes convincing proof. When a shy, timid wallflower is told in hypnosis. and *believes or "thinks"* that he is a bold, self-confident orator, his reaction patterns are changed *instantly.* He currently acts as he currently believes. His attention is given over completely to the positive desired goal—and no thought or consideration whatsoever is given to past failures.

Dorothea Brande tells in her charming book, *Wake Up and Live,* how this one idea enabled her to become more productive and successful as a writer, and to draw upon talents and abilities she never knew she had. She had been both curious and amazed after witnessing a demonstration in hypnosis. Then she happened to read one sentence written by psychologist F. M. H. Myers which she says changed her whole life. The sentence by Myers explained that the talents and abilities displayed by hypnotic subjects were due to a "purgation of memory" of past failures, while in the hypnotic state. If this were possible under hypnosis, Miss Brande asked herself—if ordinary people carried around within themselves talents, abilities, powers, which were held in and not used merely because of memories of past failures—why couldn't a person in the wakeful state use these same powers by ignoring past failures and "acting as if it were impossible to fail?" She determined to try it. She would act on the assumption that the powers and abilities were there—and that she could use them—if only she would go ahead and "ACT AS IF"—instead of in a tentative half-hearted way. Within a year her production as a writer had increased many times. So had her sales. A rather surprising result was that she discovered a talent for public speaking, became much in demand as a lecturer—and enjoyed it, whereas previously she had not only shown no talent for lecturing, but disliked it intensely.

Bertrand Russell's Method

In his book *The Conquest of Happiness,* Bertrand Russell says, "I was not born happy. As a child, my favorite hymn was: 'Weary of earth and laden with sin.' . . . In adolescence, I hated life and was continually on the verge of suicide, from which, however, I was restrained by the desire to know more mathematics. Now, on the contrary, I enjoy life; I might almost say that with every year that passes I enjoy it more . . . very largely it is due to diminishing preoccupation with myself. Like others who had a Puritan education, I had a habit of meditating on my sins, follies, and shortcomings. I seemed to myself—no doubt justly—a miserable specimen. Gradually I learned to be indifferent to myself and my deficiencies; I came to center my attention upon external objects: the state of the world, various branches of knowledge, individuals for whom I felt affection." (Bertrand Russell, *The Conquest of Happiness,* New York, Liveright Publishing Corporation.)

In the same book, he describes his method for changing automatic reaction patterns based upon false beliefs. "It is quite possible to overcome infantile suggestions of the unconscious, and even to change the contents of the unconscious, by employing the right kind of technique. Whenever you begin to feel remorse for an act which your reason tells you is not wicked, examine the causes of your feeling of remorse, and convince yourself in detail of their absurdity. Let your conscious beliefs be so vivid and emphatic that they make an impression upon your unconscious strong enough to cope with the impressions made by your nurse or your mother when you were an infant. Do not be content with an alteration between moments of rationality and moments of irrationality. Look into the irrationality closely with a determination not to respect it and not to let it dominate you. When it thrusts foolish thoughts or feelings into your consciousness, pull them up by the roots, examine them, and reject them. Do not allow yourself to remain a vacillating creature, swayed half by reason and half by infantile folly. . . .

"But if the rebellion is to be successful in bringing individual happiness and in enabling a man to live consistently by one standard, not to vacillate between two, it is necessary that he should think and feel deeply about what his reason tells him. Most men, when they have thrown off superficially the superstitions of their childhood, think that there is no more to be done. They do not realize that these superstitions are still lurking underground. When a rational conviction has been arrived at, it is necessary to dwell upon it, to follow out its consequences, to search out in oneself whatever beliefs inconsistent with the new conviction might otherwise survive. . . . What I suggest is that a man should make up his mind with emphasis as to what he rationally believes, and should never allow contrary irrational beliefs to pass unchallenged or obtain a hold over him, however brief. This is a question of reasoning with himself in those moments in which he is tempted to become infantile, but the reasoning, if it is sufficiently emphatic, may be very brief."

Ideas Are Changed, Not by "Will," But by Other Ideas

It can be seen that Bertrand Russell's technique of searching out ideas which are inconsistent with some deeply felt conviction, is essentially the same as the method tested clinically with such amazing success by Prescott Lecky. Lecky's method consisted of getting the subject to "see" that some negative concept of his was *inconsistent* with some other deeply held belief. Lecky believed that it was inherent in the very nature of "mind" itself, that all ideas and concepts which make up the total content of "personality" must *seem to be* consistent with each other. If the inconsistency of a given idea is consciously recognized, *it must be rejected.*

One of my patients was a salesman who was "scared to death" when calling upon "big shots." His fear and nervousness were overcome in just one counselling session, during which I asked him, "Would you physically get down on all fours and crawl into the man's office, prostrating yourself before a superior personage?"

"I should say not!" he bristled.

"Then, why do you mentally cringe and crawl?"

Another question: "Would you go into a man's office

with your hand out like a beggar, and beg for a dime for a cup of coffee?"

"Certainly not."

"Can't you see that you are doing essentially the same thing, when you go in overly concerned with whether or not he will approve of you? Can't you see that you have your hand out—literally begging for his approval and acceptance of you as a person?"

Lecky found that there were two powerful "levers" for changing beliefs and concepts. There are "standard" convictions which are strongly held by nearly everyone. These are (1) the feeling or belief that one is capable of doing his share, holding up his end of the log, exerting a certain amount of independence and (2) the belief that there is "something" inside you which should not be allowed to suffer indignities.

Examine and Re-evaluate Your Beliefs

One of the reasons that the power of rational thinking goes unrecognized is that it is so seldom used.

Trace down the belief about yourself, or the belief about the world, or other people, which is behind your negative behavior. Does "something always happen" to cause you to miss out just when success seems within your grasp? Perhaps you secretly feel "unworthy" of success or that you do not deserve it. Are you ill at ease around other people? Perhaps you believe you are inferior to them, or that other people per se are hostile and unfriendly. Do you become anxious and fearful for no good reason in a situation that is relatively safe? Perhaps you believe that the world you live in is a hostile, unfriendly, dangerous place, or that you "deserve punishment."

Remember that both behavior and feeling spring from belief. To root out the belief which is responsible for your feeling and behavior—ask yourself, "why?" Is there some task which you would like to do, some channel in which you would like to express yourself, but you hang back feeling that "I can't"? Ask yourself "WHY?"

"Why do I believe that I can't?"

Then ask yourself—"Is this belief based upon an actual fact—or upon an assumption—or a false conclusion?"

Then ask yourself the questions:

1. Is there any rational reason for such a belief?
2. Could it be that I am mistaken in this belief?
3. Would I come to the same conclusion about some other person in a similar situation?
4. Why should I continue to act and feel as if this were true if there is no good reason to believe it?

Don't just pass these questions by casually. Wrestle with them. Think *hard* on them. Get emotional about them. Can you see that you have cheated yourself and sold yourself short—not because of a "fact"—but only because of some stupid belief? If so, try to arouse some indignation, or even anger. Indignation and anger can sometimes act as liberators from false ideas. Alfred Adler "got mad" at himself and at his teacher and was enabled to throw off a negative definition of himself. This experience is not uncommon.

An old farmer said he quit tobacco for good one day when he discovered he had left his tobacco home and started to walk the two miles for it. On the way, he "saw" that he was being "used" in a humiliating way by a habit. He got mad, turned around, went back to the field, and never smoked again.

Clarence Darrow, the famous attorney, said his success started the day that he "got mad" when he attempted to secure a mortgage for $2,000 to buy a house. Just as the transaction was about to be completed, the lendor's wife spoke up and said, "Don't be a fool—he will never make enough money to pay it off." Darrow himself had had serious doubts about the same thing. But "something happened" when he heard her remark. He became indignant

—both at the woman and at himself, and determined he would be a success.

A businessman friend of mine had a very similar experience. A failure at 40, he continually worried about "how things would come out," about his own inadequacies, and whether or not he would be able to complete each business venture. Fearful and anxious, he was attempting to purchase some machinery on credit, when the man's wife objected. She did not believe he would ever be able to pay for it. At first his hopes were dashed. But then he became indignant. Who was he to be pushed around like that? Who was he to skulk through the world, continually fearful of failure? The experience awakened "something" within him—some "new self"—and at once he saw that this woman's remark, as well as his own opinions of himself, were an affront to this "something." He had no money, no credit, and no "way" to accomplish what he wanted. But he found a way—and within three years was more successful than he had ever dreamed of being—not in one business, but in three.

The Power of Deep Desire

Rational thought, to be effective in changing belief and behavior, must be accompanied by deep feeling and desire.

Picture to yourself what you would like to be and have, and assume for the moment that such things might be possible. Arouse a deep desire for these things. Become enthusiastic about them. Dwell upon them—and keep going over them in your mind. Your present negative beliefs were formed by thought plus feelings. Generate enough emotion, or deep feeling, and your new thoughts and ideas will cancel them out.

If you will analyze this you will see that you are using a process you have often used before—worry! The only difference is you change your goals from negative to positive. When you worry, you first of all picture some undesirable future outcome, or goal, very vividly in your imagination. You use no effort or will power. But you keep dwelling upon the "end result." You keep thinking about it—dwelling upon it—picturing it to yourself as a "possibility." You play with the idea that it "might happen."

This constant repetition, and thinking in terms of "possibilities," makes the end result appear more and more "real" to you. After a time, appropriate emotions are automatically generated—fear, anxiety, discouragement—all these are appropriate to the undesirable end result you are worrying about. Now change the "goal picture"—and you can as easily generate "good emotions." Constantly picturing to yourself, and dwelling upon a desirable end result will also make the possibility seem more real—and again appropriate emotions of enthusiasm, cheerfulness, encouragement, and happiness will automatically be generated. "In forming 'good' emotional habits, and in breaking 'bad' ones," said Dr. Knight Dunlap, "we have to deal primarily with thought and thought habits. 'As a man thinketh in his heart so is he.' "

What Rational Thought Can and Cannot Do

Remember that your automatic mechanism can as easily function as a "Failure Mechansim" as a "Success Mechanism," depending upon the data you give it to process, and the goals you set for it. It is basically a goal-striving mechanism. The goals it works upon are up to you. Many of us unconsciously and unwittingly, by holding negative attitudes and habitually picturing failure to ourselves in our imagination—set up goals of failure.

Also remember that your automatic mechanism does not reason about, nor question, the data you feed it. It merely processes it and reacts appropriately to it.

It is very important that the automatic mechanism be given true facts concerning the environment. This is the job of conscious rational thought: *to know the truth,* to form correct evaluations, *estimations,* opinions. In this connection most of us are prone to under-estimate ourselves and over-estimate the nature of the difficulty facing us. "Always think of what you have to do as easy and it will become so," said Emile Coué. "I have made extensive experiments to discover the common causes of that conscious effort which freezes the thinking mind," says psychologist Daniel W. Josselyn. "Practically always it seems to be due to the tendency to exaggerate the difficulty and importance of your mental labors, to take them too seriously and fear they will find you incapable. People who are eloquent in casual conversation become imbeciles when they mount the speaker's platform. You simply must learn that if you can interest the neighbor you can interest all the neighbors, or the world, and not be frozen by magnitudes." (Daniel W. Josselyn: *Why Be Tired?* New York, Longmans, Green & Co., Inc.)

You Never Know Until You Try

It is the job of rational, conscious thought to examine and analyze incoming messages, to accept those which are true and reject those which are untrue. Many people are bowled over by the chance remark of a friend—"You do not look so well this morning." If they are rejected or snubbed by someone, they blindly "swallow" the "fact" that this means they are an inferior person. Most of us are subjected to negative suggestions every day. If our conscious mind is working and on the job, we do not have to accept them blindly. "It ain't necessarily so," is a good motto.

It is the job of the conscious rational mind to form logical and correct conclusions. "I failed once in the past, so I will probably fail in the future," is neither logical nor rational. To conclude "I can't" in advance, without trying, and in the absence of any evidence to the contrary, is not rational. We should be more like the man who was asked if he could play the piano. "I don't know," he said.

"What do you mean you don't know?" "I have never tried."

Decide What You Want—Not What You Don't Want

It is the job of conscious rational thought to decide what you want, select the goals you wish to achieve—and concentrate upon these rather than upon what you do not want. To spend time and effort concentrating upon what you do not want is not rational. When President Eisenhower was General Eisenhower in World War II he was asked what would have been the effect upon the allied cause, if the invasion troops had been thrown back into the sea from the beaches of Italy. "It would have been very bad," he said, "but I never allow my mind to think in that way."

Keep Your Eye on the Ball

It is the job of your conscious mind to pay *strict attention* to the task at hand, to what you are doing and what is going on around you so that these incoming sensory messages can keep your automatic mechanism currently advised of the environment and allow it to respond spontaneously. In baseball parlance you must "keep your eye on the ball."

It is *not* the job of your conscious rational mind, however, to create or to "do" the job at hand. We get into trouble when we either neglect to use conscious thinking in the way that it is meant to be used, or when we attempt to use it in a way that it was never meant to be used. We cannot squeeze creative thought out of the Creative Mechanism by making conscious effort. We cannot "do" the job to be done by making strained conscious efforts. And because we try and cannot, we become concerned, anxious, frustrated. The automatic mechanism is unconscious. We cannot see the wheels turning. We cannot know what is taking place beneath the surface. And because it works spontaneously in reacting to present and current needs, we can have no intimation or certified guarantee in advance that it will come up with the answer. We are forced into a position of trust. And only by trusting and acting do we receive signs and wonders. In short, conscious rational thought selects the goal, gathers information, concludes, evaluates, estimates and starts the wheels in motion. *It is not, however, responsible for results*. We must learn to do our work, act upon the best assumptions available, and *leave results to take care of themselves*.

Points to Remember
(Fill in)

1.
2.
3.
4.
5.

CASE HISTORY:

CHAPTER SIX

Relax and Let Your
Success Mechanism Work for You

"STRESS" has recently become a popular word in our language. We speak of this as the age of stress. Worry, anxiety, insomnia, stomach ulcers have become accepted as a necessary part of the world in which we live.

Yet, I am convinced that it does not have to be that way.

We could relieve ourselves of a vast load of care, anxiety and worry, if we could but recognize the simple truth, that our Creator made ample provisions for us to live successfully in this or any other age by providing us with a built-in creative mechanism.

Our trouble is that we ignore the automatic creative mechanism and try to do everything and solve all our problems by conscious thought, or "forebrain thinking."

The forebrain is comparable to the "operator" of an electronic brain, or any other type of servo-mechanism. It is with the forebrain that we think "I," and feel our sense of identity. It is with the forebrain that we exercise imagination, or set goals. We use the forebrain to gather information, make observations, evaluate incoming sense-data, form judgments.

But the forebrain cannot create. It cannot "do" the job to be done, any more than the operator of an electronic brain can "do" the work.

It is the job of the forebrain to pose problems and to

identify them—but by its very nature it was never engineered to solve problems.

Don't Be Too Careful

Yet that is precisely what modern man tries to do—solve all his problems by conscious thought.

Jesus told us that a man cannot add one cubit to his stature by "taking thought." Today Dr. Wiener tells us that man cannot even perform such a simple operation as picking up a cigarette from a table by conscious thought or "will."

Because modern man does depend almost entirely upon his forebrain he becomes too careful, too anxious, and too fearful of "results," and the advice of Jesus to "take no thought for the morrow," or of St. Paul to be "careful in nothing," is regarded as impractical nonsense.

Yet, this is precisely the advice that William James, dean of American psychologists, gave us years ago, if we would but have listened to him. In his little essay "The Gospel of Relaxation," he said that modern man was too tense, too concerned for results, too anxious (this was in 1899), and that there was a better and easier way. "If we wish our trains of ideation and volition to be copious and varied and effective, we must form the habit of freeing them from the inhibitive influence of reflection upon them, of egoistic preoccupation about their results. Such a habit, like other habits, can be formed. Prudence and duty and self-regard, emotions of ambition and emotions of anxiety, have, of course, a needful part to play in our lives. But confine them as far as possible to the occasions when you are making your general resolutions and deciding on your plans of campaign, and keep them out of the details. *When once a decision is reached and execution is the order of the day,* dismiss absolutely all responsibility and care about the outcome. Unclamp, in a word, your intellectual and practical machinery, and let it run free; and the service it will do you will be twice as good." (William James, *On Vital Reserves,* New York, Henry Holt and Co., Inc.)

Victory by Surrender

Later, in his famous Gifford Lectures, James cited example after example of persons who had tried unsuccessfully for years to rid themselves of anxieties, worries, inferiorities, guilt feelings, by making conscious efforts, only to find that success finally came when they gave up the struggle consciously, and stopped trying to solve their problems by conscious thought. "Under these circumstances," said James, "the way to success, as vouched for by innumerable authentic personal narrations, is by . . . surrender . . . passivity, not activity—relaxation, not intentness, should be now the rule. Give up the feeling of responsibility, let go your hold, resign the care of your destiny to higher powers, be genuinely indifferent as to what becomes of it all. . . . It is but giving your private convulsive self a rest, and finding that a greater Self is there. The results, slow or sudden, or great or small, of the combined optimism and expectancy, the regenerative phenomena which ensue on the abandonment of effort, remain firm facts of human nature." (William James, *The Varieties of Religious Experience,* New York, Longmans, Green and Company.)

The Secret of Creative Thinking and Creative Doing

Proof of the fact that what we have been saying is true can be seen in the experience of writers, inventors, and other creative workers. Invariably, they tell us that creative ideas are not consciously thought out by forebrain thinking, but come automatically, spontaneously, and somewhat like a bolt out of the blue, when the conscious mind has let go of the problem and is engaged in thinking of something else. These creative ideas do not come willy-nilly without some preliminary conscious thought about the problem. All the evidence points to the conclusion that in order to receive an "inspiration" or a "hunch," the person must first of all be intensely interested in solving a particular problem, or securing a particular answer. He must think about it consciously, gather all the information he can on the subject, consider all the possible courses of action. And above all, he must have a burning desire to solve the problem. But, after he has defined the problem, sees in his imagination the desired end result, secured all the information and facts that he can, then additional struggling, fretting and worrying over it do not help, but seem to hinder the solution.

Fehr, the famous French scientist, said that practically all his good ideas came to him when not actively engaged in work on a problem and that most of the discoveries of his contemporaries were made when they were away from their work bench, so to speak.

It is well known that when Thomas A. Edison was stymied by a problem, he would lie down and take a short nap.

Charles Darwin, telling how an intuitional flash came to him suddenly, after months of conscious thinking had failed to give him the ideas he needed for *The Origin of Species,* wrote, "I can remember the very spot in the road, whilst in my carriage, when to my joy the solution occurred to me."

Lenox Riley Lohr, former president of the National Broadcasting Company, once wrote an article telling how ideas which had helped him in business, came to him. "Ideas, I find, come most readily when you are doing something that keeps the mind alert without putting too much strain upon it. Shaving, driving a car, sawing a plank, or fishing or hunting, for instance. Or engaging with some friend in stimulating conversation. Some of my best ideas came from information picked up casually and entirely unrelated to my work." ("Anyone Can Be an Idea Man," the *American Magazine,* March, 1940.)

C. G. Suits, the Chief of Research at General Electric, said that nearly all the discoveries in research laboratories came as hunches during a period of relaxation, following a period of intensive thinking and fact-gathering.

Bertrand Russell said, "I have found, for example, that, if I have to write upon some rather difficult topic, the best plan is to think about it with very great intensity—the greatest intensity of which I am capable—for a few hours or days, and at the end of that time give orders, so to speak, that the work is to proceed underground. After some months I return consciously to the topic and find that the work has been done. Before I had discovered this technique, I used to spend the intervening months worrying because I was making no progress; I arrived at the solution none the sooner for this worry, and the intervening months were wasted, whereas now I can devote them to other pursuits." (Bertrand Russell, *The Conquest of Happiness,* New York, Liveright Publishing Corporation.)

You Are a "Creative Worker"

The mistake we make is assuming that this process of "unconscious cerebration" is reserved for writers, inventors and "creative workers." We are all creative workers, whether we are housewives working in a kitchen, school teachers, students, salesmen or businessmen. We all have the same "success mechanism" within us, and it will work in solving personal problems, running a business, or selling goods, just as it will in writing a story or inventing. Bertrand Russell recommended that the same method he used in his writing be employed by his readers in solving their mundane personal problems. Dr. J. B. Rhine of Duke University has said that he is inclined to think that what we call "genius" is a process; a natural way in which the human mind works to solve any problem. but that we mistakenly apply the term "genius" only when the process is used to write a book or paint a picture.

The Secret of "Natural" Behavior and Skill

The Success Mechanism within you can work in the same way to produce "creative doing" as it does to produce "creative ideas." Skill in any performance, whether it be in sports. in playing the piano, in conversation, or in selling merchandise, consists not in painfully and consciously thinking out each action as it is performed, but in relaxing. and letting the job do itself through you. Creative performance is spontaneous and "natural" as opposed to self-conscious and studied. The most skilled pianist in the world could never play a simple composition if he tried to consciously think out just which finger should strike which key—*while he was playing.* He has given conscious thought to this matter previously—while learning, and has practiced until his actions become automatic and habit-like. He was able to become a skilled performer only when he reached the point where he could cease conscious effort and turn the matter of playing over to the unconscious habit mechanism which is a part of the Success Mechanism.

Don't Jam Your Creative Machinery

Conscious effort inhibits and "jams" the automatic creative mechanism. The reason some people are self-conscious and awkward in social situations is simply that they are too consciously concerned, too anxious, to do the right thing. They are painfully conscious of every move they make. Every action is "thought-out." Every word spoken is calculated for its effect. We speak of such persons as "inhibited," and rightly so. But it would be more true were we to say that the "person" is not inhibited;

but that the person has "inhibited" his own creative mechanism. If these people could "let go," stop trying, not care, and give no thought to the matter of their behavior, they could act creatively, spontaneously, and "be themselves."

FIVE RULES FOR FREEING YOUR CREATIVE MACHINERY

1. *"Do your worrying before you place your bet, not after the wheel starts turning."*

I am indebted to a business executive, whose weakness was roulette, for the above expression which "worked like magic" in helping him overcome worry, and at the same time function more creatively and successfully. I happened to quote to him the advice of William James, mentioned earlier, to the effect that emotions of anxiety have their place in planning and deciding upon a course of action, but that, "When once a decision is reached and execution is the order of the day, dismiss absolutely all responsibility and care about the outcome. Unclamp, in a word, your intellectual and practical machinery, and let it run free."

Several weeks later he burst into my office as enthusiastic over his "discovery" as a schoolboy who has discovered his first love. "It hit me all of a sudden," he said, "during a visit to Las Vegas. I've been trying it and it works."

"What hit you and what works?" I asked.

"That advice of William James. It didn't make too much of an impression when you told me, but while I was playing roulette it came back to me. I noticed any number of people who appeared not to worry at all before placing their bets. Apparently the odds meant nothing to them. But once the wheel started turning, they froze up, and began to worry whether their number would come up or not. How silly, I thought. If they want to worry, or be concerned, or figure odds, the time to do that is *before* the decision is made to place a bet. There is something you can do about it then, by thinking about it. You can figure out the best odds possible, or decide not to take the risk at all. But after the bets are placed and the wheel starts turning—you might as well relax and enjoy it—thinking about it is not going to do one bit of good, and is wasted energy.

"Then I got to thinking that I myself had been doing exactly the same thing in my business and in my personal life. I often made decisions or embarked upon courses of action, without adequate preparation, without considering all the risks involved, and the best possible alternative. But after I had set the wheels in motion, so to speak, I continually worried over how it would come out, whether I had done the right thing. I made a decision right then that in the future I would do all my worrying, all my fore-brain thinking, *before* a decision was made, and that after making a decision, and setting the wheels in motion, I would 'dismiss absolutely all care or responsibility about the outcome.' Believe it or not, it works. I not only feel better, sleep better, and work better, but my business is running much smoother.

"I also discovered that the same principle works in a hundred different little personal ways. For example, I used to worry and fume about having to go to the dentist, and other unpleasant tasks. Then I said to myself, 'This is silly. You know the unpleasantness involved before you make the decision to go. If the unpleasantness is all *that* important to cause so much concern, and not worth the worry involved, you can simply decide not to go. But, if the decision is that the trip is worth a little unpleasantness, and a definite decision is made to go—then forget about it. Consider the risk before the wheel starts turning.' I used to worry the night before I had to make a speech at a board meeting. Then I said to myself, 'I'm either going to make the speech or I'm not. If the decision is to make it, then there's no need in considering not making it

—or trying to mentally run away from it.' I have discovered that much nervousness and anxiety is caused by mentally trying to escape or run away from something that you have decided to go through with physically. If the decision is made to go through with it—not to run away physically—why mentally keep considering or hoping for escape. I used to detest social gatherings and go along only to please my wife, or for business reasons. I went, but mentally I resisted it, and was usually pretty grumpy and uncommunicative. Then I decided that if the decision was to go along physically, I might as well go along mentally—and dismiss all thought of resistance. Last night I not only went to what I would formerly have called a stupid social gathering, but I was surprised to find myself thoroughly enjoying it."

2. *Form the habit of consciously responding to the present moment.*

Consciously practice the habit of "taking no anxious thought for tomorrow," by *giving all your attention to the present moment.*

Your creative mechanism cannot function or work tomorrow. It can only function in the present—today. Make long range plans for tomorrow. But don't try to *live* in tomorrow, or in the past. Creative living means *responding* and *reacting* to environment spontaneously. Your creative mechanism can respond appropriately and successfully to present environment—only if you have your full attention upon present environment—and give it information concerning what is happening now. Plan all you want for the future. Prepare for it. But don't worry about *how you will react* tomorrow, or even five minutes from now. Your creative mechanism will react appropriately in the "now" if you pay attention to what is happening now. It will do the same tomorrow. It cannot react successfully to what *may* happen—but to what *is* happening.

Live in Daytight Compartments

Dr. William Osler said that this simple habit, which could be formed like any other habit, was the sole secret of his happiness and success in life. Live life in "day-tight compartments," he advised his students. Look neither forward nor backward beyond a 24-hour cycle. Live today as best you can. By living today well you do the most within your power to make tomorrow better. If you have not read his excellent little essay, "A Way of Life," in which he describes the advantages of this habit, I urge you to do so. (William Osler, *A Way of Life,* Harper & Brothers, New York.)

William James, commenting upon this same philosophy as a cardinal principle of both psychology and religion for curing worry, said, "Of Saint Catherine of Genoa it is said that 'she took cognizance of things, only as they were presented to her in succession, moment by moment.' To her holy soul, the divine moment was the present moment . . . and when the present moment was estimated in itself and in its relations, and when the duty that was involved in it was accomplished, it was permitted to pass away as if it had never been, and to give way to the faces and duties of the moment which came after."

Alcoholics Anonymous uses the same principle when they say, "Don't try to stop drinking forever—merely say, 'I will not drink today.' "

Stop—Look—and Listen!

Practice becoming more consciously aware of your present environment. What sights, sounds, odors are present in your environment *right now* that you are not conscious of?

Consciously practice *looking* and *listening.* Become alert to the feel of objects. How long since you have really felt the pavement beneath your feet as you walk? The American Indian and the early pioneers had to be alert to the sights and sounds and feels in their environment in order to survive. So does modern man, but for a different reason: Not because of physical dangers, but because of the dangers of "nervous disorders" which come from confused thinking, from failure to live creatively and spontaneously, and to respond appropriately to environment.

This becoming more aware of what is happening *now*, and attempting to respond *only* to what is happening now, has almost magical results in relieving the "jitters." The next time you feel yourself tensing up, becoming jittery and nervous—pull yourself up short and say, "What is there *here* and *now* that I should respond to? that I can *do something* about?" A great deal of nervousness is caused from unwittingly "trying" to do something that cannot be done here or now. You are geared for action or for "doing" which cannot take place.

Keep constantly in mind that the job of your creative mechanism is to respond appropriately to *present environment*—here and now. Many times, if we do not "stop and think" about this, we continue to react automatically to some past environment. We do not react to the present moment, and the present situation, but to some similar event out of the past. In short we do not react to reality —but to a fiction. Full recognition of this, and realization of what you're doing, can frequently bring about an amazingly quick "cure."

Don't Fight Strawmen out of the Past

For example, a patient of mine became jittery and anxious in business meetings, theaters, church, or in any formal gathering. "Groups of people" were the common denominator. Without realizing it, he was attempting to react to some environment out of his past where "groups of people" were a significant factor. He remembered that when a child in elementary school, he had wet his pants, and a cruel teacher had called him up in front of the class and humiliated him. He reacted with feelings of humiliation and shame. Now, one factor in the situation —"groups of people"—was reacted to as if it were the entire past situation. When he was able to "see" that he was "acting as if" he were a 10-year-old schoolboy, as if every gathering was an elementary school class, and as if every group leader was the cruel school teacher, his anxiety disappeared.

Other typical examples are the woman who responds to every man she meets "as if" he were some individual man out of her past; the man who reacts to every person in authority "as if" he were some individual authority out of his past.

3. *Try to do only one thing at a time.*

Another cause of confusion, and the resulting feelings of nervousness, hurry, and anxiety, is the absurd habit of trying to do many things at one time. The student studies and watches TV simultaneously. The businessman, instead of concentrating upon and only trying to "do" the one letter that he is presently dictating, is thinking in the back of his mind of all the things he *should* accomplish today, or perhaps this week, and unconsciously trying mentally to accomplish them all at once. The habit is particularly insidious because it is seldom recognized for what it is. When we feel jittery, or worried, or anxious in thinking of the great amount of work that lies before us, the jittery feelings are not caused by the work, but by our mental attitude—which is "I ought to be able to do this all at once." We become nervous because we are trying to do the impossible, and thereby making futility and frustration inevitable. The truth is: We can only "do" one thing at a time. Realizing this, fully convincing ourselves of this simple and obvious truth, enables us to mentally stop trying to "do" the things that lie "next," and to concentrate all our awareness, all our responsiveness, on this one thing we are doing now. When we work with this attitude, we are relaxed, we are free from the feelings of hurry and anxiety, and we are *able to concentrate* and think at our best.

The Lesson of the Hourglass

Dr. James Gordon Gilkey preached a sermon in 1944 called "Gaining Emotional Poise," which was reprinted in *Reader's Digest* and became a classic almost overnight. He had found, through many years of counselling, that one of the main causes of breakdown, worry, and all sorts of other personal problems, was this bad mental habit of feeling that you should be doing many things now. Looking at the hourglass on his desk, he had an inspiration. Just as only one grain of sand could pass through the hourglass, so could we only do one thing at a time. It is not the job, but the way we insist upon thinking of the job that causes the trouble.

Most of us feel hurried and harried, said Dr. Gilkey, because we form a false mental picture of our duties, obligations and responsibilities. There seem to be a dozen different things pressing in upon us at any given moment; a dozen different things to do; a dozen different problems to solve; a dozen different strains to endure. No matter how hurried or harried our existence may be, said Dr. Gilkey, this mental picture is entirely false. Even on the busiest day the crowded hours come to us one moment at a time; no matter how many problems, tasks or strains we face, they always come to us in *single file,* which is the only way they *can* come. To get a true mental picture, he suggested visualizing an hourglass, with the many grains of sand dropping *one by one*. This mental picture will bring emotional poise, just as the false mental picture will bring emotional unrest.

Another similar mental device which I have found very helpful to my patients is telling them: "Your success mechanism can help you do any job, perform any task, solve any problem. Think of yourself as 'feeding' jobs and problems to your success mechanism as a scientist 'feeds' a problem to an electronic brain. The 'hopper' to your success mechanism can handle only one job at a time. Just as an electronic brain cannot give the right answer if three different problems are mixed up and fed in at the same time, neither can your own success mechanism. Ease off on the pressure. Stop trying to cram into the machinery more than one job at a time."

4. *Sleep on it.*

If you have been wrestling with a problem all day without making any apparent progress, try dismissing it from your mind, and put off making a decision until you've had a chance to "sleep on it." Remember that your creative mechanism works best when there is not too much interference from your conscious "I." In sleep, the creative mechanism has an ideal opportunity to work independently of conscious interference, if you have previously started the wheels turning.

Remember the fairy story about the Shoemaker and the Elves? The shoemaker found that if he cut out the leather, and laid out the patterns before retiring, little elves came and actually put the shoes together for him while he was sleeping.

Many creative workers have used a very similar technique. Mrs. Thomas A. Edison has said that each evening her husband would go over in his mind those things which he hoped to accomplish the next day. Sometimes, he would make a list of the jobs he wanted to do, and problems which he hoped to solve.

Sir Walter Scott is reported to have said to himself, whenever his ideas would not jell, "Never mind, I shall have it at seven o'clock tomorrow morning."

V. Bechterev said, "It happened several times when I concentrated in the evening on a subject which I had put into poetic shape, that in the morning, I had only to take my pen and the words flowed, as it were, spontaneously. I had only to polish them later."

Edison's well-known "cat-naps" were far more than mere respites from fatigue. Joseph Rossman, in the *Psychology of Invention*, says, "When stumped by something, he would stretch out in his Menlo workshop and, half-dozing, get an idea from his dream mind to help him around the difficulty."

J. B. Priestley dreamed three essays, complete in every detail—"The Berkshire Beast," "The Strange Outfitter," and "The Dream."

Archbishop Temple of Canterbury has said: "All decisive thinking goes on behind the scenes; I seldom know when it takes place . . . much of it certainly during sleep." Henry Ward Beecher once preached every day for 18 months. His method? He kept a number of ideas "hatching" and each night before retiring would select an "incubating idea" and "stir it up" by thinking intensely about it. The next morning it would have fitted itself together for a sermon.

Kekule's discovery of the secret of the benzine molecule during sleep, Otto Loewi's Nobel Prize-winning discovery (that active chemicals are involved in the action of nerves), and Robert Louis Stevenson's "Brownies," which he said gave him all his plot ideas while sleeping, are all well known. Less well known is the fact that many businessmen use the same technique. For example, Henry Cobbs, who started his business in the early 1930's with a ten-dollar bill and now operates a multi-million-dollar mail order fruit business in North Miami, Florida, keeps a notebook by his bedside to jot down creative ideas immediately upon wakening.

Vic Pocker arrived in this country from Hungary with no money and unable to speak English. He got a job as a welder, went to night school to learn English, and saved his money. His savings were wiped out in the depression. But in 1932 he started a small welding shop of his own, which he called Steel Fabricators. Today that small business has grown into a profitable million-dollar firm. "I've discovered you have to make your own breaks," he says. "Sometimes in my dreams I get ideas for licking problems, and wake up all excited. Many's the time I've gotten out of bed at 2 A.M. and gone down to the shop to see if an idea would work."

5. *Relax while you work.*

Practice Exercise: In Chapter Four you learned how to induce physical and mental relaxation while resting. Continue with the daily practice in relaxation and you will become more and more proficient. In the meantime, you can induce something of "that relaxed feeling," and the relaxed attitude, while going about your daily activities, if you will form the habit of mentally *remembering* the nice relaxed feeling that you induced. Stop occasionally during the day, it need only take a moment, and *remember in detail* the sensations of relaxation. Remember how your arms felt, your legs, back, neck, face. Sometimes forming a mental picture of yourself lying in bed, or sitting relaxed and limp in an easy chair helps to recall the relaxed sensations. Mentally repeating to yourself several times, "I feel more and more relaxed," also helps. Practice this remembering faithfully several times each day. You will be surprised at how much it reduces fatigue, and how much better you are able to handle situations. For by relaxing, and maintaining a relaxed attitude, you remove those excessive states of concern, tension and anxiety, which interfere with the efficient operation of your creative mechanism. In time, your relaxed attitude will become a habit, and you will no longer need to consciously practice it.

Points to Remember
(Fill in)

1.
2.
3.
4.
5.

Case History or Example:

CHAPTER SEVEN

You Can Acquire
the Habit of Happiness

IN this chapter I want to discuss with you the subject of happiness, not from a philosophical, but from a medical standpoint. Dr. John A. Schindler's definition of happiness is, "A state of mind in which our thinking is pleasant a good share of the time." From a medical standpoint, and also from an ethical standpoint, I do not believe that simple definition can be improved upon. It is what we are talking about in this chapter.

Happiness is Good Medicine

Happiness is native to the human mind and its physical machine. We think better, perform better, feel better, and are healthier when we are happy. Even our physical sense organs work better. Russian psychologist K. Kekcheyev tested people when they were thinking pleasant and unpleasant thoughts. He found that when thinking pleasant thoughts they could see better, taste, smell and hear better, and detect finer differences in touch. Dr. William Bates proved that eyesight improves immediately when the individual is thinking pleasant thoughts, or visualizing pleasant scenes. Margaret Corbett has found that memory is greatly improved, and that the mind is relaxed, when the subject is thinking pleasant thoughts.

Psychosomatic medicine has proved that our stomachs, liver, heart, and all our internal organs function better when we are happy. Thousands of years ago wise old King Solomon said in his Proverbs: "A merry heart doeth good like a medicine, but a broken spirit drieth up the bones." It is significant, too, that both Judaism and Christianity prescribe joy, rejoicing, thankfulness, cheerfulness as a *means towards* righteousness and the good life.

Harvard psychologists studied the correlation between happiness and criminality and concluded that the old Dutch proverb, "Happy people are never wicked," was scientifically true. They found that a majority of criminals came from unhappy homes, had a history of unhappy human relationships. A ten-year study of frustration at Yale University brought out that much of what we call immorality and hostility to others is brought about by our own unhappiness. Dr. Schindler has said that unhappiness is the sole cause of all psychosomatic ills and that happiness is the only cure. The very word "disease" means a state of unhappiness—"dis-ease." A recent survey showed that by and large, optimistic, cheerful businessmen who "looked on the bright side of things" were more successful than pessimistic businessmen.

It appears that in our popular thinking about happiness we have managed to get the cart before the horse. "Be good," we say, "and you will be happy." "I would be happy," we say to ourselves, "if I could be successful and healthy." "Be kind and loving to other people and you will be happy." It might be nearer the truth if we said, "Be happy—and you will be good, more successful, healthier, feel and act more charitably towards others."

Common Misconceptions About Happiness

Happiness is not something that is earned or deserved. Happiness is not a moral issue, any more than the circulation of the blood is a moral issue. Both are necessary to health and well-being. Happiness is simply a "state of mind in which our thinking is pleasant a good share of the time." If you wait until you "deserve" to think pleasant thoughts, you are likely to think unpleasant thoughts concerning your own unworthiness. "Happiness is not the reward of virtue," said Spinoza, "but virtue itself; nor do we delight in happiness because we restrain our lusts; but, on the contrary, because we delight in it, therefore are we able to restrain them." (Spinoza, *Ethics*.)

The Pursuit of Happiness Is Not Selfish

Many sincere people are deterred from seeking happiness because they feel that it would be "selfish" or "wrong." Unselfishness does make for happiness, for it not only gets our minds directed outward away from ourselves and our introspection, our faults, sins, troubles (unpleasant thoughts), or pride in our "goodness," but it also enables us to express ourselves creatively, and fulfill ourselves in helping others. One of the most pleasant thoughts to any human being is the thought that he is needed, that he is important enough to help and add to the happiness of some other human being. However, if we make a moral issue out of happiness and conceive of it as something to be earned as a sort of reward for being unselfish, we are very apt to feel guilty about wanting happiness. Happiness comes from being and acting unselfishly—as a natural accompaniment to the *being* and *acting*, not as a "pay off" or prize. If we are rewarded for being unselfish, the next logical step is to assume that the more self-abnegating and miserable we make ourselves, the more happy we will be. The premise leads to the absurd conclusion that the way to be happy is to be unhappy.

If there is any moral issue involved it is on the side of happiness rather than unhappiness. "The attitude of unhappiness is not only painful, it is mean and ugly," says William James. "What can be more base and unworthy than the pining, puling, mumping mood, no matter by what outward ills it may have been engendered? What is more injurious to others? What less helpful as a way out of the difficulty? It but fastens and perpetuates the trouble which occasioned it, and increases the total evil of the situation."

Happiness Does Not Lie in the Future but the Present

"We are never living, but only hoping to live; and, looking forward always to being happy, it is inevitable that we never are so," said Pascal.

I have found that one of the commonest causes of unhappiness among my patients is that they are attempting to live their lives on the deferred payment plan. They do not live, nor enjoy life now, but wait for some future event or occurrence. They will be happy when they get married, when they get a better job, when they get the house paid for, when they get the children through college, when they have completed some task or won some victory. Invariably, they are disappointed. Happiness is a mental habit, a mental attitude, and if it is not learned and practiced in the present it is never experienced. It cannot be made contingent upon solving some external problem. When one problem is solved another appears to take its place. Life is a series of problems. If you are to be happy at all, you must be happy—period! not happy "because of."

"I have now reigned above fifty years in victory or peace," said the Caliph Abdelraham, "beloved by my subjects, dreaded by my enemies, and respected by my allies. Riches and honors, power and pleasure, have waited on my call, nor does any earthly blessing appear to have been wanting to my felicity. In this situation, I have diligently numbered the days of pure and genuine happiness which have fallen to my lot; they amount to fourteen."

Happiness Is a Mental Habit Which Can be Cultivated and Developed

"Most people are about as happy as they make up their minds to be," said Abraham Lincoln.

"Happiness is purely internal," says psychologist Dr. Matthew N. Chappell. "It is produced, not by objects, but by ideas, thoughts, and attitudes which can be developed and constructed by the individual's own activities, irrespective of the environment."

No one, other than a saint, can be 100 per cent happy all the time. And, as George Bernard Shaw quipped, we would probably be miserable if we were. But we can, by taking thought, and making a simple decision, be happy and think pleasant thoughts a large share of the time, regarding that multitude of little events and circumstances of daily living which now make us unhappy. To a large extent we react to petty annoyances, frustrations, and the like with grumpiness, dissatisfaction, resentment and irritability, purely out of habit. We have *practiced* reacting that way so long, it has become habitual. Much of this habitual unhappiness-reaction originated because of some event which we *interpreted* as a blow to our self-esteem. A driver honks his horn at us unnecessarily; someone interrupts and doesn't pay attention while we're talking; someone doesn't come through for us as we think he should. Even impersonal events can be interpreted, and reacted to, as affronts to our self-esteem. The bus we wanted to catch had to be late; it had to go and rain when we had planned to play golf; traffic had to get into a snarl just when we needed to catch the plane. We react with anger, resentment, self-pity—or in other words, *unhappiness*.

Stop Letting Things Push You Around

The best cure I have found for this sort of thing is to use unhappiness' own weapon—self-esteem. "Have you

ever been to a TV show and seen the master of cere-
monies manipulate the audience?" I asked a patient. "He
brings out a sign which says 'applause' and everyone
applauds. He brings out another which says 'laughter' and
everyone laughs. They act like sheep—as if they were
slaves, and meekly react as they are told to react. You
are acting the same way. You are letting outward events
and other people dictate to you how you shall feel and
how you shall react. You are acting as an obedient slave
and obeying promptly when some event or circumstance
signals to you—'Be angry'—'Get upset'—or 'Now is the
time to feel unhappy.' "

Learning the happiness habit, you become a master
instead of a slave, or as Robert Louis Stevenson said,
"The habit of being happy enables one to be freed, or
largely freed, from the domination of outward conditions."

Your Opinion Can Add to Unhappy Events

Even in regard to tragic conditions, and the most adverse environment, we can usually manage to be *happier,*
if not completely happy, by not adding to the misfortune
our own feelings of self-pity, resentment, and our own
adverse opinions.

"How can I be happy?" the wife of an alcoholic
husband asked me. "I don't know," I said, "but you can
be *happier* by resolving not to add resentment and self-
pity to your misfortune."

"How can I possibly be happy?" asked a businessman,
"I have just lost $200,000 on the stock market. I am
ruined and disgraced."

"You can be *happier*," I said, "by not adding your own
opinion to the facts. It is a fact that you lost $200,000. It
is your opinion that you are ruined and disgraced."

I then suggested that he memorize a saying of Epictetus,
which has always been a favorite of mine—"Men are dis-

turbed," said the sage, "not by things that happen, but by their opinion of the things that happen."

When I announced that I wanted to be a doctor, I was told that this could not be, because my folks had no money. It was a fact that my mother had no money. It was only an opinion that I could never be a doctor. Later, I was told I could never take post-graduate courses in Germany, and that it was impossible for a young plastic surgeon to hang out his own shingle and go into business for himself in New York. I did all these things—and one of the things that helped me was that I kept reminding myself that all these "impossibles" were opinions, not facts. I not only managed to reach my goals—but I was happy in the process—even when I had to pawn my overcoat to buy medical books, and do without lunch in order to purchase cadavers. I was in love with a beautiful girl. She married someone else. These were facts. But I kept reminding myself that it was merely my opinion that this was a "catastrophe" and that life was not worth living. I not only got over it, but it turned out that it was one of the luckiest things that ever happened to me.

The Attitude That Makes for Happiness

It has been pointed out earlier that since man is a *goal-striving* being, he is functioning naturally and normally when he is oriented toward some positive goal and striving toward some desirable goal. Happiness is a symptom of normal, natural functioning and when man is functioning as a goal-striver, he tends to feel fairly happy, regardless of circumstances. My young business executive friend was very unhappy because he had lost $200,000. Thomas A. Edison lost a laboratory worth millions in a fire, with no insurance. "What in the world will you do?" someone asked. "We will start rebuilding tomorrow morning," said Edison. He maintained an aggressive attitude, he was still goal-oriented despite his misfortune. And because he did maintain an aggressive goal-striving attitude, it is a good bet that he was never unhappy about his loss.

Psychologist H. L. Hollingworth has said that happiness *requires* problems, plus a mental attitude that is ready to meet distress with action toward a solution.

"Much of what we call evil is due entirely to the way men take the phenomenon," said William James. "It can so often be converted into a bracing and tonic good by a simple change of the sufferer's inner attitude from one of fear to one of fight; its sting can so often depart and turn into a relish when, after vainly seeking to shun it, we agree to face about and bear it cheerfully; that a man is simply bound in honor, with reverence to many of the facts that seem at first to disconcern his peace, to adopt this way of escape. Refuse to admit their badness; despise their power; ignore their presence; turn your attention the other way; and so far as you yourself are concerned at any rate, though the facts may still exist, their evil character exists no longer. Since you make them evil or good by your own thoughts about them, it is the ruling of your thoughts which proves to be your principal concern." (William James, *The Varieties of Religious Experience,* New York, Longmans, Green & Co.)

Looking back on my own life I can see that some of the happiest years were those when I was struggling through as a medical student, and living from hand to mouth in my early days of practice. Many times I was hungry. I was cold and ill-clad. I worked hard a minimum of about 12 hours a day. Many times I did not know from month to month where the money was coming from to pay my rent. But I did have a goal. I had a consuming desire to reach it, and a determined persistence which kept me working toward it.

I related all this to the young business executive and suggested that the real cause of his unhappy feeling was not that he had lost $200,000, but that he had lost his goal; he had lost his aggressive attitude, and was yielding passively rather than reacting aggressively.

"I must have been crazy," he told me later, "to let you convince me that losing the money was not what was making me unhappy—but I'm awfully glad that you did." He stopped moaning about his misfortune, "faced about," got himself another goal—and started working toward it. Within five years he not only had more money than ever before in his life, but for the first time he was in a business that he enjoyed.

Practice Exercise: Form the habit of reacting aggressively and positively toward threats and problems. Form the habit of keeping goal-oriented all the time, regardless of what happens. Do this by practicing a positive aggressive attitude, both in actual everyday situations which come up, and also in your imagination. See yourself in your imagination taking positive, intelligent action toward solving a problem or reaching a goal. See yourself reacting to threats, not by running away or evading them, but by meeting them, dealing with them, grappling with them in an aggressive and intelligent manner. "Most people are brave only in the dangers to which they accustom themselves, either in imagination or practice," said Bulwer-Lytton, the English novelist.

Systematically Practice "Healthy-Mindedness"

"The measure of mental health is the disposition to find good everywhere," said that most famous moralist, Ralph Waldo Emerson.

The idea that happiness, or keeping one's thoughts pleasant most of the time, can be deliberately and systematically cultivated by practicing in a more or less cold-blooded manner, strikes many of my patients as rather incredible, if not ludicrous, when I first suggest it. Yet, experience has shown not only that this can be done, but that it is about the only way that the "habit of happiness" can be cultivated. In the first place happiness isn't something that happens to you. It is something you yourself do and determine upon. If you wait for happiness to catch up with you, or "just happen," or be brought to you by others, you are likely to have a long wait. No one can decide what your thoughts shall be but yourself. If you wait until circumstances "justify" your thinking pleasant thoughts, you are also likely to wait forever. Every day is a mixture of good and evil—no day or circumstance is completely 100 per cent "good." There are ments and "facts" present in the world, and in our personal lives at all times, which "justify" either a pessimistic and grumpy outlook, or an optimistic and happy outlook, depending upon our choice. It is largely a matter of selection, attention, and decision. Nor is it a matter of being either intellectually honest or dishonest. Good is as "real" as evil. It is merely a matter of to what we choose to give primary attention—and what thoughts we hold in the mind.

Deliberately choosing to think pleasant thoughts is more than a palliative. It can have very practical results. Carl Erskine, the famous baseball pitcher, has said that bad thinking got him into more spots than bad pitching. "One sermon has helped me overcome pressure better than the advice of any coach," he said. "Its substance was that, like a squirrel hoarding chestnuts, we should store up our moments of happiness and triumph so that in a crisis we can draw upon these memories for help and inspiration. As a kid I used to fish at the bend of a little country stream just outside my home town. I can vividly remember this spot in the middle of a big, green pasture surrounded by tall, cool trees. Whenever tension builds up both on or off the ballfield now, I concentrate on this relaxing scene, and the knots inside me loosen up." (Norman Vincent Peale, ed., *Faith Made Them Champions,* Englewood Cliffs, N.J., Prentice-Hall, 1954.)

Gene Tunney tells how concentrating on the wrong "facts" almost caused him to lose his first fight with Jack Dempsey. He awoke one night from a nightmare. "The vision was of myself, bleeding, mauled and helpless, sinking to the canvas and being counted out. I couldn't stop trembling. Right there I had already lost that ring match which meant everything to me—the championship. . . . What could I do about this terror? I could guess the cause. I had been thinking about the fight in the wrong way. I had been reading the newspapers, and all they had said was how Tunney would lose. Through the newspapers I was losing the battle in my own mind.

"Part of the solution was obvious. Stop reading the papers. Stop thinking of the Dempsey menace, Jack's killing punch and ferocity of attack. *I simply had to close the doors of my mind* to destructive thoughts—and divert my thinking to other things."

A Salesman Who Needed Surgery on His Thoughts Rather Than His Nose

A young salesman had made up his mind to quit his job when he consulted me about an operation on his nose. His nose was slightly larger than normal, but certainly not "repulsive" as he insisted. He felt that prospects were secretly laughing at his nose or repulsed because of it. It was a "fact" that he had a large nose. It was a "fact" that three customers had called in to complain of his rude and hostile behavior. It was a fact that his boss had placed him on probation, and that he hadn't made a sale in two weeks. Instead of an operation on his nose, I suggested he perform surgery on his own thinking. For thirty days he was to "cut out" all these negative thoughts. He was to completely ignore all the negative and unpleasant "facts" in his situation, and deliberately focus his attention upon pleasant thoughts. At the end of thirty days he not only felt better, but he found that prospects and customers had become much more friendly, his sales were steadily increasing, and his boss had publicly congratulated him in a sales meeting.

A Scientist Tests the Theory of Positive Thinking

Dr. Elwood Worcester, in his book, *Body, Mind and Spirit,* relates the testimony of a world-famous scientist:

"Up to my fiftieth year I was an unhappy, ineffective man. None of the works on which my reputation rests were published. . . . I lived in a constant sense of gloom and failure. Perhaps my most painful symptom was a blinding headache which recurred usually two days of the week, during which I could do nothing.

"I had read some of the literature of New Thought, which at the time appeared to be buncombe, and some statement of William James on the directing of attention to what is good and useful and ignoring the rest. One saying of his stuck in my mind, 'We might have to give up our philosophy of evil, but what is that in comparison with gaining a life of goodness?', or words to that effect. Hitherto these doctrines had seemed to me only mystical theories, but realizing that my soul was sick and growing worse and that my life was intolerable, I determined to put them to the proof. . . . I decided to limit the period of conscious effort to one month, as I thought this time long enough to prove its value or worthlessness to me. During this month I resolved to impose certain restrictions on my thoughts. If I thought of the past, I would try to let my mind dwell only on its happy, pleasing incidents, the bright days of my childhood, the inspiration of my teachers and the slow revelation of my life-work. In thinking of the present, I would deliberately turn my attention to its desirable elements, my home, the opportunities my solitude gave me to work, and so on, and I resolved to make the utmost use of these opportunities and to ignore the fact that they seemed to lead to nothing. In thinking of the future I determined to regard every worthy and possible ambition as within my grasp. Ridiculous as this seemed at the time, in view of what has come to me since,

I see that the only defect of my plan was that it aimed too low and did not include enough."

He then tells how his headaches ceased within one week, and how he felt happier and better than ever before in his life. But, he adds:

"The outward changes of my life, resulting from my change of thought have surprised me more than the inward changes, yet they spring from the latter. There were certain eminent men, for example, whose recognition I deeply craved. The foremost of those wrote me, out of a clear sky, and invited me to become his assistant. My works have all been published, and a foundation has been created to publish all that I may write in the future. The men with whom I have worked have been very helpful and cooperative toward me chiefly on account of my changed disposition. Formerly they would not have endured me. . . . As I look back over all these changes, it seems to me that in some blind way I stumbled on a path of life and set forces to working for me which before were against me." (Elwood Worcester and Samuel McComb, *Body, Mind and Spirit,* New York, Charles Scribner's Sons.)

How an Inventor Used "Happy-Thoughts"

Professor Elmer Gates of the Smithsonian Institution was one of the most successful inventors this country has ever known, and a recognized genius. He made a daily practice of "calling up pleasant ideas and memories" and believed that this helped him in his work. If a person wants to improve himself, he said, "Let him summon those finer feelings of benevolence and usefulness, which are called up only now and then. Let him make this a regular exercise like swinging dumbbells. Let him gradually increase the time devoted to these psychical gymnastics, and at the end of a month he will find the change in himself surprising. The alteration will be apparent in his actions and thoughts. Morally speaking, the man will be a great improvement of his former self."

How to Learn the Happiness Habit

Our self-image and our habits tend to go together. Change one and you will automatically change the other. The word "habit" originally meant a garment, or clothing. We still speak of riding habits, and habiliments. This gives us an insight into the true nature of habit. Our habits are literally garments worn by our personalities. They are not accidental, or happenstance. We have them because *they fit us*. They are consistent with our self-image and our entire personality pattern. When we consciously and deliberately develop new and better habits, our self-image tends to outgrow the old habits and grow into the new pattern.

I can see many patients cringe when I mention changing habitual action patterns, or acting out new behavior patterns until they become automatic. They confuse "habit" with "addiction." An addiction is something you feel compelled to, and which causes severe withdrawal symptoms. Treatment of addiction is beyond the scope of this book.

Habits, on the other hand, are merely reactions and responses which we have learned to perform automatically without having to "think" or "decide." They are performed by our Creative Mechanism.

Fully 95 per cent of our behavior, feeling, and response is habitual.

The pianist does not "decide" which keys to strike. The dancer does not "decide" which foot to move where. The reaction is automatic and unthinking.

In much the same way our attitudes, emotions and beliefs tend to become habitual. In the past we "learned" that certain attitudes, ways of feeling and thinking were "appropriate" to certain situations. Now, we tend to think, feel and act the same way whenever we encounter what we interpret as "the same sort of situation."

What we need to understand is that these habits, unlike addictions, can be modified, changed, or reversed, simply by taking the trouble to make a *conscious decision*—and then by practicing or "acting out" the new response or behavior. The pianist can consciously decide to strike a different key, if he chooses. The dancer can consciously "decide" to learn a new step—and there is no agony about it. It does require constant watchfulness and practice until the new behavior pattern is thoroughly learned.

PRACTICE EXERCISE

Habitually, you put on either your right shoe first or your left shoe. Habitually, you tie your shoes by either passing the right-hand lace around behind the left-hand lace, or vice versa. Tomorrow morning determine which shoe you put on first and how you tie your shoes. Now, consciously decide that for the next 21 days you are going to form a new habit by putting on the other shoe first and tying your laces in a different way. Now, each morning as you decide to put on your shoes in a certain manner, let this simple act serve as a reminder to change other habitual ways of thinking, acting and feeling throughout that one day. Say to yourself as you tie your shoes, "I am beginning the day in a new and better way." Then, consciously decide that throughout the day:

1. I will be as cheerful as possible.
2. I will try to feel and act a little more friendly toward other people.
3. I am going to be a little less critical and a little more tolerant of other people, their faults, failings and mistakes. I will place the best possible interpretation upon their actions.
4. Insofar as possible, I am going to act as if success were inevitable, and I already am the sort of personality I

want to be. I will practice "acting like" and "feeling like" this new personality.

5. I will not let my own opinion color facts in a pessimistic or negative way.

6. I will practice smiling at least three times during the day.

7. Regardless of what happens, I will react as calmly and as intelligently as possible.

8. I will ignore completely and close my mind to all those pessimistic and negative "facts" which I can do nothing to change.

Simple? Yes. But each of the above habitual ways of acting, feeling, thinking does have beneficial and constructive influence on your self-image. Act them out for 21 days. "Experience" them, and see if worry, guilt, hostility have not been diminished and if confidence has not been increased.

Points to Remember
(Fill in)

1.
2.
3.
4.
5.

CHAPTER EIGHT

Ingredients of the "Success-Type" Personality and How to Acquire Them

JUST as a doctor learns to diagnose disease from certain symptoms, failure and success can also be diagnosed. The reason is that a man does not simply "find" success or "come to" failure. He carries their seeds around in his personality and character.

I have found one of the most effective means of helping people achieve an adequate or "successful" personality is to first of all give them a graphic picture of what the successful personality looks like. Remember, the creative guidance mechanism within you is a goal-striving mechanism, and the first requisite for using it is to have a clear-cut goal or target to shoot for. A great many people want to "improve" themselves, and long for a "better personality," who have no clear-cut idea of the direction in which improvement lies, nor what constitutes a "good personality." A good personality is one which enables you to deal effectively and appropriately with environment and reality, and to gain satisfaction from reaching goals which are important to you.

Time and again, I have seen confused and unhappy people "straighten themselves out," when they were given a goal to shoot for and a straight course to follow. There was the advertising man in his early forties, for example, who felt strangely insecure and dissatisfied with himself after receiving an important promotion.

New Roles Require New Self-Images

"It doesn't make sense," he said. "I've worked for this, and dreamed about it. It's just what I've always wanted. I know I can do the work. And yet, for some reason my self-confidence is shaken. I suddenly wake up, as if from a dream, and ask myself—'What in the world is a small potatoes like me doing in a job like this?' " He had become super-sensitive to his appearance, and thought perhaps that his "weak chin" might be the cause of his discomfort. "I don't *look* like a business executive," he said. He felt plastic surgery might be the answer to his problem.

There was the housewife, whose children were "running her crazy" and whose husband irritated her so much that she "teed off on him" at least twice a week for no cause. "What is the matter with me?" she asked. "My children are really nice kids I should be proud of. My husband is really a nice guy, and I'm always ashamed of myself afterwards." She felt that a "face lift" might give her more confidence, and cause her family to "appreciate her more."

The trouble with these people, and many more like them, is not their physical appearance but their self-image. They find themselves in a new role, and are not sure what kind of a person they are supposed to "be" in order to live up to that role. Or, they have never developed a clear-cut self-image of themselves in any role.

The Picture of Success

In this chapter I am going to give you the same "prescription" that I would give you should you come to my office.

I have found that an easy-to-remember picture of the

successful personality is contained in the letters of the word "Success" itself:

The "Success-type" personality is composed of:

S–ense of direction
U–nderstanding
C–ourage
C–harity
E–steem
S–elf-Confidence
S–elf-Acceptance.

(1) SENSE OF DIRECTION:

The advertising executive "straightened himself out" and regained his confidence within a short time, once he saw clearly that for several years he had been motivated by strong personal goals which *he wanted* to attain, including securing his present position. These goals, which were important *to him,* kept him on the track. However, once he got the promotion, he ceased to think in terms of what he wanted, but in terms of what others expected of him, or whether he was living up to other people's goals and standards. He was like the skipper of a ship who had relinquished his hold upon the wheel, and hoped that he would drift in the right direction. He was like a mountain climber, who as long as he looked upward to the peak he wished to scale, felt and acted courageously and boldly. But when he got to the top, he felt there was nowhere else to go, and began to look down, and became afraid. He was now on the defensive, defending his present position, rather than acting like a goal-striver and going on the offensive to attain his goal. He regained control when he set himself new goals and began to think in terms of, "What do I want out of this job? What do I want to achieve? Where do I want to go?"

"Functionally, a man is somewhat like a bicycle," I

told him. "A bicycle maintains its poise and equilibrium only so long as it is going forward towards something. You have a good bicycle. Your trouble is you are trying to maintain your balance sitting still, with no place to go. It's no wonder you feel shaky."

We are engineered as goal-seeking mechanisms. We are built that way. When we have no personal goal which we are interested in and which "means something" to us, we are apt to "go around in circles," feel "lost" and find life itself "aimless," and "purposeless." We are built to conquer environment, solve problems, achieve goals, and we find no real satisfaction or happiness in life without obstacles to conquer and goals to achieve. People who say that life is not worthwhile are really saying that they themselves have no personal goals which are worthwhile.

Prescription: Get yourself a goal worth working for. Better still, get yourself a project. Decide what *you want* out of a situation. Always have something ahead of you to "look forward to"—to work for and hope for. Look forward, not backward. Develop what one of the automobile manufacturers calls "the forward look." Develop a "nostalgia for the future" instead of for the past. The "forward look" and a "nostalgia for the future" can keep you youthful. Even your body doesn't function well when you stop being a goal-striver and "have nothing to look forward to." This is the reason that very often when a man retires, he dies shortly thereafter. When you're not goal-striving, not looking forward, you're not really "living." In addition to your purely personal goals, have at least one impersonal goal—or "cause" which you can identify yourself with. Get interested in some project to help your fellow man—not out of a sense of duty, but because you *want to*.

(2) UNDERSTANDING:

Understanding depends upon good communication. Communication is vital to any guidance system or computer. You cannot react appropriately if the information you act upon is faulty or misunderstood. Many doctors believe that "confusion" is the basic element in neurosis. To deal effectively with a problem, you must have some understanding of its true nature. Most of our failures in human relations are due to "misunderstandings."

We expect other people to react and respond and come to the same conclusions as we do from a given set of "facts" or "circumstances." We should remember what we said in an earlier chapter—no one reacts to "things as they are," but to his own mental images. Most of the time the other person's reaction or position is not taken in order to make us suffer, nor to be hardheaded, nor malicious, but because he "understands" and interprets the situation differently from us. He is merely responding appropriately to what—*to him*—seems to be the truth about the situation. To give the other person credit for being sincere, if mistaken, rather than willful and malicious, can do much to smooth out human relations and bring about better understanding between people. Ask yourself, "How does this appear—to him?" "How does he interpret this situation?" "How does he *feel* about it?" Try to understand *why* he might "act the way he does."

Fact vs. Opinion

Many times we create confusion when we add our own opinion to facts and come up with the wrong conclusion. FACT: A husband cracks his knuckles. OPINION: The wife concludes, "He does that because he thinks it will annoy me." FACT: The husband sucks his teeth after eating. OPINION: The wife concludes, "If he had any regard for me, he would improve his manners." FACT: Two friends are whispering when you walk up. Suddenly they stop talking and look somewhat embarrassed. OPINION: They must have been gossiping about me.

The housewife, mentioned earlier, was able to understand that her husband's annoying mannerisms were not deliberate and willful acts on his part for the purpose of annoying her. When she stopped reacting *just as if* she had been personally insulted, she was able to pause, analyze the situation, and select an appropriate response.

Be Willing to See the Truth

Oftentimes, we color incoming sensory data by our own fears, anxieties, or desires. But to deal effectively with environment we must be willing to acknowledge the truth about it. Only when we understand what it is can we respond appropriately. We must be able to see the truth, and to accept the truth, good or bad. Bertrand Russell said one reason Hitler lost World War II was that he did not fully understand the situation. Bearers of bad news were punished. Soon no one dared tell him the truth. Not knowing the truth, he could not act appropriately.

Many of us are individually guilty of the same error. We do not like to admit to ourselves our errors, mistakes, shortcomings, or ever admit we have been in the wrong. We do not like to acknowledge that a situation is other than we would like it to be. So we kid ourselves. And because we will not see the truth, we cannot act appropriately. Someone has said that it is a good exercise to daily admit one painful fact about ourselves to ourselves. The Success-type personality not only does not cheat and lie to other people, he learns to be honest with himself. What we call "sincerity" is itself based upon self-understanding and self-honesty. For no man can be sincere who lies to himself by "rationalizing," or telling himself "rational-lies."

Prescription: Look for and seek out true information concerning yourself, your problems, other people, or the situation, whether it is good news or bad news. Adopt the motto—"It doesn't matter who's right, but what's right." An automatic guidance system corrects its course from negative feedback data. It acknowledges errors in order to correct them and stay on course. So must you. Admit your mistakes and errors but don't cry over them. Correct them and go forward. In dealing with other people try to see the situation from their point of view as well as your own.

(3) COURAGE:

Having a goal and understanding the situation are not enough. You must have the courage to act, for only by actions can goals, desires and beliefs be translated into realities.

Admiral William F. Halsey's personal motto was a quotation from Nelson, "No Captain can do very wrong if he places his Ship alongside that of an Enemy." " 'The best defense is a strong offense,' is a military principle," said Halsey, "but its application is wider than war. All problems, personal, national, or combat, become smaller if you don't dodge them, but confront them. Touch a thistle timidly, and it pricks you; grasp it boldly and its spines crumble." (William Nichols, *Words to Live By*, Simon and Schuster, New York.)

Someone has said that FAITH is not believing something in spite of the evidence. It is the COURAGE to do something regardless of the consequences.

Why Not Bet on Yourself?

Nothing in this world is ever absolutely certain or guaranteed. Often the difference between a successful man and a failure is not one's better abilities or ideas, but the courage that one has to bet on his ideas, to take a calculated risk—and to act.

We often think of courage in terms of heroic deeds on the battlefield, in a shipwreck, or similar crisis. But everyday living requires courage, too, if it is to be effective.

Standing still, failure to act, causes people who are faced with a problem to become nervous, feel "stymied," "trapped," and can bring on a host of physical symptoms.

I tell such people: "Study the situation thoroughly, go over in your imagination the various courses of action possible to you and the consequences which can and may follow from each course. Pick out the course which gives the most promise—and go ahead. If we wait until we are absolutely certain and sure before we act we will never do anything. Any time you act you can be wrong. Any decision you make can turn out to be the wrong one. But we must not let this deter us from going after the goal we want. You must daily have the courage to risk making mistakes, risk failure, risk being humiliated. A step in the wrong direction is better than staying "on the spot" all your life. Once you're moving forward you can correct your course as you go. Your automatic guidance system cannot guide you when you're stalled, "standing still."

Faith and Courage Are "Natural Instincts"

Have you ever wondered why the "urge" or desire to gamble seems to be instinctive in human nature? My own theory is that this universal "urge" is an instinct, which, when used correctly, urges us to bet on ourselves, to take a chance on our own creative potentialities. When we have faith and act with courage—that is exactly what we're doing—gambling on, taking a chance on, our own creative God-given talents. It is also my theory that people who frustrate this natural instinct, by refusing to live creatively and act with courage, are the people who develop "gambling fever" and become addicts of gambling tables. A man who will not take a chance on himself must bet on something. And the man who will not act with courage sometimes seeks the feeling of courage from a bottle. Faith and courage are natural human instincts and we feel a need to express them—in one way or another.

Prescription: Be willing to make a few mistakes, to suffer a little pain to get what you want. Don't sell yourself short. "Most people," says General R. E. Chambers, Chief of the Army's Psychiatry and Neurology Consultant Division, "don't know how brave they really are. In fact, many potential heroes, both men and women, live out their lives in self-doubt. If they only knew they had these deep resources, it would help give them the self-reliance to meet most problems, even a big crisis." You've got the resources. But you never know you've got them until you act—and give them a chance to work for you.

Another helpful suggestion is to practice acting boldly and with courage in regard to "little things." Do not wait until you can be a big hero in some dire crisis. Daily living also requires courage—and by practicing courage in little things, we develop the power and talent to act courageously in more important matters.

(4) CHARITY:

Successful personalities have some interest in and regard for other people. They have a respect for others' problems and needs. They respect the dignity of human personality and deal with other people as if they were human beings, rather than as pawns in their own game. They recognize that every person is a child of God and is a unique individuality which deserves some dignity and respect.

It is a psychologic fact that our feelings about ourselves tend to correspond to our feelings about other people. When a person begins to feel more charitably about others, he invariably begins to feel more charitably toward himself. The person who feels that "people are not very important" cannot have very much deep-down self-respect and self-regard—for he himself is "people" and with what judgment he considers others, he himself is unwittingly judged in his own mind. One of the best known methods of getting over a feeling of guilt is to stop condemning other people in your own mind—stop judging them—stop blaming them and hating them for their mistakes. You will develop a better and more adequate self-image when you begin to feel that other people are more worthy.

Another reason that Charity toward other people is symptomatic of the successful personality is because it means that the person is dealing with reality. People *are* important. People cannot for long be treated like animals or machines, or as pawns to secure personal ends. Hitler found this out. So will other tyrants wherever they may be found—in the home, in business, or in individual relationships.

Prescription: The prescription for charity is three-fold: (1) Try to develop a genuine appreciation for people by realizing the truth about them; they are children of God, unique personalities, creative beings. (2) Take the trouble to stop and think of the other person's feelings, his viewpoints, his desires and needs. Think more of what the other fellow wants, and how he must feel. A friend of mine kids his wife by telling her, whenever she asks him, "Do you love me?"—"Yes, whenever I stop and think about it." There is a lot of truth in this. We cannot feel anything about other people unless we "stop and think" about them. (3) Act as if other people are important and treat them accordingly. In your treatment of people have regard for their feelings. We tend to feel about objects in accordance with the way we treat them.

(5) ESTEEM:

Several years ago I wrote a contribution to the "Words to Live By" feature of *This Week Magazine* on the words of Carlyle, "Alas! the fearful Unbelief is unbelief in yourself." At that time I said:

"Of all the traps and pitfalls in life, self-*dis*esteem is the deadliest, and the hardest to overcome; for it is a pit designed and dug by our own hands, summed up in the phrase, 'It's no use—I can't do it.'

"The penalty of succumbing to it is heavy—both for the individual in terms of material rewards lost, and for society in gains and progress unachieved.

"As a doctor I might also point out that defeatism has still another aspect, a curious one, which is seldom recognized. It is more than possible that the words quoted above are Carlyle's own confession of the secret that lay behind his own craggy assertiveness, his thunderous temper and waspish voice and his appalling domestic tyranny.

"Carlyle, of course, was an extreme case. But isn't it on those days when we are most subject to the 'fearful Unbelief,' when we most doubt ourselves and feel inadequate to our task—isn't it precisely then that we are most difficult to get along with?"

We simply must get it through our heads that holding a low opinion of ourselves is not a virtue, but a vice. Jealousy, for example, which is the scourge of many a marriage, is nearly always caused by self-doubt. The person with adequate self-esteem doesn't feel hostile toward others, he isn't out to prove anything, he can see facts more clearly, isn't as demanding in his claims on other people.

The housewife who felt that a face lift might cause her husband and children to appreciate her more, really needed to appreciate herself more. Middle-age, plus a few wrinkles and a few grey hairs had caused her to lose self-esteem. She then became super-sensitive to innocent remarks and actions of her family.

Prescription: Stop carrying around a mental picture of yourself as a defeated, worthless person. Stop dramatizing yourself as an object of pity and injustice. Use the practice exercises in this book to build up an adequate self-image.

The word "esteem" literally means to appreciate the worth of. Why do men stand in awe of the stars, and the moon, the immensity of the sea, the beauty of a flower or a sunset, and at the same time downgrade themselves? Did not the same Creator make man? Is not man himself the most marvelous creation of all? This appreciation of your own worth is not egotism unless you assume that you made yourself and should take some of the credit. Do not downgrade the product merely because you haven't used it correctly. Don't childishly blame the product for your own errors like the schoolboy who said, "This typewriter can't spell."

But the biggest secret of self-esteem is this: Begin to appreciate other people more; show respect for *any* human being merely because he is a child of God and therefore a "thing of value." Stop and think when you're dealing with people. You're dealing with a unique, individual creation of the Creator of all. Practice treating *other* people as if they had some value—and surprisingly enough your own self-esteem will go up. For real self-esteem is not derived from the great things you've done, the things you own, the mark you've made—but an appreciation of yourself for what you *are*—a child of God. When you come to this realization, however, you must necessarily conclude that all other people are to be appreciated for the same reason.

(6) SELF-CONFIDENCE:

Confidence is built upon an experience of success. When we first begin any undertaking, we are likely to have little confidence, because we have not learned from experience that we can succeed. This is true of learning to ride a bicycle, speak in public, or perform surgery. It is literally true that success breeds success. Even a small success can be used as a stepping stone to a greater one. Managers of boxers are very careful to match them carefully so they can have a graduated series of successful experiences. We can use the same technique, starting gradually, and experiencing success at first on a small scale.

Another important technique is to form the habit of remembering past successes, and forgetting failures. This is the way both an electronic computer and the human brain are supposed to operate. Practice improves skill and success in basketball, golf, horseshoe pitching, or salesmanship, not because "repetition" has any value in itself. If it did we would "learn" our errors instead of our "hits." A person learning to pitch horseshoes, for example, will miss the stake many more times than he will hit it. If mere repetition were the answer to improved skill, his practice should make him more expert at missing since that is what he has practiced most. However, although his misses may outnumber hits ten to one, through practice his misses gradually diminish and his hits come more and more frequently. This is because the computer in his brain remembers and reinforces his successful attempts, and forgets the misses.

This is the way that both an electronic computer and our own success mechanisms learn to succeed.

Yet, what do most of us do? We destroy our self-confidence by remembering past failures and forgetting all about past successes. We not only remember failures, we impress them on our minds with emotion. We condemn ourselves. We flay ourselves with shame and remorse (both are highly egotistical, self-centered emotions). And self-confidence disappears.

It doesn't matter how many times you have failed in the past. What matters is the successful attempt, which should be remembered, reinforced, and dwelt upon. Charles Kettering has said that any young man who wants to be a scientist must be willing to fail 99 times before he succeeds once, and suffer no ego damage because of it.

Prescription: Use errors and mistakes as a way to learning—then dismiss them from your mind. Deliberately remember and picture to yourself past successes. Everyone has succeeded *sometime* at *something*. Especially, when beginning a new task, call up the *feelings* you experienced in some past success, however small it might have been.

Dr. Winfred Overholser, Superintendent of St. Elizabeth's Hospital, has said that recalling brave moments is a very sound way to restore belief in yourself; that too many people are prone to let one or two failures blot out all good memories. If we will systematically relive our brave moments in memory, he says, we will be surprised to see we had more courage than we thought. Dr. Overholser recommends the practice of vividly remembering our past successes and brave moments as an invaluable aid whenever self-confidence is shaken.

(7) SELF-ACCEPTANCE:

No real success or genuine happiness is possible until a person gains some degree of self-acceptance. The most miserable and tortured people in the world are those who are continually straining and striving to convince themselves and others that they are something other than what they basically are. And there is no relief and satisfaction like that that comes when one finally gives up the shams and pretenses and is willing to be himself. Success, which comes from self-expression, often eludes those who strive and strain to "be somebody," and often comes, almost of its own accord, when a person becomes willing to relax and—"Be Himself."

Changing your self-image does not mean changing your *self,* or improving your self, but changing your own *mental picture,* your own *estimation,* conception, and realization of that self. The amazing results which follow from developing an adequate and realistic self-image, come about, not as a result of self-transformation, but from self-realization, and self-revelation. Your "self," right now, is what it has always been, and all that it can ever be. You did not create it. You cannot change it. You can, however, realize it, and make the most of *what already is* by gaining a true mental picture of your actual self. There is no use straining to "be somebody." You are what you are—now. You *are* somebody, not because you've made a million dollars, or drive the biggest car in your block, or win at bridge—but because God created you in His own image.

Most of us are better, wiser, stronger, more competent —*now,* than we realize. Creating a better self-image does not *create* new abilities, talents, powers—it releases and utilizes them.

We can change our personality, but not our basic self. Personality is a tool, an outlet, a focal point of the "self" that we use in dealing with the world. It is the sum total of our habits, attitudes, learned skills, which we use as a *method* of expressing ourselves.

"You" Are Not Your Mistakes

Self-acceptance means accepting and coming to terms with ourselves now, just as we are, with all our faults, weaknesses, shortcomings, errors, as well as our assets and strengths. Self-acceptance is easier, however, if we realize that these negatives *belong* to us—they *are* not us. Many people shy away from healthy self-acceptance because they insist upon identifying themselves with their mistakes. You may have made a mistake, but this does not mean that you *are* a mistake. You may not be expressing yourself properly and fully, but this does not mean you yourself are "no good."

We must recognize our mistakes and shortcomings before we can correct them.

The first step toward acquiring knowledge is the recognition of those areas where you are ignorant. The first step toward becoming stronger is the recognition that you are weak. And all religions teach that the first step toward salvation is the self-confession that you are a sinner. In the journey toward the goal of ideal self-expression, we must use negative feed-back data to correct course, as in any other goal-striving situation.

This requires admitting to ourselves—*and accepting the fact,* that our personality, our "expressed self," or what some psychologists call our "actual self," is always imperfect and short of the mark.

No one ever succeeds during a lifetime in fully expressing or bringing into actuality all the potentialities of the Real Self. In our Actual, expressed Self, we never exhaust all the possibilities and powers of the Real Self. We can always learn more, perform better, behave better. The Actual Self is necessarily imperfect. Throughout life it is always *moving toward* an ideal goal, but never arriving. The Actual Self is not a static but a dynamic thing. It is never completed and final, but always in a state of growth.

It is important that we learn to accept this Actual Self, with all its imperfections, because it is the only vehicle we have. The neurotic rejects his Actual Self and hates it because it is imperfect. In its place he tries to create a fictitious ideal self which is already perfect, has already "arrived." Trying to maintain the sham and fiction is not only a terrific mental strain, but he continually invites disappointment and frustration when he tries to operate in a real world with a fictitious self. A stage coach may not be the most desirable transportation in the world, but a real stage coach will still take you coast to coast more satisfactorily than will a fictitious jet air-liner.

Prescription: Accept yourself as you are—and start from there. Learn to emotionally tolerate imperfection in yourself. It is necessary to intellectually recognize our shortcomings, but disastrous to hate ourselves because of them. Differentiate between your "self" and your behavior. "You" are not ruined or worthless because you made a mistake or got off course, any more than a typewriter is worthless which makes an error, or a violin which sounds a sour note. Don't hate yourself because you're not perfect. You have lots of company. No one else is, either, and those who try to pretend they are are kidding themselves.

You Are "Somebody"—Now!

Many people hate and reject themselves because they feel and experience perfectly natural biological desires. Others reject themselves because they do not conform to the current fashion or standard for physical proportions. I can remember in the 1920's when many women felt ashamed of themselves because they had breasts. The boyish figure was in vogue and bosoms were taboo. Today, many young girls develop anxieties because they do not have 40 inch busts. In the 1920's women used to come to me and in effect say—"Make me somebody, by reducing the size of my breasts." Today, the plea is, "Make me somebody, by increasing the size of my breasts." This seeking for identity—this desire for selfhood—this urge to be "somebody" is universal, but we make a mistake when we seek it in conformity, in the approval of other people, or in material things. It is a gift of God. You *are*—period. Many people say in effect to themselves, "Because I am skinny, fat, short, too tall, etc.—I am nothing." Say to yourself instead, "I may not be perfect, I may have faults and weaknesses, I might have gotten off the track, I may have a long way to go—but I *am something* and I will make the most of that something."

"It is the young man of little faith who says, 'I am nothing,'" said Edward W. Bok. "It is the young man of true conception who says, 'I am everything,' and then goes to prove it. That does not spell conceit or egotism, and if people think it does, let them think so. Enough for us to know that it means faith, trust, confidence, the human expression of the God within us. He says, 'Do my work.' Go and do it. No matter what it is. Do it, but do it with a zest; a keenness; a gusto that surmounts obstacles and brushes aside discouragement."

Accept yourself. Be yourself. You cannot realize the potentialities and possibilities inherent in that unique and special something which is "YOU" if you keep turning your back upon it, feeling ashamed of it, refusing to recognize it.

Points to Remember
(Fill in)

1.
2.
3.
4.
5.
6.
7.

CHAPTER NINE

The Failure Mechanism:
How to Make It Work *For* You
Instead of *Against* You

STEAM boilers have pressure gauges which show when the pressure is reaching the danger point. By *recognizing* the potential danger, corrective action can be taken—and safety assured. Dead-end streets, blind alleys, and impassable roads *can* cause you inconvenience and delay your arrival at your destination *if* they are not clearly marked and recognized for what they are. However, if you can read the signposts, and take proper corrective action, detour signs, dead-end street signs, and the like, can help you reach your destination easier and more efficiently.

The human body has its own "red light" signals and "danger signs," which doctors refer to as symptoms or syndromes. Patients are prone to regard symptoms as malevolent; a fever, a pain, etc., is "bad." Actually, these negative signals function *for* the patient, and for his benefit, *if* he recognizes them for what they are, and takes corrective action. They are the pressure gauges and red lights which help maintain the body in health. The pain of appendicitis may seem "bad" to the patient, but actually it operates for the patient's survival. If he felt no pain he would take no action toward having the appendix removed.

The failure-type personality also has its symptoms. We need to be able to recognize these failure symptoms in ourselves so that we can do something about them. When we learn to recognize certain personality traits as signposts to failure, these symptoms then act automatically as "negative feedback," and help guide us down the road to creative accomplishment. However, we not only need to become "aware" of them. Everyone "feels" them. We need to recognize them as "undesirables," as things which we do not want, and most important of all convince ourselves deeply and sincerely that these things do not bring happiness.

No one is immune to these negative feelings and attitudes. Even the most successful personalities experience them at times. The important thing is to recognize them for what they are, and take positive action to correct course.

The Picture of Failure

Again, I have found that patients can remember these negative feedback signals, or what I call the "Failure Mechanism," when they associate them with the letters that make up the word "Failure." They are:

> F–rustration, hopelessness, futility
> A–ggressiveness (misdirected)
> I–nsecurity
> L–oneliness (lack of "oneness")
> U–ncertainty
> R–esentment
> E–mptiness.

Understanding Brings Cure

No one sits down and deliberately, with malice aforethought, decides to develop these negative traits just to be perverse. They do not "just happen." Nor are they an indication of the imperfection of human nature. Each of these negatives was originally adopted as a "way" to solve a difficulty or a problem. We adopt them because we mistakenly see them as a "way" out of some difficulty. They have *meaning* and *purpose,* although based upon a mistaken premise. They constitute a "way of life" for us. Remember, one of the strongest urges in human nature is to react appropriately. We can cure these failure symptoms, not by will power, but by understanding—by being able to "see" that they do not work and that they are inappropriate. The truth can set us free from them. And when we can see the truth, then the same instinctive forces which caused us to adopt them in the first place, will work in our behalf in eradicating them.

(1) FRUSTRATION:

Frustration is an emotional feeling which develops whenever some important goal cannot be realized or when some strong desire is thwarted. All of us must necessarily suffer some frustration by the very fact of being human and therefore imperfect, incomplete, unfinished. As we grow older we should learn that all desires cannot be satisfied immediately. We also learn that our "doing" can never be as good as our intentions. We also learn to accept the fact that perfection is not necessary nor required, and that approximations are good enough for all practical purposes. We learn to tolerate a certain amount of frustration without becoming upset about it.

It is only when a frustrating experience brings excessive emotional feelings of deep dissatisfaction and futility that it becomes a symptom of failure.

Chronic frustration usually means that the goals we have set for ourselves are unrealistic, or the image we have of ourselves is inadequate, or both.

Practical Goals vs. Perfectionistic Goals

To his friends, Jim S. was a successful man. He had risen from stock clerk to vice-president of his company. His golf score was in the low eighties. He had a beautiful wife and two children who loved him. But, nevertheless, he felt chronically frustrated because none of these measured up to his unrealistic goals. He himself was not perfect in every particular, but he *should* be. He *should* be chairman of the board by now. He *should* be shooting in the low seventies. He *should* be such a perfect husband and father, that his wife would never find cause to disagree with him, and his children never misbehave. Hitting the bull's-eye was not good enough. He had to hit the infinitesimal speck in the center of the bull's-eye. "You should use the same technique in all your affairs that Jackie Burke recommends in putting," I told him. "That is, not to feel that you have to pinpoint the ball right to the cup itself on a long putt, but to aim at an area the size of a washtub. This takes off the strain, relaxes you, enables you to perform better. If it's good enough for the professionals, it should be good enough for you."

His Self-fulfilling Prophecy Made Failure Certain

Harry N. was somewhat different. He had won none of the external symbols of success. Yet, he had had many opportunities, all of which he muffed. Three times he had been on the verge of landing the job he wanted and each time "something happened"—something was always defeating him just when success seemed within his grasp. Twice he had been disappointed in love affairs.

His self-image was that of an unworthy, incompetent, inferior person who had no right to succeed, or to enjoy the better things in life, and unwittingly he tried to be true to that role. He felt he was not the sort of person to be successful, and always managed to do something to make this self-fulfilling prophecy come true.

Frustration as a Way of Solving Problems Does Not Work

Feelings of frustration, discontent, dissatisfaction are *ways* of solving problems that we all "learned" as infants. If an infant is hungry he expresses discontent by crying. A warm, tender hand then appears magically out of nowhere and brings milk. If he is uncomfortable, he again expresses his dissatisfaction with the status quo, and the same warm hands appear magically again and solve his problem by making him comfortable. Many children continue to get their way, and have their problems solved by over-indulgent parents, by merely expressing their feelings of frustration. All they have to do is *feel* frustrated and dissatisfied and the problem is solved. This way of life "works" for the infant and for some children. It *does not work* in adult life. Yet many of us continue to try it, by feeling discontented and expressing our grievances against life, apparently in the hope that life itself will take pity—rush in and solve our problem for us—if only we feel badly enough. Jim S. was unconsciously using this childish technique in the hope that some magic would bring him the perfection he craved. Harry N. had "practiced" feeling frustrated and defeated so much that feelings of defeat became habitual with him. He projected them into the future and expected to fail. His habitual defeatist feelings helped create a picture of himself as a defeated person. Thoughts and feelings go together. Feelings are the soil that thoughts and ideas grow in. This is the reason that you have been advised throughout this book to imagine how you would *feel* if you succeeded—and then feel that way now.

(2) AGGRESSIVENESS:

Excessive and misdirected aggressiveness follows frustration as night follows day. This was proved conclusively by a group of Yale scientists some years ago in their book, *Frustration and Aggressiveness* (John Dollard, et al., Yale University Press, New Haven).

Aggressiveness itself is not an abnormal behavior pattern as some psychiatrists once believed. Aggressiveness, and emotional steam, are very necessary in reaching a goal. We must go out after what we want in an aggressive rather than in a defensive or tentative manner. We must grapple with problems aggressively. The mere fact of having an important goal is enough to create emotional steam in our boiler and bring aggressive tendencies into play. However, trouble ensues when we are blocked or frustrated in achieving our goal. The emotional steam is then dammed up, seeking an outlet. Misdirected, or unused, it becomes a destructive force. The worker who wants to punch his boss in the nose but doesn't dare, goes home and snaps at his wife and kids or kicks the cat. Or he may turn his aggressiveness upon himself in much the same way that a certain scorpion in South America will sting itself and die of its own poison, when angered.

Don't Lash Out Blindly—Concentrate Your Fire

The failure-type personality does not direct his aggressiveness toward the accomplishment of a worthwhile goal. Instead it is used in such self-destructive channels as ulcers, high blood pressure, worry, excessive smoking, compulsive overwork, or it may be turned upon other persons in the form of irritability, rudeness, gossip, nagging, fault-finding.

Or, if his goals are unrealistic and impossible, the solution of this type person, when he meets defeats, is to "try harder than ever." When he finds that he is butting his head up against a stone wall, he unconsciously figures that the solution to his problem is to butt his head even harder.

The answer to aggression is not to eradicate it, but to understand it, and provide proper and appropriate channels for its expression. Recently Dr. Konrad Lorentz, the famous Viennese M.D. and animal sociologist, told psychiatrists at the Postgraduate Center for Psychotherapy, New York City, that the study of animal behavior for many years has shown that aggressive behavior is basic and fundamental, and that an animal cannot feel or express affection, until channels have been provided for the expression of aggression. Dr. Emanuel K. Schwartz, assistant Dean of the center, said that Dr. Lorentz's discoveries have tremendous implications for man and may require us to revaluate our total view of human relations. They indicate, he said, that providing a proper outlet for aggression is as important, if not more so, than providing for love and tenderness.

Knowledge Gives You Power

Merely understanding the mechanism involved helps a person handle the frustration-aggression cycle. Misdirected aggression is an attempt to hit *one* target (the original goal) by lashing out at any target. It doesn't work. You don't solve one problem by creating another. If you feel like snapping at someone, stop and ask yourself—"Is this merely my own frustration at work? What has frustrated me?" When you see that your response is inappropriate, you have gone a long way toward controlling it. It also takes much of the sting away when someone is rude to you, if you realize that it is probably not a willful act, but an automatic mechanism at work. The other fellow is letting off steam which he could not use in achieving some goal. Many automobile accidents are caused by the frustration-aggression mechanism. The next time someone is rude to you in traffic, try this: Instead of becoming aggressive and thus a menace yourself, say to yourself: "The poor fellow has nothing against me personally. Maybe his wife burned the toast this morning, he can't pay the rent, or his boss chewed him out."

Safety-valves for Emotional Steam

When you are blocked in achieving some important goal, you are somewhat like a steam locomotive with a full head of steam with nowhere to go. You need a safety-valve for your excess of emotional steam. All types of physical exercise are excellent for draining off aggression. Long brisk walks, push-ups, dumbbell exercises, are good. Especially good are those games where you hit or smash something—golf, tennis, bowling, punching the bag. Many frustrated women intuitively recognize the value of heavy muscular exercise in draining off aggressiveness, when they feel an urge to rearrange all the furniture in the house after becoming upset. Another good device is to vent your spleen in writing. Write a letter to the person who has frustrated or angered you. Pull out all the stops. Leave nothing to the imagination. *Then burn the letter.*

The best channel of all for aggression is to use it up as it was intended to be used—in working toward some goal. Work remains one of the best therapies, and one of the best tranquilizers for a troubled spirit.

(3) INSECURITY:

The feeling of insecurity is based upon a concept or belief of inner inadequacy. If you feel that you do not "measure up" to what is required, you feel insecure. A great deal of insecurity is not due to the fact that our inner resources are actually inadequate, but due to the fact that we use a false measuring stick. We compare our actual abilities to an imagined "ideal," perfect, or absolute self.

Thinking of yourself in terms of absolutes induces insecurity.

The insecure person feels that he should be "good"—period. He should be "successful"—period. He should be "happy," competent, poised—period. These are all worthy goals. But they should be thought of, at least in their absolute sense, as goals to be achieved, as something to reach for, rather than as "shoulds."

Since man is a goal-striving mechanism, the self realizes itself fully only when man is moving forward towards something. Remember our comparison with the bicycle in a previous chapter? Man maintains his balance, poise, and sense of security only as he is moving forward—or seeking. When you think of yourself as having *attained* the goal, you become static, and you lose the security and equilibrium you had when you were moving towards something. The man who is convinced that he is "good" in the absolute sense, not only has no incentive to do better, but he feels insecure because he must defend the sham and pretense. "The man who thinks he has 'arrived' has about used up his usefulness to us," the president of a large business said to me. When someone called Jesus "good" he admonished him, "Why callest thou me good? There is but one good and that is the Father." St. Paul is generally regarded as a "good" man, yet his own attitude was, "I count myself not to have *achieved* . . . but I press on toward the goal."

Keep Your Feet on Solid Ground

It *is* insecure, trying to stand on the top of a pinnacle. Mentally, get down off your high-horse and you will feel more secure.

This has very practical applications. It explains the "underdog psychology" in sports. When a championship team begins to think of itself as "the champions," they no longer have something to fight for, but a status to defend. The champions are defending something, trying to prove something. The underdogs are fighting to do something and often bring about an upset.

I used to know a boxer who fought well until he won the championship. In his next fight he lost the championship and looked bad doing so. After losing the title, he fought well again and regained the championship. A wise manager said to him, "You can fight as well as champion as when you're the contender if you'll remember one thing. When you step into that ring you aren't *defending* the championship—you're *fighting* for it. You haven't got it—you've laid it on the line when you crawl through the ropes."

The mental attitude which engenders insecurity is a "way." It is a way of substituting sham and pretense for reality. It is a way of proving to yourself and others your superiority. But it is self-defeating. If you *are* perfect and superior *now*—then there is no need to fight, grapple and try. In fact, if you are caught trying real hard, it may be considered evidence that you are not superior—so you "don't try." You lose your fight—your Will to Win.

(4) LONELINESS:

All of us are lonely at times. Again, it is a natural penalty we pay for being human and individual. But it is the extreme and chronic feeling of loneliness—of being cut off and alienated from other people—that is a symptom of the failure mechanism.

This type of loneliness is caused by an alienation from life. It is a loneliness from your real self. The person who is alienated from his real self has cut himself off from the basic and fundamental "contact" with life. The lonely person often sets up a vicious cycle. Because of his feeling of alienation from self, human contacts are not very satisfying, and he becomes a social recluse. In doing so, he cuts himself off from one of the pathways to finding himself, which is to lose oneself in social activities with other people. Doing things with other people and enjoying things with other people, helps us to forget ourselves. In stimulating conversation, in dancing, playing together, or in working together for a common goal, we become interested in something other than maintaining our own shams and pretenses. As we get to know the other fellow, we feel less need for pretense. We "unthaw" and become more natural. The more we do this the more we feel we can afford to dispense with the sham and pretense and feel more comfortable just being ourselves.

Loneliness Is a "Way" That Doesn't Work

Loneliness is a way of self-protection. Lines of communication with other people—and especially any emotional ties—are cut down. It is a way to protect our idealized self against exposure, hurt, humiliation. The lonely personality is *afraid* of other people. The lonely person often complains that he has no friends, and there are no people to mix with. In most cases, he unwittingly arranges things in this manner because of his passive attitude, that it is up to other people to come to him, to make the first move, to see that he is entertained. It never occurs to him that he should contribute something to any social situation.

Regardless of your feelings, force yourself to mix and mingle with other people. After the first cold plunge, you will find yourself warming up and enjoying it if you persist. Develop some social skill that will add to the happiness of other people: dancing, bridge, playing the piano, tennis, conversation. It is an old psychological axiom that constant exposure to the object of fear immunizes against the fear. As the lonely person continues to force himself into social relations with other human beings—not in a passive way, but as an active contributor—he will gradually find that most people are friendly, and that he is accepted. His shyness and timidity begin to disappear. He feels more comfortable in the presence of other people and with himself. The experience of their acceptance of him enables him to accept himself.

(5) UNCERTAINTY:

Elbert Hubbard said, "The greatest mistake a man can make is to be afraid of making one."

Uncertainty is a "way" of avoiding mistakes, and responsibility. It is based upon the fallacious premise that if no decision is made, nothing can go wrong. Being "wrong" holds untold horrors to the person who tries to conceive of himself as perfect. He is never wrong, and always perfect in all things. If he were ever wrong his picture of a perfect, all powerful self would crumble. Therefore, decision-making becomes a life-or-death matter.

One "way" is to avoid as many decisions as possible, and prolong them as much as possible. Another "way" is to have a handy scapegoat to blame. This type of person makes decisions—but he makes them hastily, prematurely, and is well-known for going off half-cocked. Making decisions offers him no problem at all. He is perfect. It is impossible for him to be wrong in any case. Therefore, why consider facts or consequences? He is able to maintain this fiction when his decisions backfire, simply by convincing himself it was someone else's fault. It is easy to see why both types fail. One is continually in hot water from impulsive and ill-considered actions, the other is stymied because he will not act at all. In other words, the "Uncertainty" way of being right doesn't work.

Nobody Is Right All the Time

Realize that it is not required that a man be 100 per cent right at all times. No baseball batter has ever had a 1000 average. If he is right three times out of ten he is considered good. The great Babe Ruth, who holds the record for the most home runs, also holds the record for the most strike-outs. It is in the nature of things that we progress by acting, making mistakes, and correcting course. A guided torpedo literally arrives at its target by making a series of mistakes and continually correcting its course. You cannot correct your course if you are standing still. You cannot change or correct "nothing." You must consider the known facts in a situation, imagine possible consequences of various courses of action, choose one that seems to offer the best solution—and bet on it. You can correct your course as you go.

Only "Little Men" Are "Never Wrong"

Another help in overcoming uncertainty is to realize the role that self-esteem, and the protection of self-esteem, play in indecisiveness. Many people are indecisive because they fear loss of self-esteem if they are proved wrong. Use self-esteem for yourself, instead of against yourself, by convincing yourself of this truth: Big men and big personalities make mistakes and admit them. It is the little man who is afraid to admit he has been wrong.

"No man ever became great or good except through many and great mistakes," said Gladstone. "I have learned more from my mistakes than from my successes," said Sir Humphry Davy. "We learn wisdom from failure much more than from success; we often discover what will do, by finding out what will not do; and probably he who never made a mistake never made a discovery."— Samuel Smiles. "Mr. Edison worked endlessly on a problem, using the method of elimination. If a person asked him whether he were discouraged because so many attempts proved unavailing, he would say, 'No, I am not discouraged, because every wrong attempt discarded is another step forward.' "—Mrs. Thomas A. Edison.

(6) RESENTMENT:

When the failure-type personality looks for a scapegoat or excuse for his failure, he often blames society, "the system," life, the "breaks." He resents the success and happiness of others because it is proof to him that life is short-changing him and he is being treated unfairly. Resentment is an attempt to make our own failure palatable by explaining it in terms of unfair treatment, injustice. But, as a salve for failure, resentment is a cure that is worse than the disease. It is a deadly poison to the spirit, makes happiness impossible, uses up tremendous energy which could go into accomplishment. A vicious cycle is often set up. The person who always carries a grievance, and has a chip on his shoulder, does not make the best companion or co-worker. When co-workers do not warm up to him, or the boss attempts to point out deficiencies in his work, he has additional reasons for feeling resentful.

Resentment Is a "Way" That Fails

Resentment is also a "way" of making us feel important. Many people get a perverse satisfaction from feeling "wronged." The victim of injustice, the one who has been unfairly treated, is morally superior to those who caused the injustice.

Resentment is also a "way," or an attempt, to wipe out or eradicate a real or fancied wrong or injustice which has already happened. The resentful person is trying to "prove his case" before the court of life, so to speak. If he can feel resentful enough, and thereby "prove" the injustice, some magic process will reward him by making "not so" the event or circumstance which caused the resentment. In this sense resentment is a mental resistance to, a non-acceptance of, something which has already happened. The word itself comes from two Latin words: "re" meaning back, and "sentire" meaning to feel. Resentment is an emotional rehashing, or re-fighting of some event in the past. You cannot win, because you are attempting to do the impossible—change the past.

Resentment Creates an Inferior Self-Image

Resentment, even when based upon real injustices and wrongs, is not the way to win. It soon becomes an emotional habit. Habitually feeling that you are a victim of injustice, you begin to picture yourself in the role of a victimized person. You carry around an inner feeling which is looking for an external peg to hang itself on. It is then easy to see "evidence" of injustice, or fancy you have been wronged, in the most innocent remark or neutral circumstance.

Habitual resentment invariably leads to self-pity, which is the worst possible emotional habit anyone can develop. When these habits have become firmly ensconced, a person does not feel "right" or "natural" when they are absent. They then literally begin to search for and look for "injustices." Someone has said that such people feel good only when they are miserable.

Emotional habits of resentment and self-pity also go with an ineffective, inferior self-image. You begin to picture yourself as a pitiful person, a victim, who was meant to be unhappy.

The Real Cause of Resentment

Remember that your resentment is not caused by other persons, events, or circumstances. It is caused by your own emotional response—your own reaction. You alone have power over this, and you can control it if you firmly convince yourself that resentment and self-pity are not ways to happiness and success, but ways to defeat and unhappiness.

As long as you harbor resentment, it is literally impossible for you to picture yourself as a self-reliant, independent, self-determining person who is "the Captain of his soul, the master of his Fate." The resentful person turns over his reins to other people. They are allowed to dictate how he shall feel, how he shall act. He is wholly dependent upon other people, just as a beggar is. He makes unreasonable demands and claims upon other people. If everyone else should be dedicated to making you happy, you will be resentful when it doesn't work out that way. If you feel that other people "owe" you eternal gratitude, undying appreciation, or continual recognition of your superlative worth, you will feel resentment when these "debts" are not paid. If life owes you a living, you become resentful when it isn't forthcoming.

Resentment is therefore inconsistent with creative goal-striving. In creative goal-striving, *you* are the actor, not the passive recipient. *You* set your goals. No one owes you anything. You go out after your own goals. You become responsible for your own success and happiness. Resentment doesn't fit into this picture, and because it doesn't it is a "failure mechanism."

(7) EMPTINESS:

Perhaps as you read this chapter you thought of someone who had been "successful" in spite of frustration, misdirected aggressiveness, resentment, etc. But do not be too sure. Many people acquire the outward symbols of success but when they go to open the long-sought-for treasure chest, they find it empty. It is as if the money they have strained so hard to attain, turns to counterfeit in their hands. Along the way, they *lost the capacity to enjoy*. And when you have lost the capacity to enjoy, no amount of wealth or anything else can bring success or happiness. These people win the nut of success but when they crack it open it is empty.

A person who has the capacity to enjoy still alive within him finds enjoyment in many ordinary and simple things in life. He also enjoys whatever success in a material way he has achieved. The person in whom the capacity to enjoy is dead can find enjoyment in nothing. No goal is worth working for. Life is a terrible bore.

Nothing is worthwhile. You can see these people by the hundreds night after night knocking themselves out in night clubs trying to convince themselves they are enjoying it. They travel from place to place, become entangled in a whirl of parties, hoping to find enjoyment, always finding an empty shell. The truth is that joy is an accompaniment of creative function, of creative goal-striving. It is possible to win a fake "success," but when you do you are penalized with an empty joy.

Life Becomes Worthwhile When You Have Worthwhile Goals

Emptiness is a symptom that you are not living creatively. You either have no goal that is important enough to you, or you are not using your talents and efforts in striving toward an important goal. It is the person who has no purpose of his own who pessimistically concludes, "Life has no purpose." It is the person who has no goal worth working for who concludes, "Life is not worthwhile." It is the person with no important job to do who complains, "There is nothing to do." The individual who is *actively engaged* in a struggle, or in striving toward an important goal, does not come up with pessimistic philosophies concerning the meaninglessness or the futility of life.

Emptiness Is Not a "Way" That Wins

The failure mechanism is self-perpetuating, unless we step in and break the vicious cycle. Emptiness, when once experienced, can become a "way" of avoiding effort, work, and responsibility. It becomes an excuse, or a justification for non-creative living. If all is vanity, if there is no new thing under the sun, if there is no joy to be found anyway—why bother? Why try? If life is just a treadmill —if we work 8 hours a day so we can afford a house to sleep in, so we can sleep 8 hours to become rested for another day's work—why get excited about it? All these intellectual "reasons" vanish, however, and we do experience joy and satisfaction, when once we get off the treadmill, stop going around and around in circles, and select some goal worth striving for—and go after it.

Emptiness and an Inadequate Self-Image Go Together

Emptiness may also be the symptom of an inadequate self-image. It is impossible to psychologically accept something that you feel does not belong to you—or is not consistent with your self. The person who holds an unworthy and undeserving self-image may hold his negative tendencies in check long enough to achieve a genuine success—then be unable to accept it psychologically and enjoy it. He may even feel guilty about it—as if he had stolen it. His negative self-image may even spur such a person on to achievement by the well-known principle of over-compensation. But I do not subscribe to the theory that one should be proud of his inferiority complex, or thankful for it, because it sometimes leads to the external symbols of success. When "success" finally comes such a person feels little sense of satisfaction or accomplishment. He is unable to "take credit" in his own mind for his accomplishments. To the world he is a success. He himself still feels inferior, undeserving, almost as if he was a thief and had stolen the "status symbols" which he thought were so important. "If my friends and associates really knew what a phony I am," he will say.

This reaction is so common that psychiatrists refer to it as the "success syndrome"—the man who feels guilty, insecure and anxious, when he realizes he has "succeeded." This is the reason that "success" has become a bad word. Real success never hurt anyone. Striving for goals which are important to you, not as status symbols, but because they are consistent with your own deep inner wants, is healthful. Striving for real success—for *your* success— through creative accomplishment, brings a deep inner satisfaction. Striving for a phony success to please others brings a phony satisfaction.

Glance at Negatives, But Focus on Positives

Automobiles come equipped with "negative indicators" placed directly in front of the driver, to tell you when the battery is not charging, when the engine is becoming too hot, when the oil pressure is becoming too low, etc. To ignore these negatives might ruin your car. However, there is no need to become unduly upset if some negative signal flashes. You merely stop at a service station or a garage, and take positive action to correct. A negative signal does not mean the car is no good. All cars overheat at times.

However, the driver of the automobile does not look at the control panel exclusively and continuously. To do so might be disastrous. He must focus his gaze through the windshield, look where he is going, and keep his primary attention on his goal—*where he wants to go*. He merely glances at the negative indicators from time to time. When he does, he does not fix upon them or dwell upon them. He quickly focuses his sight ahead of him again and concentrates on the positive goal of where he wants to go.

How to Use Negative Thinking

We should adopt a somewhat similar attitude about our own negative symptoms. I am a firm believer in "negative thinking" when used correctly. We need to be *aware* of negatives so that we can steer clear of them. A golfer needs to know where the bunkers and sandtraps are— but he doesn't think continuously about the bunker— where he doesn't want to go. His mind "glances" at the bunker, but dwells upon the green. Used correctly this type of "negative thinking" can work for us to lead us to success, if: (1) We are sensitive to the negative to the extent that it can alert us to danger. (2) We recognize the negative for what it is—something undesirable—something we don't want—something that does not bring genuine happiness. (3) We take immediate corrective action and substitute an opposite factor from the Success Mechanism. Such practice will in time create a sort of automatic reflex which becomes a part of our inner guidance system. Negative feedback will act as a sort of automatic control, to help us "steer clear" of failure and guide us to success.

Points to Remember
(Fill in)

1.

2.

3.

4.

5.

6.

7.

CHAPTER TEN

How to Remove Emotional Scars
Or
How to Give Yourself
An Emotional Face Lift

WHEN you receive a physical injury, such as a cut on the face, your body forms scar tissue which is both tougher and thicker than the original flesh. The purpose of the scar tissue is to form a protective cover or shell, nature's way of insuring against another injury in the same place. If an ill-fitting shoe rubs against a sensitive part of your foot, the first result is pain and sensitiveness. But again, nature protects against further pain and injury by forming a callus, a protective shell.

We are inclined to do very much the same thing whenever we receive an emotional injury, when someone "hurts" us, or "rubs us the wrong way." We form emotional or spiritual "scars" for self-protection. We are very apt to become hardened of heart, callous toward the world, and to withdraw within a protective shell.

When Nature Needs an Assist

In forming scar tissue, it is nature's intention to be helpful. In our modern society, however, scar tissue, especially on the face, can work against us instead of for us. Take George T., for example, a promising young at-

149

torney. He was affable, personable, and well on his way
to a successful career, when he had an automobile accident which left him with a horrible scar from midway on
his left cheek to the left corner of his mouth. Another
cut, just over his right eye, pulled his upper eyelid up
tightly when it healed, which gave him a grotesque "glar-
ing" appearance. Every time he looked in the bathroom
mirror he saw a repulsive image. The scar on his cheek
gave him a perpetual "leer," or what he called an "evil
look." After leaving the hospital he lost his first case in
court, and was sure that his "evil" and grotesque appearance had influenced the jury. He felt that old friends
were repelled and repulsed by his appearance. Was it
only his imagination that even his own wife flinched
slightly when he kissed her?

George T. began to turn down cases. He started drinking during the day. He became irritable, hostile, and
something of a recluse.

The scar tissue on his face formed a tough protection
against future automobile accidents. But the society in
which George lived, physical injuries to his face were not
the primary hazard. He was more vulnerable than ever to
social "cuts," injuries and hurts. His scars were a liabil-
ity instead of an asset.

Had George been a primitive man and suffered facial
scars from an encounter with a bear or a saber-toothed
tiger, his scars would have probably made him more
acceptable to his fellows. Even in fairly recent times old
soldiers have proudly displayed their "scars of battle,"
and today in the outlawed duelling societies in Germany,
a saber scar is a mark of distinction.

In George's case, nature had good intentions, but nature
needed an assist. I gave George back his old face by plastic surgery which removed the scar tissue and restored his
features.

Following surgery, the personality change in him was
remarkable. He became his good-natured, self-confident
self again. He stopped drinking. He gave up his lone-

wolf attitude, moved back into society, and became a member of the human race again. He literally found a "new life."

This new life, however, was brought about only indirectly by plastic surgery on physical tissue. The real curative agent was the removal of the emotional scars, the security against social "cuts," the healing of emotional hurts and injuries, and the restoration of his self-image as an acceptable member of society, which—in his case—surgery made possible.

How Emotional Scars Alienate You From Life

Many people have inner emotional scars who have never suffered physical injuries. And the result on personality is the same. These people have been hurt or injured by someone in the past. To guard against future injury *from that source* they form a spiritual callus, an emotional scar to protect their ego. This scar tissue, however, not only "protects" them from the individual who originally hurt them—it "protects" them against all other human beings. An emotional wall is built through which neither friend nor foe can pass.

A woman, who has been "hurt" by one man, takes a vow never to trust *any man* again. A child who has had his ego sliced up by a despotic and cruel parent or teacher, may take a vow never to trust *any authority* in the future. A man who has had his love rejected by *one woman* may take a vow never to become emotionally involved with *any human being* in the future.

As in the case of a facial scar, excessive protection against the original source of injury can make us more vulnerable, and do us even more damage in other areas. The emotional wall that we build as protection against *one person,* cuts us off from all other human beings, and from our real selves. As we have pointed out previously, the person who feels "lonely" or out of touch with other human beings, also feels out of touch with his real self and with life.

Emotional Scars Help Make Juvenile Delinquents

Psychiatrist Bernard Holland has pointed out that although juvenile delinquents appear to be very independent and have the reputation of being braggarts, particularly about how they hate everyone in authority, they protest too much. Underneath this hard exterior shell, says Dr. Holland, "is a soft vulnerable inner person who wants to be dependent upon others." However, they cannot get close to anyone because they will not trust anyone. Sometime in the past they were hurt by a person important to them, and they dare not leave themselves open to be hurt again. They always have their defenses up. To prevent further rejection and pain, they attack first. Thus, they drive away the very people who would love them, if given half a chance, and could help them.

Emotional Scars Create a Marred and Ugly Self-Image

Emotional scars to our ego also have another adverse effect. They lead to the development of a scarred, marred, self-image; the picture of a person not liked or accepted by other human beings; the picture of a person who can't get along well in the world of people in which he lives.

Emotional scars prevent you from creative living, or being what Dr. Arthur W. Combs calls a "self-fulfilled person." Dr. Combs, professor of educational psychology and counseling at the University of Florida, says that the goal of every human being should be to become a "self-fulfilled person." This, he says, is not something you're born with, but must be achieved. Self-fulfilled persons have the following characteristics:

1. They see themselves as liked, wanted, acceptable and able individuals.

2. They have a high degree of acceptance of themselves as they are.
3. They have a feeling of oneness with others.
4. They have a rich store of information and knowledge.

The person with emotional scars not only has a self-image of an unwanted, unliked, and incapable person, he also has an image of the world in which he lives as a hostile place. His primary relationship with the world is one of hostility, and his dealings with other people are not based upon giving and accepting, cooperating, working with, enjoying with, but upon concepts of overcoming, combating, and protecting from. He can neither be charitable towards others nor himself. Frustration, aggression, and loneliness are the price he pays.

Three Rules for Immunizing Yourself
Against Emotional Hurts

(1) BE TOO BIG TO FEEL THREATENED:

Many people become "hurt" terribly by tiny pin-pricks or what we call social "slights." Everyone knows someone in the family, office, or circle of friends who is so thin-skinned and "sensitive" that others must be continually on guard, lest offense be taken at some innocent word or act.

It is a well-known psychologic fact that the people who become offended the easiest, have the lowest self-esteem. We are "hurt" by those things we conceive of as threats to our ego or self-esteem. Fancied emotional thrusts which go by unnoticed by the person with wholesome self-esteem slice these people up terribly. Even the real "digs" and "cuts" which inflict a terrible injury to the ego of the person with low self-esteem, do not make a dent in the ego of the person who thinks well of himself. It is the person who feels undeserving, doubts his own capabilities, and has a poor opinion of himself who becomes jealous at the drop of a hat. It is the person who secretly doubts his own worth and who feels insecure within himself, who sees threats to his ego where there are none, that exaggerates and over-estimates the potential damage from real threats.

We all need a certain amount of emotional toughness and ego-security to protect us from real and fancied ego-threats. It wouldn't be wise for our physical body to be covered over completely with a hard callus, or a shell like a turtle's. We would be denied the pleasure of all sensual feeling. But our body does have a layer of outer skin, the epidermis, for the purpose of protecting us from invasion of bacteria, small bumps and bruises, and small pin-pricks. The epidermis is thick enough and tough enough to offer protection against small wounds, but not so thick and hard that it interferes with all feeling. Many people have no epidermis on their ego. They have only the thin, sensitive inner skin. They need to become thicker-skinned, emotionally tougher, so that they will simply ignore petty cuts and minor ego threats.

Also, they need to build up their self-esteem, get a better and more adequate self-image of themselves so that they will not feel threatened by every chance remark or innocent act. A big strong man does not feel threatened by a small danger; a little man does. In the same way a healthy strong ego, with plenty of self-esteem, does not feel itself threatened by every innocent remark.

Healthy Self-Images Do Not Bruise Easily

The person who feels his self-worth is threatened by a slighting remark, has a small weak ego and a small amount of self-esteem. He is "self-centered," self-concerned, hard to get along with and what we call "egotistic." But we do not cure a sick or weak ego by beating it down, undermining it, or making it even weaker through "self-abnegation" or trying to become "selfless." Self-esteem is as necessary to the spirit as food is to the body. The cure for self-centeredness, self-concern, "egotism" and all the ills that go with it, is the development of a healthy strong ego by building up self-esteem. When a person has adequate self-esteem little slights offer no threat at all—they are simply "passed over" and ignored. Even deeper emotional wounds are likely to heal faster and cleaner, with no festering sores to poison life and spoil happiness.

(2) A SELF-RELIANT, RESPONSIBLE ATTITUDE MAKES YOU LESS VULNERABLE:

As Dr. Holland has pointed out, the juvenile delinquent with the hard outer shell has a soft, vulnerable inner person who *wants to be dependent* upon others, and wants to be loved by others.

Salesmen tell me that the person who apparently puts up the most sales resistance at the outset, is frequently an "easy" sell once you get past his defenses; that people who feel called upon to put up "No salesmen allowed" signs, do so because they know they are soft touches and need protection.

The person with the hard, gruff exterior, usually develops it because instinctively he realizes that he is so soft inside that he needs protection.

The person who has little or no self-reliance, who feels emotionally dependent upon others, makes himself most vulnerable to emotional hurts. Every human being wants and needs love and affection. But the creative, self-reliant person also feels a need to *give love*. His emphasis is as much or more on the giving as on the getting. He doesn't expect love to be handed to him on a silver platter. Nor does he have a compulsive need that "everybody" must love him and approve of him. He has sufficient ego-security to tolerate the fact that a certain number of people will dislike him and disapprove. He feels some sense of responsibility for his life and conceives of himself primarily as one who acts, determines, gives, goes after what he wants, rather than as a person who is the passive recipient of all the good things in life.

The passive-dependent person turns his entire destiny over to other people, circumstances, luck. Life owes him a living and other people owe him consideration, appreciation, love, happiness. He makes unreasonable demands and claims on other people and feels cheated, wronged, hurt, when they aren't fulfilled. Because life just isn't built that way, he is seeking the impossible and leaving himself "wide open" to emotional hurts and injuries. Someone has said that the neurotic personality is forever "bumping into" reality.

Develop a more self-reliant attitude. Assume responsibility for your own life and emotional needs. Try *giving* affection, love, approval, acceptance, understanding, to other people, and you will find them coming back to you as a sort of reflex action.

(3) RELAX AWAY EMOTIONAL HURTS:

I once had a patient ask me: "If the forming of scar tissue is a natural and automatic thing, why doesn't scar tissue form when a plastic surgeon makes an incision?"

The answer is that if you cut your face and it "heals naturally," scar tissue will form, because there is a certain amount of tension in the wound and just underneath the wound which pulls the surface of the skin back, creates a "gap" so to speak, which is filled in by scar tissue. When a plastic surgeon operates, he not only pulls the skin together by sutures, he also cuts out a small amount of flesh underneath the skin so that there is no tension present. The incision heals smoothly, evenly, and with no distorting surface scar.

It is interesting to note that the same thing happens in the case of an emotional wound. If there is no tension present, there is no disfiguring emotional scar left.

Have you ever noticed how easy it is to "get your feelings hurt," or "take offense," when you are suffering tensions brought about by frustration, fear, anger, or—depression.

We go to work feeling out of sorts, or down in the dumps, or with self-confidence shaken because of some adverse experience. A friend comes by and makes a joking remark. Nine times out of ten we would laugh, think it funny, "think nothing about it," and make a good-natured crack in return. But not today. Today, we are suffering tensions of self-doubt, insecurity, anxiety. We "take" the remark in the wrong way, become offended and hurt, and an emotional scar begins to form.

This simple, everyday experience illustrates very well the principle that we are injured and hurt emotionally—not so much by other people or what they say or don't say—but by *our own attitude* and *our own response*.

Relaxation Cushions Emotional Blows

When we "feel hurt" or "feel offended," the *feeling* is entirely a matter of our own response. In fact the feeling *is* our response.

It is our own responses that we have to be concerned about—not other people's. We can tighten up, become angry, anxious, or resentful and "feel hurt." Or, we can make no response, remain relaxed and feel no hurt. Scientific experiments have shown that it is absolutely impossible to feel fear, anger, anxiety, or negative emotions of any kind while the muscles of the body are kept perfectly relaxed. We have to "do something" to feel fear, anger, anxiety. "No man is hurt but by himself," said Diogenes.

"Nothing can work me damage except myself," said St. Bernard. "The harm that I sustain I carry about with me, and am never a real sufferer but by my own fault."

You alone are responsible for your responses and reactions. You do not *have* to respond at all. You can remain relaxed and free from injury.

Thought Control Brought These People New Life

At Shirley Center, Massachusetts, results attained by group psychotherapy have surpassed results obtained by classic psychoanalysis and in a much shorter time. Two things are emphasized: "Group Training in Thought Control" and daily relaxation periods. The aim is "re-education intellectually and emotionally, in order to find the way into a kind of life that will be fundamentally successful and happy." (Winfred Rhoades, "Group Training in Thought Control for Relieving Nervous Disorders," *Mental Hygiene,* 1935.)

Patients, in addition to "intellectual re-education" and advice on thought control, are taught to relax by lying in a comfortable position while the director paints them a pleasant word picture of some placid, calm outdoor scene. The patients are also asked to practice relaxation daily at home, and to carry the calm peaceful feeling with them throughout the day.

One woman patient, who found a new way of life at the center, wrote, "I had seven years of sickness, I could not sleep. I had a hot temper. I was a miserable person to live with. For years I thought I had a mutt of a husband. When he came home after a single drink, and was perhaps fighting the craving, I would get excited and use harsh words and drive him to a spree instead of helping him in his fight. Now I say nothing and keep calm. That helps him and he and I get along swell. I was living my life antagonistically. I exaggerated little troubles. I was at the point of suicide. When I came to the class I began to realize that it was not the world that was wrong with me. I am now healthier than ever before and happier. In the old days I didn't ever relax, even in my sleep. Now I don't bustle around as I used to, and I get the same amount of work done and don't get tired out as I used to."

HOW TO REMOVE OLD EMOTIONAL SCARS

We can prevent, and immunize ourselves against, emotional scars by practicing the three foregoing rules. But what about the old emotional scars which were formed in the past—the old hurts, grudges, grievances against life, resentments?

Once an emotional scar has formed, there is but one thing to do and that is to remove it by surgery, the same as a physical scar.

Give Yourself a Spiritual Face Lift

In removing old emotional scars, you alone can do the operation. You must become your own plastic surgeon—and give yourself a spiritual face lift. The results will be new life and new vitality, a new-found peace of mind and happiness.

To speak of an emotional face lift and the use of "mental surgery" is more than a simile.

Old emotional scars cannot be doctored or medicated. They must be "cut out," given up entirely, eradicated. Many people apply various kinds of salve or balm to old emotional wounds, but this simply does not work. They may self-righteously forego overt and physical revenge, yet "take it out" or "get even" in many subtle ways. A typical example is the wife who discovers her husband's infidelity. Upon the advice of her minister and/or psychiatrist she agrees she should "forgive" him. Accordingly she does not shoot him. She does not leave him. In all overt behavior she is a "dutiful" wife. She keeps his house neatly. She prepares his meals well, and so on. But she makes his life hell on earth in many subtle ways by the coldness of her heart and by flaunting her moral superiority. When he complains, her answer is, "Well, dear, I did forgive you—but I cannot forget." Her very "forgiveness" becomes a thorn in his side, because she is conscious of the fact that it is proof of her moral superiority. She would have been more kind to him, and been happier herself, had she refused this type of forgiveness and left him.

Forgiveness Is a Scalpel
Which Removes Emotional Scars

" 'I can forgive, but I cannot forget,' is only another way of saying 'I will not forgive,' " said Henry Ward Beecher. "Forgiveness ought to be like a cancelled note—torn in two, and burned up, so that it never can be shown against one."

Forgiveness, when it is real and genuine and complete, *and forgotten*—is the scalpel which can remove the pus from old emotional wounds, heal them, and eliminate scar tissue.

Forgiveness which is partial, or half-hearted, works no better than a partially completed surgical operation on the face. Pretended forgiveness, which is entered into as a duty, is no more effective than a simulated facial surgery.

Your forgiveness should be forgotten, as well as the wrong which was forgiven. Forgiveness which is remembered, and dwelt upon, re-infects the wound you are attempting to cauterize. If you are too proud of your forgiveness, or remember it too much, you are very apt to feel that the other person owes you something for forgiving him. You forgive him one debt, but in doing so, he incurs another, much like the operators of small loan companies who cancel one note and make out a new one every two weeks.

Forgiveness Is Not a Weapon

There are many common fallacies regarding forgiveness, and one of the reasons that its therapeutic value has not been more recognized is the fact that *real* forgiveness has been so seldom tried. For example, many writers have told us that we should forgive to make us "good." We have seldom been advised to forgive that we might be happy. Another fallacy is that forgiveness places us in a superior position, or is a method of winning out over our enemy. This thought has appeared in many glib phrases such as—"Don't merely try to 'get even'—forgive your enemy and you 'get ahead' of him." Tillotson, the former Archbishop of Canterbury, tells us, "A more glorious victory cannot be gained over another man, than this, that when the injury began on his part, the kindness should begin on ours." This is just another way of saying that forgiveness itself can be used as an effective weapon of revenge—which it can. Revengeful forgiveness, however, is not therapeutic forgiveness.

Therapeutic forgiveness cuts out, eradicates, cancels, makes the wrong as if it had never been. Therapeutic forgiveness is like surgery.

Give Up Grudges as You Would a Gangrenous Arm

First, the "wrong"—and particularly our own feeling of condemnation of it—must be seen as an undesirable thing rather than a desirable thing. Before a man can agree within himself to have his arm amputated, he must cease to see his arm as a desirable thing to be retained, but as an undesirable, damaging and threatening thing to be given up.

In facial surgery there can be no partial, tentative, or halfway measures. The scar tissue is cut out, completely and entirely. The wound is allowed to heal cleanly. And care is taken to see that the face will be *restored* in every particular, just as it was before injury and just as if the injury had never been.

You Can Forgive—If You're Willing

Therapeutic forgiveness is not difficult. The only difficulty is to secure your own willingness to give up and do without your sense of condemnation—your willingness to cancel out the debt, with no mental reservations.

We find it difficult to forgive only because we like our sense of condemnation. We get a perverse and morbid enjoyment out of nursing our wounds. As long as we can condemn another, we can feel superior to him.

No one can deny that there is also a perverse sense of satisfaction in feeling sorry for yourself.

Your Reasons for Forgiveness Are Important

In therapeutic forgiveness we cancel out the debt of the other person, not because we have decided to be generous, or do him a favor, or because we are a morally superior person. We cancel the debt, mark it "null and void," not because we have made the other person "pay" sufficiently for his wrong—but because we have come to recognize that the debt itself is not valid. True forgiveness comes only when we are able to see, and emotionally accept, that there is and was *nothing for us to forgive*. We should not have condemned or hated the other person in the first place.

Not long ago I went to a luncheon also attended by a number of clergymen. The subject of forgiveness came up in general, and the case of the adulterous woman whom Jesus forgave in particular. I listened to a very learned discussion of why Jesus was able to "forgive" the woman, how he forgave her, how his forgiveness was a rebuke to the church men of his time who were ready to stone her, etc. etc.

Jesus Didn't "Forgive" the Adulterous Woman

I resisted the temptation to shock these gentlemen by pointing out that actually Jesus never forgave the woman at all. Nowhere in the narrative, as it appears in the New Testament, are the words "forgive" or "forgiveness" used, or even hinted at. Nor can they be reasonably implied from the facts as given in the story. We are told merely that after her accusers had left, Jesus asked the woman— "Hath no man condemned thee?" When she answered in the negative, he said, "Neither do I condemn thee— go and sin no more."

You cannot forgive a person unless you have first condemned him. Jesus never condemned the woman in the first place—so there was nothing for him to forgive. He recognized her sin, or her mistake, but did not feel called upon to hate her for it. He was able to see, before the fact, what you and I must see after the fact in practicing forgiveness: that we ourselves err when we hate a person because of his mistakes, or when we condemn him, or classify him as a certain type of person, confusing his person with his behavior; or when we mentally incur a debt that the other person must "pay" before being restored to our good graces, and our emotional acceptance.

Whether you "ought" to do this, or whether you "should" do it, or can reasonably be expected to do it, is a matter which is outside the scope of this book, and my own field. I can only tell you as a doctor that if you *will* do it, you will be far happier, healthier and attain more peace of mind. However, I would like to point out that this is what therapeutic forgiveness is, and that it is the only type of forgiveness that really "works." And if forgiveness is anything less than this, we might as well stop talking about it.

Forgive Yourself as Well as Others

Not only do we incur emotional wounds from others, most of us inflict them upon ourselves.

We beat ourselves over the head with self-condemnation, remorse and regret. We beat ourselves down with self-doubt. We cut ourselves up with excessive guilt.

Remorse and regret are attempts to emotionally live in the past. Excessive guilt is an attempt to make right *in the past* something we did wrong or thought of as wrong in the past.

Emotions are used correctly and appropriately when they help us to respond or react appropriately to some reality in the present environment. Since we cannot live in the past, we cannot appropriately react emotionally to the past. The past can be simply written off, closed, forgotten, insofar as our emotional reactions are concerned. We do not need to take an "emotional position" one way or the other regarding detours that might have taken us off course in the past. The important thing is our present direction and our present goal.

We need to recognize our own errors as mistakes. Otherwise we could not correct course. "Steering" or "guidance" would be impossible. But it is futile and fatal to hate or condemn ourselves for our mistakes.

You Make Mistakes—Mistakes Do Not Make "You"

Also, in thinking of our own mistakes (or those of others) it is helpful, and realistic, to think in terms of what we *did* or *did not do,* rather than in terms of what the mistakes *made us.*

One of the biggest mistakes we can make is to confuse our behavior with our "self" . . . to conclude that because we *did* a certain act it characterizes us as a certain sort of person. It clarifies thinking if we can see that mistakes involve something we *do*—they refer to actions, and to be realistic we should use verbs denoting action, rather than nouns denoting a state of being in describing them.

For example, to say "I *failed*" (verb form) is but to recognize an error, and can help lead to future success.

But to say, "I am a *failure*" (noun form) does not describe what *you did,* but what *you think the mistake did to you.* This does not contribute to learning, but tends to "fixate" the mistake and make it permanent. This has been proved over and over in clinical psychologic experiments.

We seem to recognize that all children, in learning to walk, will occasionally fall. We say "he fell" or he "stumbled." We do not say "he is a faller" or he is a "stumbler."

However, many parents do fail to recognize that all children, in learning to talk, also make mistakes or "non-fluences"—hesitation, blocking, repetition of syllables and words. It is a common experience for an anxious, concerned parent to conclude, "He is a stutterer." Such an attitude, or a judgment—not of the child's *actions* but of the child himself, gets across to the child and he begins to think of himself as a stutterer. His learning is fixated, the stutter tends to become permanent.

According to Dr. Wendell Johnson, the nation's foremost authority on stuttering, this sort of thing is *the* cause of stuttering. He has found that the parents of non-stutterers are more likely to use descriptive terms ("He did not speak"), whereas the parents of stutterers were inclined to use judgmental terms ("He *could* not speak"). Writing in the *Saturday Evening Post,* January 5, 1957, Dr. Johnson said, "Slowly we began to comprehend the vital point that had been missed for so many centuries. Case after case had developed after it had been diagnosed as stuttering by over-anxious persons unfamiliar with the facts of normal speech development. The parents rather than the child, the listeners rather than the speakers, seemed to be the ones most requiring understanding and instruction."

Dr. Knight Dunlap, who made a 20 year study of habits, their making, unmaking, and relation to learning, discovered that the same principle applied to virtually all "bad habits," including bad emotional habits. It was essential, he said, that the patient learn to stop blaming himself, condemning himself, and feeling remorseful over his habits—if he were to cure them. He found particularly damaging the conclusion "I am ruined," or "I am worthless," because the patient had done, or was doing, certain acts.

So remember "You" make mistakes. Mistakes don't make "You"—anything.

Who Wants to Be an Oyster?

One final word about preventing and removing emotional hurts. To live creatively, we must be willing to be *a little vulnerable*. We must be willing to be *hurt a little*—if necessary, in creative living. A lot of people need a thicker and tougher emotional skin than they have. But they need only a tough emotional hide or epidermis—not a shell. To trust, to love, to open ourselves to emotional communication with other people is to run the risk of being hurt. If we are hurt once, we can do one of two things. We can build a thick protective shell, or scar tissue, to prevent being hurt again, live like an oyster, and not be hurt. Or we can "turn the other cheek," remain vulnerable and go on living creatively.

An oyster is never "hurt." He has a thick shell which protects him from everything. He is isolated. An oyster is secure, but not creative. He cannot "go after" what he wants—he must wait for it to come to him. An oyster knows none of the "hurts" of emotional communication with his environment—but neither can an oyster know the joys.

An Emotional Face Lift Makes You Look and Feel Younger

Try giving yourself a "Spiritual Face Lift." It is more than a play on words. It opens you up to more life, more vitality, the "stuff" that youth is made of. You'll feel younger. You'll actually look younger. Many times I have seen a man or woman apparently grow five or ten years younger in appearance after removing old emotional scars. Look around you. Who are the youthful looking people you know over the age of forty? The grumpy? Resentful? The pessimistic? The ones who are "soured on the world," or the cheerful, optimistic, good-natured people?

Carrying a grudge against someone or against life can bring on the old age stoop, just as much as carrying a heavy weight around on your shoulders would. People with emotional scars, grudges, and the like are living in the past, which is characteristic of old people. The youthful attitude and youthful spirit which erases wrinkles from the soul and the face, and puts a sparkle in the eye, looks to the future and has a great expectation to look forward to.

So, why not give yourself a face lift? Your do-it-yourself kit consists of relaxation of negative tensions to prevent scars, therapeutic forgiveness to remove old scars, providing yourself with a tough (but not a hard) epidermis instead of a shell, creative living, a willingness to be a *little vulnerable,* and a nostalgia for the future instead of the past.

Points to Remember
(Fill in)

1.

2.

3.

4.

5.

6.

7.

CHAPTER ELEVEN

How to Unlock
Your Real Personality

"PERSONALITY," that magnetic and mysterious something that is easy to recognize but difficult to define, is not so much something that is acquired from without, as something that is *released,* from within.

What we call "personality" is the outward evidence of that unique and individual creative self, made in the image of God—that spark of divinity within us—or what might be called the free and full expression of your real self.

This real self within every person *is* attractive. It *is* magnetic. It does have a powerful impact and influence upon other people. We have the feeling that we are in touch with something real—and basic—and it does something to us. On the other hand, a phony is universally disliked and detested.

Why does everyone love a baby? Certainly not for what the baby can *do,* or what he *knows,* or what he *has,* but simply because of what he *is.* Every infant has "personality plus." There is no superficiality, no phoniness, no hypocrisy. In his own language, which consists of either crying or cooing, the baby expresses his real feelings. He "says what he means." There is no guile. The baby is certainly honest. He exemplifies to the nth degree the psychologic dictum—"Be yourself." He has no qualms about expressing himself. He is not in the least inhibited.

Everyone Has Personality Locked Up Within Him

Every human being *has* the mysterious something we call personality.

When we say that a person "has a good personality" what we really mean is that he has freed and released the creative potential within him and is able to express his real self.

"Poor personality" and "inhibited personality" are one and the same. The person with a "poor personality" does not express the creative self within. He has restrained it, handcuffed it, locked it up and thrown away the key. The word "inhibit" literally means to stop, prevent, prohibit, restrain. The inhibited personality has imposed restraint upon the expression of the real self. For one reason or another he is afraid to express himself, afraid to be himself, and has locked up his real self within an inner prison.

The symptoms of inhibition are many and varied: shyness, timidity, self-consciousness, hostility, feelings of excessive guilt, insomnia, nervousness, irritability, inability to get along with others.

Frustration is characteristic of practically every area and activity of the inhibited personality. His real and basic frustration is his failure to "be himself" and his failure to adequately express himself. But this basic frustration is likely to color and overflow into all that he does.

Excessive Negative Feedback is the Key to Inhibition

The science of Cybernetics gives us a new insight into the inhibited personality, and shows us the way toward disinhibition, freedom, and how to release our spirits from self-imposed prisons.

Negative feedback in a servo-mechanism is equivalent to *criticism*. Negative feedback says in effect, "You are wrong—you are off course—you need to take corrective action to get back on the beam."

The purpose of negative feedback, however, is to *modify response,* and change the course of *forward action,* not to *stop it altogether.*

If negative feedback is working properly, a missile or a torpedo reacts to "criticism" just enough to correct course, and keeps going forward toward the target. This course will be, as we have previously explained, a series of zig-zags.

However, if the mechanism is too sensitive to negative feedback, the servo-mechanism overcorrects. Instead of progressing toward the target, it will perform exaggerated lateral zig-zags, or stop all forward progress altogether.

Our own built-in servo-mechanism works in the same way. We must have negative feedback in order to operate purposely, in order to steer our way, or be guided to a goal.

Excessive Negative Feedback Equals Inhibition

Negative feedback always says in effect, "Stop what you're doing, or the way you're doing it—*and do something else."* Its purpose is to modify response, or change the degree of forward action—not to stop all action. Negative feedback does not say, "stop—period!" It says, "What you are doing is wrong," but it does not say, "it is wrong to do anything."

Yet, where negative feedback is excessive, or where our own mechanism is *too sensitive* to negative feedback, the result is not modification of response—but total inhibition of response.

Inhibition and excessive negative feedback are one and the same. When we over-react to negative feedback or criticism, we are likely to conclude that not only is our present course slightly off-beam, or wrong, but that it is wrong for us even to want to go forward.

A woodsman, or a hunter, often guides himself back to his automobile by picking out some prominent landmark near his car—such as an extra tall tree which can be seen for miles. When he is ready to return to his car, he looks for his tree (or target) and starts walking towards it. From time to time the tree may be lost from his view, but as soon as he is able he "checks course" by comparing his direction with the location of the tree. If he finds that his present course is taking him 15 degrees to the left of the tree, he must recognize that what he is doing is "wrong." He immediately corrects his course and again walks directly towards the tree. *He does not, however, conclude that it is wrong for him to walk.*

Yet, many of us are guilty of just so foolish a conclusion. When it comes to our attention that our *manner of expression* is off course, missing the mark, or "wrong"— we conclude that *self-expression* itself is wrong, or that success for us (reaching our particular tree) is wrong.

Keep in mind that excessive negative feedback has the effect of interfering with, or stopping completely, the appropriate response.

Stuttering as a Symptom of Inhibition

Stuttering offers a good illustration of how excessive negative feedback brings on inhibition, and interferes with appropriate response.

While most of us are not consciously aware of the fact, when we talk we receive negative feedback data through our ears by listening to or "monitoring" our own voice. This is the reason that totally deaf individuals seldom speak well. They have no way of knowing whether their voice is coming out as a shriek, a scream, or an unintelligible mumble. This is also the reason that persons born deaf, do not learn to talk at all, except with special tutoring. If you sing, perhaps you have been surprised to find that you could not sing on key, or in harmony with others, while suffering temporary deafness or partial deafness because of a cold.

Thus, negative feedback itself is no bar or handicap to speech. On the contrary, it *enables* us to speak and speak correctly. Voice teachers advise that we record our own voices on a tape recorder, and listen back to them, as a method of improving tone, enunciation, etc. By doing this we become aware of errors in speech that we had not noticed before. We are able to see clearly what it is we are doing "wrong"—and we can make correction.

However, if negative feedback is to be effective in helping us to talk better, it should (1) be more or less automatic or subconscious, (2) it should occur spontaneously, *or while we're talking* and (3) response to feedback should not be so sensitive as to result in inhibition.

If we are consciously overcritical of our speech, or if we are *too careful* in trying to avoid errors in advance, rather than reacting spontaneously, stuttering is likely to result.

If the stutterer's excessive feedback can be toned down, or if it can be made spontaneous rather than anticipatory, improvement in speech will be immediate.

Conscious Self-Criticism Makes You Do Worse

This has been proved by Dr. E. Colin Cherry of London, England. Writing in the British scientific journal, *Nature,* Dr. Cherry stated his belief that stuttering was caused by "excessive monitoring." To test his theory he equipped 25 severe stutterers with earphones through which a loud tone drowned out the sound of their own voices. When asked to read aloud from a prepared text under these conditions, which eliminated self-criticism, the improvement was "remarkable." Another group of severe stutterers was trained in "shadow-talk"—to follow as closely as possible, and attempt to "talk with" a person reading from a text, or a voice on radio or TV. After brief practice the stutterers learned to "shadow-talk" easily—and most of them were able to speak normally and correctly under these conditions, which obviated "advance criticism" and literally forced them to speak spontaneously—or to synchronize speaking and "correcting." Additional practice in "shadow-talk" enabled the stutterers to learn how to speak correctly at all times.

When excessive negative feedback, or self-criticism, was eliminated, inhibition disappeared and performance improved. When there was no time for worry, or too much "carefulness" in advance, expression immediately improved. This gives us a valuable clue as to how we may disinhibit or release a locked up personality, and improve performance in other areas.

Excessive "Carefulness"
Leads to Inhibition and Anxiety

Have you ever tried to thread a needle?

If so, and if you are inexperienced at it, you may have noticed that you could hold the thread steady as a rock *until* you approached the eye of the needle and *attempted* to insert it into the very small opening. Each time you tried to place the thread through the small opening, your hand unaccountably shook and the thread missed the mark.

Attempting to pour a liquid into the mouth of a very small-necked bottle often results in the same kind of behavior. You can hold your hand perfectly steady, until you try to accomplish your *purpose,* then for some strange reason you quiver and shake.

In medical circles, we call this "purpose tremor."

It occurs, as above, in normal people when they try too hard, or are "too careful" not to make an error in accomplishing some purpose. In certain pathological conditions, such as injury to certain areas of the brain, this "purpose tremor" can become very pronounced. A patient, for example, may be able to hold his hand steady as long as he is not trying to accomplish anything. But let him try to insert his door-key into the lock on his front door, and his hand may "zigzag" back and forth as much as six to ten inches. He may be able to hold a pen steady enough until he attempts to sign his name. Then his hand tremors uncontrollably. If he is ashamed of this, and becomes even more "careful" not to make an error in the presence of strangers, he may not be able to sign his name at all.

These people can be helped, and often remarkably, by training in relaxation techniques where they learn to relax from excessive effort and "purposing" and not to be overly-careful in trying to avoid errors or "failures."

Excessive carefulness, or being too anxious not to make an error is a form of excessive negative feedback. As in the case of the stutterer, who attempts to anticipate possible errors and be overly-careful not to make them—the result is inhibition and deterioration of performance. Excessive carefulness and anxiety are close kin. Both have to do with too much concern for possible failure, or doing the "wrong thing," and making too much of a conscious effort to do right.

"I don't like these cold, precise, perfect people, who, in order not to speak wrong, never speak at all, and in order not to do wrong, never do anything," said Henry Ward Beecher.

William James's Advice to Students and Teachers

"Who are the scholars who get 'rattled' in the recitation-room?" asked the sage. "Those who think of the possibilities of failure and feel the great importance of the act." James continues: "Who are those who do recite well? Often those who are most indifferent. *Their* ideas reel themselves out of their memories of their own accord. Why do we hear the complaint so often that the social life in New England is either less rich and expressive or more fatiguing than it is in some other parts of the world? To what is the fact, if fact it be, due unless to the over-active conscience of the people, afraid of either saying something too trivial and obvious, or something insincere, or something unworthy of one's interlocutor, or something in some way or other not adequate to the occasion? How can conversation possibly steer itself through such a sea of responsibilities and inhibitions such as this? On the other hand, conversation does flourish and society is refreshing, and neither dull on the one hand nor exhausting from its effort on the other, wherever people forget their scruples and take the brakes off their hearts, and let their tongues wag as automatically and irresponsibly as they will.

"They talk much in pedagogic circles today about the duty of the teacher to prepare for every lesson in advance. To some extent this is useful. But we Yankees are assuredly not those to whom such a general doctrine should be preached. We are only too careful as it is. The advice I should give to most teachers would be in the words of one who is himself an admirable teacher. Prepare yourself in the subject so well that it shall always be on tap; then in the class-room trust your spontaneity and fling away all further care.

"My advice to students, especially to girl students, would be somewhat similar. Just as a bicycle chain may be too tight, so may one's carefulness and conscientious-ness be so tense as to hinder the running of one's mind. Take, for example, periods when there are many succes-sive days of examination impending. One ounce of good nervous tone in an examination is worth many pounds of anxious study for it in advance. If you want really to do your best in an examination, fling away the book the day before, say to yourself, 'I won't waste another minute on this miserable thing, and I don't care an iota whether I succeed or not.' Say this sincerely, and feel it, and go out and play, or go to bed and sleep, and I am sure the results next day will encourage you to use the method permanently." (William James, *On Vital Reserves,* New York, Henry Holt and Co., Inc.)

"Self-consciousness" Is Really "Others Consciousness"

The cause-and-effect relationship between excessive negative feedback and what we call "self-consciousness" can be readily seen.

In any sort of social relationship we constantly receive negative feedback data from other people. A smile, a frown, a hundred different subtle clues of approval or disapproval, interest or lack of interest, continually advise us of "how we're doing," whether we're getting across, whether we're hitting or missing the mark, so to speak. In any sort of social situation there is a constant interaction going on between speaker and listener, actor and observer. And without this constant communication, back and forth, human relations and social activities would be virtually impossible. And if not impossible, certainly dull, boring, non-inspiring and dead, without "sparks."

Good actors and actresses and public speakers can sense this communication from the audience, and it helps them to perform better. Persons with "good personalities," who are popular and magnetic in social situations, can sense this communication from other people and they automatically and spontaneously react and respond to it in a creative way. The communication from other people is used as negative feedback, and enables the person to perform better socially. Unless a person can respond to this communication from other people, he is a "cold fish" type—the "reserved" personality who does not warm up to other people. Without this communication you become a social dud—the hard-to-get-to-know type who interests no one.

However, this type of negative feedback, to be effective, should be creative. That is, it should be more or less subconscious and automatic, and spontaneous, rather than consciously contrived or thought about.

"What Others Think" Creates Inhibition

When you become too consciously concerned about "what others think"; when you become too careful to consciously try to please other people; when you become too sensitive to the real or fancied disapproval of other people—then you have excessive negative feedback, inhibition, and poor performance.

Whenever you constantly and consciously monitor your every act, word, or manner, again you become inhibited and self-conscious.

You become too careful to make a good impression, and in so doing choke off, restrain, inhibit your creative self and end up making a rather poor impression.

The way to make a good impression on other people is: Never consciously "try" to make a good impression on them. Never act, or fail to act purely for consciously contrived effect. Never "wonder" consciously what the other person is thinking of you, how he is judging you.

How a Salesman Cured Self-consciousness

James Mangan, the famous salesman, author, and lecturer, says that when he first left home he was painfully self-conscious, especially when eating in the dining room of a "ritzy" or high-class hotel. As he walked through the dining room he felt that every eye was upon him, judging him, critical of him. He was painfully conscious of his every movement, motion and act—the way he walked, the way he sat down, his table manners and the way he ate his food. And all these actions seemed stiff and awkward. Why was he so ill at ease? he asked himself. He knew he had good table manners and knew enough social etiquette to get by. Why had he never felt self-conscious and ill at ease when eating in the kitchen with Ma and Pa?

He decided it was because when he was eating with Ma

and Pa, he did not think or bother to wonder how he was acting. He was neither careful nor self-critical. He was not concerned about producing an effect. He had felt composed, relaxed, and had done all right.

James Mangan cured his self-consciousness by remembering how he had felt, and how he had acted, when he "was going to the kitchen to eat with Ma and Pa." Then, when he walked into a ritzy dining room, he would *imagine* or pretend that he "was going to eat with Ma and Pa"—and act that way.

Poise Comes When You Ignore Excessive Negative Feedbacks

Mangan also found that he could overcome his "stage fright" and self-consciousness when calling upon big shots, or in any other social situation, by saying to himself, "I'm going to eat with Ma and Pa," conjuring up in his imagination how he had felt and how he had acted— and then "acting that way." In his book, *The Knack of Selling Yourself,* Mangan advises salesmen to use the "I'm going home to eat supper with my Ma and Pa! I've been through this a thousand times—nothing new can happen here," attitude in all sorts of new and strange situations.

"This attitude of being immune to strangers or strange situations, this total disregard for all the unknown or unexpected has a name. It is called *poise*. Poise is the deliberate shunting aside of all fears arising from new and uncontrollable circumstances." (James Mangan, *The Knack of Selling Yourself,* The Dartnell Corp., Chicago.)

You Need to Be More Self-conscious

The late Dr. Albert Edward Wiggam, famous educator, psychologist, and lecturer, said that in his early years he was so painfully self-conscious he found it all but impossible to recite in school. He avoided other people, and could not talk to them without hanging his head. He constantly fought his self-consciousness and tried hard to overcome it, all to no avail. Then one day he got a new idea. His trouble was not "self-consciousness" at all. It was really excessive "others consciousness." He was too painfully sensitive to what others might think of everything he said or did, every move he made. This tied him up in knots—he could not think clearly, and he could think of nothing to say. He did not feel this way when alone with himself. When alone, he was perfectly calm and relaxed, at ease, poised, and he could think of lots of interesting ideas and things to say. And, he was also perfectly aware of and at home with his self.

Then he stopped fighting and trying to conquer his "self-consciousness," and instead concentrated on developing more self-consciousness: feeling, acting, behaving, thinking *as he did when he was alone,* without any regard to how some other person might feel about or judge him. This total disregard for the opinion and judgement of other people did not result in his becoming callous, arrogant, or entirely insensitive to others. There is no danger of entirely eradicating negative feedback, no matter how hard you may try. But this effort in the opposite direction did tone down his overly sensitive feedback mechanism. He got along better with other people, and went on to make his living counseling people and making public speeches to large groups, "without the slightest degree of self-consciousness."

"Conscience Doth Make Cowards of Us All"

So said Shakespeare. And so say modern-day psychiatrists and enlightened ministers.

Conscience itself is a *learned* negative feedback mechanism having to do with morals and ethics. If the learned and stored data is correct (concerning what is "right" and what is "wrong") and if the feedback mechanism is not overly sensitive, but realistic, the result is (just as with any other goal-striving situation) we are relieved from the burden of having to "decide" constantly as to what is right and wrong. Conscience steers us, or guides us, down the "straight and narrow" to the goal of correct, appropriate and realistic behavior insofar as ethics and morals are concerned. Conscience works automatically and subconsciously, as does any other feedback system.

However, as Dr. Harry Emerson Fosdick says, "Your conscience can fool you." Your conscience itself *can be wrong*. It depends upon your own basic beliefs concerning right and wrong. If your basic beliefs are true, realistic and sensible, conscience becomes a valuable ally in dealing with the real world and in sailing upon the ethical sea. It acts as a compass which "keeps you out of trouble" as a mariner's compass keeps him off the reefs. But if your basic beliefs are themselves wrong, untrue, unrealistic, or nonsensible, these "declinate" your compass and get it off true north, just as magnetic bits of metal can disturb the compass of the mariner, and guide him into trouble rather than away from it.

Conscience can mean many things to many people. If you are brought up to believe, as some people are, that it is sinful to wear buttons on your clothes, your conscience will bother you when you do. If you are brought up to believe that cutting off another human's head, shrinking it, and hanging it on your wall is right, proper, and a sign of manhood—then you will feel guilty, unworthy, and undeserving if you haven't managed to shrink a head. (Head-shrinking savages would no doubt call this a "sin of omission.")

Conscience's Job Is to Make You Happy— Not Miserable

The purpose of conscience is to help make us happy and productive—not the other way around. But if we are to "let our conscience be our guide," our conscience must be based upon truth—it must point to true north. Otherwise, blindly obeying conscience can only get us into trouble, rather than out of it, and make us unhappy and unproductive into the bargain.

Self-Expression Is Not a Moral Issue

Much mischief results from our taking a "moral" position on matters which are not basically moral matters at all.

For example, self-expression, or lack of it, is not basically an ethical question, aside from the fact that it is our "duty" to use the talents which our Creator gave us.

Yet, self-expression may become morally "wrong" as far as your conscience is concerned, if you were squelched, shut-up, shamed, humiliated, or perhaps punished as a child for speaking up, expressing your ideas, "showing off." Such a child "learns" that it is "wrong" to express himself, to hold himself out as having any worthwhile ideas, or perhaps to speak at all.

If a child is punished for showing anger, or shamed too much for showing fear, or perhaps made fun of for showing love, he learns that expressing his real feelings is "wrong." Some children learn that it is sinful or wrong only to express the "bad emotions"—anger and fear. But, when you inhibit bad emotions, you also inhibit the expression of good emotions. And the yardstick for judging emotions is not "goodness" or "badness," as such, but appropriateness and inappropriateness. It is appropriate for the man who meets with the bear on the trail to experience fear. It is appropriate to experience anger if there is a legitimate need to destroy an obstacle by sheer force and destructiveness. Properly directed and controlled, anger is an important element of courage.

If every time a child comes up with an opinion, he is squelched and put in his place, he learns that it is "right" for him to be a nobody, and wrong to want to be a somebody.

Such a distorted and unrealistic conscience does indeed make cowards of us all. We can become overly sensitive, and become too carefully concerned with whether we "have a right" to succeed in even a worthwhile endeavor. We become too carefully concerned about whether or not "I deserve this." Many people, inhibited by the wrong kind of conscience, "hold back," or "take a back seat" in any kind of endeavor, even in church activities. They secretly feel it would not be "right" for them to "hold themselves out" as a leader, or "presume to be somebody," or they are overly concerned with whether other people might think they were "showing off."

Stage fright is a common and universal phenomenon. It becomes understandable when seen as excessive negative feedback coming from a "declinated conscience." Stage fright is the fear that we will be punished for speaking up, expressing our own opinion, presuming to "be somebody," or "showing off"—things which most of us learned were "wrong" and punishable as children. Stage fright illustrates how universal is the suppression and inhibition of self-expression.

Disinhibition—a Long Step in the Opposite Direction

If you are among the millions who suffer unhappiness and failure because of inhibition—you need to deliberately practice *disinhibition*. You need to practice being less careful, less concerned, less conscientious. You need to practice speaking before you think instead of thinking before you speak—acting without thinking, instead of thinking or "considering carefully" before you act.

Commonly, when I advise a patient to practice disinhibition (and the most inhibited object the most), I am likely to hear something like this: "But surely you do not think that we need to exercise no care at all, no concern, no worry about results. It seems to me that the world needs a certain amount of inhibition, otherwise we would live like savages and civilized society would collapse. If we express ourselves without *any* restraint, freely expressing our feelings, we would go around punching people in the nose who disagreed with us."

"Yes," I say, "you are correct. The world does need a certain amount of inhibition. But not you. The key words are 'a certain amount.' You have such an excessive amount of inhibition, you are like a patient running a temperature of 108 degrees, who says, 'But surely heat is necessary for health. Man is a warm-blooded animal and could not live without a certain amount of temperature—we all need temperature—yet you are telling me that I should concentrate completely and entirely on *reducing my temperature,* and ignore completely the danger of not having any temperature.' "

The stutterer, who is already so tied up with "moral tensions," excessive negative feedback, self-critical analysis, and inhibition, that he cannot talk at all, is prone to argue in the same way, when told to *totally ignore* negative feedback and self-criticism. He can cite you numerous proverbs, apothegms, and the like to prove that one should think before he speaks, that an idle and careless tongue gets you into trouble, and that one should be very careful of what he says and how he says it because "good speech is important" and "a word spoken cannot be recalled." All that he is saying in effect is that negative feedback is a useful and beneficial thing. But *not for him.* When he totally ignores negative feedback by either being deafened by a loud tone, or by "shadow talk"—he speaks correctly.

The Straight and Narrow Path Between Inhibition and Disinhibition

Someone has said that the inhibited, worry-warty, anxiously concerned personality "stutters all over."

Balance and harmony are what is needed. When the temperature has gone *too high,* the doctor attempts to lower it; when it has sunk too low, he attempts to raise it. When a person cannot sleep enough, a prescription is given to make the patient sleep more; when a person sleeps too much, a stimulant is prescribed to keep him awake, etc. It is not a question of which is "best"—a hot or cold temperature, or sleepfulness or wakefulness. The "cure" lies in taking a long step in the opposite direction. Here, the principle of cybernetics enters into the picture again. Our goal is an adequate, self-fulfilling, creative personality. The path to the goal is a course between too much inhibition and too little. When there is too much, we correct course by ignoring inhibition and practicing more disinhibition.

How to Tell Whether You Need Disinhibition

Here are the "feedback" signals which can tell you whether you are off course because of too much or too little inhibition:

If you continually get yourself into trouble because of overconfidence; if you habitually "rush in where angels fear to tread"; if you habitually find yourself in hot water because of impulsive, ill-considered actions; if projects backfire on you because you always practice "acting first and asking questions later"; if you can never admit you're wrong; if you are a loud-talker and a blabber-mouth—you probably have *too little* inhibition. You need to think more of consequences before acting. You need to stop acting like a bull in a china shop, and plan your activities more carefully.

However, the great majority of people do not fall in the above category. If you are shy around strangers; if you dread new and strange situations; if you feel inadequate, worry a lot, are anxious, overly-concerned; if you are nervous, and feel self-conscious; if you have any "nervous symptoms" such as facial tics, blinking your eyes unnecessarily, tremor, difficulty in going to sleep; if you feel ill at ease in social situations; if you hold yourself back and continually take a back seat—then, these are all symptoms showing that you have too much inhibition—you are too careful in everything, you "plan" too much. You need to practice St. Paul's advice to the Ephesians: "Be careful in nothing. . . ."

Practice Exercises: 1. Don't wonder in advance what you are "going to say." Just open your mouth and say it. Improvise as you go along. (Jesus advises us to give no thought as to what we would say if delivered up to councils, but that the spirit would advise us what to say at the time.)

2. Don't plan (take no thought for tomorrow). Don't think before you act. Act—and correct your actions as you go along. This advice may seem radical, yet it is actually the way all servo-mechanisms *must* work. A torpedo does not "think out" all its errors in advance, and attempt to correct them in advance. It must *act first*—start moving toward the goal—*then* correct any errors which may occur. "We cannot think first and act afterwards," said A. N. Whitehead. "From the moment of birth we are immersed in action, and can only fitfully guide it by taking thought."

3. Stop criticising yourself. The inhibited person indulges in self-critical analysis continually. After each action, however simple, he says to himself, "I wonder if I should have done that." After he has gotten up courage enough to say something, he immediately says to himself, "Maybe I shouldn't have said that. Maybe the other person will take it the wrong way." Stop all this tearing yourself apart. Useful and beneficial feedback works subconsciously, spontaneously, and automatically. Conscious self-criticism, self-analysis, and introspection is good and useful—if undertaken perhaps once a year. But as a continual, moment-by-moment, day-by-day, sort of second-guessing yourself, or playing Monday-morning quarterback to your past actions—it is defeating. Watch for this self-criticism—pull yourself up short and stop it.

4. Make a habit of speaking *louder* than usual. Inhibited people are notoriously soft-spoken. Raise the volume of your voice. You don't have to shout at people

and use an angry tone—just consciously practice speaking louder than usual. Loud talk in itself is a powerful disinhibitor. Recent experiments have shown that you can exert up to 15 per cent more strength, and lift more weight, if you will shout, grunt or groan loudly as you make the lift. The explanation of this is that loud shouting disinhibits—and allows you to exert *all* your strength, including that which has been blocked off and tied up by inhibition.*

5. Let people know when you like them. The inhibited personality is as afraid of expressing "good" feelings as bad ones. If he expresses love, he is afraid it will be judged sentimentality; if he expresses friendship he is afraid it will be considered fawning or apple polishing. If he compliments someone he is afraid the other will think him superficial, or suspect an ulterior motive. Totally ignore all these negative feedback signals. Compliment at least three people every day. If you like what someone is doing, or wearing, or saying—let him know it. Be direct. "I like that, Joe." "Mary, that is a very pretty hat." "Jim, that proves to me you are a swell person." And if you're married—just say to your wife, "I love you" at least twice a day.

Points to Remember
(Fill in)

1.

2.

3.

4.

5.

6.

7.

---

* Reported to the Pan American Congress on Sports Medicine by Dr. Michio Ikai of the University of Tokyo and Dr. Arthur H. Steinhaus of George Williams College, Chicago.

CHAPTER TWELVE

Do-It-Yourself Tranquilizers
Which Bring Peace of Mind

TRANQUILIZER drugs, which have become so popular during the past few years, bring peace of mind, calmness, and reduce or eliminate "nervous symptoms" by an "umbrella action." Just as an umbrella protects us from the rain, the various tranquilizers erect a "psychic screen" between us and disturbing stimuli.

No one fully understands just how the tranquilizers manage to erect this "umbrella," but we do understand why this brings tranquility.

Tranquilizers work because they greatly reduce, or eliminate, *our own response* to disturbing stimuli.

Tranquilizers do not change the environment. The disturbing stimuli are still there. We are still able to *recognize* them intellectually, but we do not *respond* to them emotionally.

Remember in the chapter on "happiness," we said that our own feelings do not depend upon externals, but upon our own attitudes, reactions and responses? Tranquilizers offer convincing evidence of this fact. In substance they reduce or tone down our over-response to negative feedback.

Over-response Is a Bad Habit Which Can Be Cured

Let us suppose that as you read this, you are sitting quietly in your den. Suddenly, the telephone rings. From habit and experience, this is a "signal" or stimulus which you have learned to obey. Without taking thought, without making a conscious decision about the matter, you respond to it. You jump up from your comfortable seat, and hurry to the telephone. The outside stimulus has had the effect of "moving" you. It has changed your mental set and your "position" or self-determined course of action. You were all set to spend an hour, sitting quietly and relaxed, reading. You were inwardly organized for this. Now, all this is suddenly changed by your response to the external stimuli in the environment.

The point I wish to make is this. You do not *have* to answer the telephone. You do not have to obey. You can, *if you choose,* totally ignore the telephone bell. You can, if you choose, continue sitting quietly and relaxed— maintaining your own original state of organization, by *refusing to respond* to the signal. Get this mental picture clearly in your mind for it can be quite helpful in overcoming the power of external stimuli to disturb you. See yourself sitting quietly, letting the phone ring, ignoring its signal, unmoved by its command. Although you are *aware* of it you no longer mind or obey it. Also, get clearly in your mind the fact that the outside signal in itself has no power over you; no power to move you. In the past you have obeyed it, responded to it, purely out of habit. You can, if you wish, form a new habit of not responding.

Also notice that your failure to respond does not consist in "doing something," or making an effort, or resisting or fighting, but in "doing nothing"—in relaxation from doing. You merely relax, ignore the signal, and let its summons go by unheeded.

How to Condition Yourself for Equanimity

In much the same way that you automatically obey or respond to the ring of the telephone, we all become conditioned to respond in a certain way to various stimuli in our environment.

The word "conditioning" in psychologic circles grew out of Pavlov's well-known experiments where he "conditioned" a dog to salivate at the sound of a bell, by ringing it just before presenting food to the dog. This procedure was repeated many times. First, the sound of the bell. A few seconds later, the appearance of food. The dog "learned" to respond to the sound of the bell by salivating in anticipation of the food. Originally, the response made sense. The bell signified that food was forthcoming, and the dog got ready by salivating. However, after the process was repeated a number of times, the dog would continue to salivate whenever the bell was rung—whether or not food was immediately forthcoming. The dog had now become "conditioned" to salivate at the mere sound of the bell. His response made no sense and served no good purpose, but he continued to respond in the same way out of habit.

There are a great many "bells," or disturbing stimuli in our various environmental situations which we have become conditioned to, and which we continue to respond to out of habit, whether or not the response makes any sense.

Many people learn to fear strangers, for example, because of parental admonitions to have nothing to do with strange people; "do not accept candy from a stranger," "do not get into a car with a stranger," etc. The response of avoiding strangers serves a good purpose in small children. But many people continue to feel ill at ease and uncomfortable in the presence of *any* stranger, even when they know that he comes as a friend instead of a foe. Strangers become "bells" and the learned response becomes fear, avoidance, or the desire to run away.

Still another person may respond to crowds, closed spaces, open spaces, persons in authority such as "the boss," by feelings of fear and anxiety. In each case the crowd, the closed space, the open space, the boss, etc., act as "bells," which say—"danger is present, run away, feel afraid." And out of habit, we continue to respond in the accustomed way. We "obey" the bell.

How to Extinguish Conditioned Responses

We can, however, extinguish the conditioned response if we make a practice of relaxing instead of responding. We can, if we wish, just as in the case of the telephone, learn to ignore the "bell," and continue to sit quietly and "let it ring." A key thought that we can carry with us to use whenever we are confronted by any disturbing stimulus is to say to ourselves, "The telephone is ringing, but I do not *have* to answer it. I can just let it ring." This thought will "key in" to your mental picture of yourself sitting quietly, relaxed, unresponding, doing nothing, letting the telephone ring unheeded, and will act as a trigger or "clue" to call up the same attitude that you had when letting the telephone ring.

If You Cannot Ignore the Response—Delay It

In the process of extinguishing a conditioning, a person may find it difficult, especially at first, to totally ignore the "bell," especially if it is rung unexpectedly. In such instances you can accomplish the same final result—extinction of the conditioning—by *delaying* your response.

A woman whom we will call Mary S., became anxious and ill at ease in the presence of crowds. She was able, by practicing the foregoing technique, to immunize or tranquilize herself against the disturbing stimuli on most occasions. However, occasionally, the desire to run away, to flee, became almost overpowering.

"Remember Scarlett O'Hara in *Gone with the Wind?*" I asked her. "Her philosophy was, 'I won't worry about that now—I'll worry about it tomorrow.'" She was able to maintain her inner equilibrium and effectively cope with her environment in spite of war, fire, pestilence, and unrequited love, by delaying the response.

Delaying the response breaks up and interferes with the automatic workings of conditioning.

"Counting to ten" when you are tempted to become angry is based upon the same principle, and is very good advice—if you count slowly, and in fact actually delay the response, rather than merely holding in your angry shouting or desk pounding. The "response" in anger consists of more than shouting or desk beating. The tension in your muscles is a response. You cannot "feel" the emotion of anger or fear if your muscles remain perfectly relaxed. Therefore, if you can delay "feeling angry" for ten seconds, delay responding at all, you can extinguish the automatic reflex.

Mary S. did extinguish her conditioned fear of crowds by delaying her response. When she felt that she simply *had* to run away, she would say to herself—"very well, but not this very minute. I will delay leaving the room for two minutes. I can refuse to obey for only two minutes!"

Relaxation Erects a Psychic Screen—or Tranquilizer

It is well to get clearly in your mind the fact that our disturbed feelings—our anger, hostility, fear, anxiety, insecurity, are caused by our own responses—not by externals. Response means tension. Lack of response means relaxation. It has been proved in scientific laboratory experiments that you absolutely cannot feel angry, fearful, anxious, insecure, "unsafe" as long as your muscles remain perfectly relaxed. All these things are, in essence, *our own feelings*. Tension in muscles is a "preparation for action"—or a "getting ready to respond." Relaxation of muscles brings about "mental relaxation," or a peaceful "relaxed attitude." Thus, relaxation is nature's own tranquilizer, which erects a psychic screen or umbrella between you and the disturbing stimulus.

Physical relaxation is a powerful "disinhibitor" for the same reason. In the last chapter we learned that inhibition results from excessive negative feedback, or rather our over-response to negative feedback. Relaxation means —no response. Therefore, in your daily practice of relaxation, you are learning disinhibition as well as providing yourself with nature's own do-it-yourself tranquilizer, which you can take with you into your daily activities. Protect yourself from disturbing stimuli by maintaining the relaxed attitude.

Build Yourself a Quiet Room in Your Mind

"Men seek retreats for themselves: houses in the country, seashores and mountains; and thou too art wont to desire such things very much," said Marcus Aurelius. "But this is altogether a mark of the most common sort of men, for it is in thy power whenever thou shalt choose to retire into thyself. For nowhere, either with more quiet or more freedom from trouble, does a man retire than into his own soul, particularly when he has within him such thoughts that by looking into them he is immediately in perfect tranquility; and I affirm that tranquility is nothing else than the good ordering of the mind. Constantly then give to thyself this retreat, and renew thyself. . . ." (*Meditations of Marcus Aurelius,* translated by George Long, Mount Vernon, N.Y., Peter Pauper Press.)

During the last days of World War II someone commented to President Harry Truman that he appeared to bear up under the stress and strain of the presidency better than any previous President; that the job did not appear to have "aged" him or sapped his vitality, and that this was rather remarkable, especially in view of the many problems which confronted him as a war-time President. His answer was, "I have a foxhole in my mind." He went on to say that just as a soldier retreated into his foxhole for protection, rest and recuperation, he periodically retired into his own mental foxhole, where he allowed nothing to bother him.

Your Own Decompression Chamber

Each of us needs a quiet room inside his own mind—a quiet center within him, like the deep of the ocean that is never disturbed, no matter how rough the waves may become upon the surface.

This quiet room within, which is built in imagination, works as a mental and emotional decompression chamber. It depressurizes you from tensions, worry, pressures, stresses and strains, refreshes you and enables you to return to your work-a-day world better prepared to cope with it.

It is my belief that each personality does already have a quiet center within, which is never disturbed, and is unmoved, like the mathematical point in the very center of a wheel or axle which remains stationary. What we need to do is to find this quiet center within us and retreat into it periodically for rest, recuperation, and renewed vigor.

One of the most beneficial prescriptions that I have ever given patients is the advice to learn to return into this quiet tranquil center. And one of the best ways that I have found for entering this quiet center is to build for yourself, in imagination, a little mental room. Furnish this room with whatever is most restful and refreshing to you: perhaps beautiful landscapes, if you like paintings; a volume of your favorite verse, if you like poetry. The colors of the walls are your own favorite "pleasant" colors, but should be chosen from the restful hues of blue, light green, yellow, gold. The room is plainly and simply furnished; there are no distracting elements. It is very neat and everything is in order. Simplicity, quietness, beauty, are the keynotes. It contains your favorite easy chair. From one small window you can look out and see a beautiful beach. The waves roll in upon the beach and retreat, but you cannot hear them, for your room is very, very quiet.

Take as much care in building this room in your imagination as you would in building an actual room. Be thoroughly familiar with every detail.

A Little Vacation Every Day

Whenever you have a few spare moments during the day—between appointments, riding the bus, retire into your quiet room. Whenever you begin to feel tension mounting, or to feel hurried or harried, retire into your quiet room for a few moments. Just a very few minutes taken from a very busy day in this manner, will more than pay for themselves. It is not time wasted, but time invested. Say to yourself, "I am going to rest a bit in my quiet room."

Then, in imagination, see yourself climbing the stairs to your room. Say to yourself, "I am now climbing the stairs—now I am opening the door—now I am inside." In imagination notice all the quiet, restful details. See yourself sitting down in your favorite chair, utterly relaxed and at peace with the world. Your room is secure. Nothing can touch you here. There is nothing to worry about. You left your worries at the foot of the stairs. There are no decisions to be made here—no hurry, no bother.

You Need a Certain Amount of Escapism

Yes, this is "escapism." So is sleep "escapism." Carrying an umbrella in the rain is escapism. Building yourself an actual house where you can retreat from the weather and the elements is escapism. And taking a vacation is escapism. Our nervous system needs a certain amount of escapism. It needs some freedom and protection from the continual bombardment of external stimuli. We need yearly vacations where we physically "vacate" the old scenes, the old duties, the old responsibilities, "get away from it all."

Your soul and your nervous system need a room for rest, recuperation and protection every bit as much as your physical body needs a physical house, and for the same reasons. Your mental quiet room gives your nervous system a little vacation every day. For the moment, you mentally "vacate" your work-a-day world of duties, responsibilities, decisions, pressures, and "get away from it all" by mentally retiring into your "No-pressure Chamber."

Pictures are more impressive to your automatic mechanism than words. Particularly so, if the picture happens to have a strong symbolic meaning. One mental picture that I have found very effective is the following:

On a visit to Yellowstone National Park, I was waiting patiently for the geyser "Old Faithful," which goes off approximately every hour. Suddenly the geyser erupted in a great mass of hissing steam, like a gigantic boiler whose safety plug had blown out. A small boy standing near me, asked his father, "What makes it do that?"

"Well," said his father, "I guess old Mother Earth is like the rest of us. She builds up a certain amount of pressure, and every once in a while just has to blow off steam to stay healthy."

Wouldn't it be wonderful, I thought to myself, if we humans could "blow off steam" harmlessly like that when emotional pressures build up inside us?

I didn't have a geyser, nor a steam valve in the top of my head, but I did have an imagination. So I began to use this mental picture when I would retire into my mental quiet room. I would remember Old Faithful, and form a mental picture of emotional steam and pressure coming out the top of my head and evaporating harmlessly. Try this mental picture on yourself when you're "wrought up" or tense. The ideas of "blowing off steam" and "blowing your top" have powerful associations built into your mental machinery.

"Clear" Your Mechanism
Before Undertaking a New Problem

If you are using an adding machine, or an electronic computer, you must "clear" the machine of previous problems before undertaking a new one. Otherwise, parts of the old problem, or the old situation, "carry over" into the new situation, and give you a wrong answer.

This exercise of retiring for a few moments into your quiet room in your mind can accomplish the same sort of "clearance" of your success mechanism, and for that reason, it is very helpful to practice it in between tasks, situations, environments, which require different moods, mental adjustments, or "mental sets."

Common examples of "carry-over," or failure to clear your mental machinery, are the following:

A business executive carries his work-a-day worries and his work-a-day "mood" home with him. All day he has been harried, hurried, aggressive, and "set to go." Perhaps he has felt a bit of frustration which tends to make him irritable. He stops working physically when he goes home. But he carries with him a residue of his aggressiveness, frustration, hurry and worry. He is still set to go and cannot relax. He is irritable with his wife and family. He keeps thinking about problems at the office, although there is nothing he can do about them.

Insomnia, Rudeness, Are Often Emotional Carry-overs

Many people carry their troubles to bed with them when they should be resting. Mentally and emotionally, they are still trying to do something about a situation, at a time when "doing" is not in order.

All during the day we have need of many different types of emotional and mental organization. You need a different "mood" and mental organization for talking with your boss, and talking with a customer. And if you have just talked with an irate and irritable customer, you need a change in set before talking with a second customer. Otherwise "emotional carry-over" from the one situation will be inappropriate in dealing with the other.

One large company found that one of their executives unknowingly answered the telephone in a harsh, angry, hostile tone. The phone rings in the midst of a knock-down, drag-out conference, or while the executive is enmeshed in frustration and hostility for one reason or another, and his angry, hostile tone of voice surprises and offends the innocent caller. This company directed all executives to pause five seconds—and smile—before picking up the phone.

Emotional Carry-over Causes Accidents

Insurance companies, and other agencies which do research on the cause of accidents, have found that emotional carry-over causes many automobile accidents. If the driver has just had a spat with his wife or his boss, if he has just experienced frustration, or if he has just left a situation which called for aggressive behavior, he is much more likely to have an accident. He carries over into his driving, attitudes and emotions which are inappropriate. He is really not angry at the other drivers. He is somewhat like a man who wakes up in the morning from a dream in which he experienced extreme anger. He realizes that the injustice heaped upon him happened only in a dream. But he is still angry—period!

Fear can carry over in the same manner.

Calmness Carries Over, Too

But the really helpful thing to know about all this is that friendliness, love, peace, quiet and calmness, also "carry over."

It is impossible, as we have said, to experience, or feel either fear, anger, or anxiety, while completely relaxed, quiet and composed. Retiring into your "quiet room" thus becomes an ideal clearance mechanism for emotions and moods. Old emotions evaporate and disappear. At the same time you experience calmness, peacefulness, and a feeling of well-being which will also "carry over" into whatever activities immediately follow. Your quiet time wipes the slate clean so to speak, clears the machine, and gives you a clean new page for the environment which is to follow.

I practice the quiet time both immediately before and after surgery. Surgery requires a high degree of concentration, calmness, control. It would be disastrous to "carry over" into the surgical situation feelings of hurry, aggressiveness, or personal worries. Therefore, I clear my mental machinery by spending a few moments completely relaxed in my quiet room. On the other hand, the high degree of concentration, purpose, and obliviousness to surroundings, which are so necessary to the surgical situation, would be most inappropriate to a social situation—whether the social situation be an interview in my office, or a grand ball. Therefore, upon leaving surgery I also make it a point to spend a couple of minutes in my quiet room, to clear the decks, so to speak, for a new type of action.

Build Your Own Psychic Umbrellas

By practicing the techniques in this chapter you can build your own psychic umbrellas, which will screen out disturbing stimuli, bring you more peace of mind, and enable you to perform better.

Above all, keep in mind, and hammer it home to yourself, that the *key* to the matter of whether you are disturbed or tranquil, fearful or composed, *is not* the external stimulus, whatever it may be, but *your own response and reaction.* Your *own response* is what "makes" you feel fearful, anxious, insecure. If you do not respond at all, but "just let the telephone ring," it is impossible for you to feel disturbed, regardless of what is happening around you. "Be like the promontory against which the waves continually break, but it stands firm and tames the fury of the water around it," said Marcus Aurelius.

The Ninety-first Psalm is a vivid word picture of a man who experiences feelings of safety and security in the very midst of terrors of the night, arrows that fly by day, plagues, intrigues, snares of enemies, danger (10,000 fall at his side), because he has found the "secret place" within his own soul and is unmoved—that is, he does not emotionally react or respond to the scare "bells" in his environment. Emotionally, he totally ignores them, much as William James recommended totally ignoring evil and unhappy "facts" to feel happy, and as James T. Mangan recommends totally ignoring adverse situations in the environment, to feel poised.

You are basically an "actor"—not a "reactor." Throughout this book we have spoken of *reacting* and *responding* appropriately to environmental factors. Man, however, is not primarily a "reactor," but an "actor." We do not merely react and respond, willy-nilly, to whatever environmental factors may be present, like a ship that goes whichever way the wind happens to blow. As goal-striving beings we first—ACT. We set our own goal, determine our own course. *Then,* within the context of this goal-striving structure—we respond and react appropriately, that is, in a manner which will further our progress and serve our own ends.

If responding and reacting to negative feedback does not take us further down the road to our own goal—or serve our ends, then there is no need to respond at all. And, if response of any kind gets us off course, or works against us—then *no response* is the appropriate response.

Your Emotional Stabilizer

In almost any goal-striving situation, our own inner stability is in itself an important goal to maintain. We must be sensitive to negative feedback data which advises us when we are off course, so that we can change direction and go forward. But at the same time, we must keep our own ship afloat and stable. Our ship must not be tossed and rocked and perhaps sunk by every passing wave, or even a serious storm. As Prescott Lecky expressed it, "The same attitude must be maintained in spite of environmental changes."

Our "letting the telephone ring" is a mental attitude which keeps our stability. It keeps us from being tossed about, knocked off course, or "shaken up," by every wave or ripple in the environment.

Stop Fighting Straw Men

Still another type of inappropriate response which causes worry, insecurity, and tension, is the bad habit of trying to respond emotionally to something which doesn't exist except in our imaginations. Not satisfied with over-responding to actual minor stimuli in the actual environment, many of us create straw men in our imaginations, and emotionally respond to our own mental pictures. In addition to those negatives which actually exist in the environment, we impose our own negatives: This or that *may* happen; *What if* such and such happens. When we worry, we form mental pictures—adverse mental pictures of what *may* exist in the environment, of what *may* happen. We then respond to these negative pictures *as if* they were present reality. Remember, your nervous system cannot tell the difference between a real experience and one that is vividly imagined.

"Doing Nothing" Is the Proper Response to an Unreal Problem

Again, you can tranquilize yourself against this sort of disturbance, not by something you "do"—but by something you don't do—your refusal to respond. *As far as your emotions are concerned,* the proper response to worry pictures is to totally ignore them. Live emotionally in the present moment. Analyze your environment—become more aware of what actually exists in your environment—and respond and react spontaneously to that. In order to do this you must give all your attention to what is happening now. You must keep your eye on the ball. Then, your response will be appropriate—and you will have no time to notice or respond to a fictitious environment.

Your First Aid Kit

Carry these thoughts with you as a sort of first aid kit:

Inner disturbance, or the opposite of tranquility, is nearly always caused by over-response, a too sensitive "alarm reaction." You create a built-in tranquilizer, or psychic screen between yourself and the disturbing stimulus, when you practice "not responding"—letting the telephone ring.

You cure old habits of over-response, you extinguish old conditioned reflexes, when you practice *delaying* the habitual, automatic, and unthinking response.

Relaxation is nature's own tranquilizer. Relaxation is non-response. Learn physical relaxation by daily practice, then when you need to practice non-response in daily activities, just "do what you're doing" when you relax.

Use the quiet room in your mind technique both as a daily tranquilizer to tone down nervous response, and to clear your emotional mechanism of "carry-over" emotions which would be inappropriate in a new situation.

Stop scaring yourself to death with your own mental pictures. Stop fighting straw men. Emotionally, respond only to what actually *is,* here and now—and ignore the rest.

Practice Exercise: Create in your imagination a vivid mental picture of yourself sitting quietly, composed, unmoved, letting your telephone ring, as outlined earlier in this chapter. Then, in your daily activities "carry over" the same peaceful, composed, unmoved attitude by remembering this mental picture. Say to yourself, "I am letting the telephone ring" whenever you are tempted to "obey" or respond to some fear-bell or anxiety-bell. Next, use your imagination to practice non-response in various sorts of situations: See yourself sitting quietly and unmoved while an associate rants and raves. See yourself going through your daily tasks one by one, calmly, composed, unhurried, in spite of the pressures of a busy day. See yourself maintaining the same constant, stable course, in spite of the various "hurry-bells" and "pressure-bells" in your environment. See yourself in various situations which have in the past upset you—only now you remain "set," settled, poised—by not responding.

Your Spiritual Thermostat

Your physical body has a built-in thermostat, itself a servo-mechanism, which maintains your inner physical temperature at a steady 98.6 degrees, regardless of the temperature in the environment. The weather around you may be freezing cold, or 110 degrees. Yet your body maintains its own climate—a steady 98.6. It is able to function properly in the environment because it does not take on itself the climate of the environment. Cold or hot —it maintains its own.

You also have a built-in spiritual thermostat which enables you to maintain an emotional climate and atmosphere in spite of the emotional weather around you. Many people do not use this spiritual thermostat because they do not know it is there; they do not know such a thing is possible, and they do not understand that they do *not have* to take on the outward climate. Yet, your spiritual thermostat is just as necessary for emotional health and well-being as your physical thermostat is for physical health. Begin using it now by practicing the techniques in this chapter.

CHAPTER THIRTEEN

How to Turn a Crisis
Into a Creative Opportunity

I KNOW a young golfer who holds the all-time course record for his home course, yet has never even placed in a really big tournament. When playing by himself, or with friends, or in small tournaments where the stakes are low, his play is flawless. Yet, each time he gets into a big tournament his game deteriorates. In the language of golfdom, "the pressure gets him."

Many baseball pitchers have pinpoint control until they find themselves in a situation where "the chips are down." Then they "choke up," lose all control, and appear to have no ability whatever.

On the other hand, many athletes perform better under pressure. The situation itself seems to give them more strength, more power, more finesse.

People Who Come into Their Own in a Crisis

For example, John Thomas, the record-breaking high-jumper from Boston University, often performs better in competition than in practice. In February, 1960, Thomas set a new world's record, clearing 7 feet 1¼ inches at the U.S. Indoor Championships. His highest previous jump in practice had been 6 feet 9¼ inches.

It isn't always the baseball player with the highest batting average who is called upon as a pinch hitter in a tough spot. The manager frequently turns down the man with the highest batting average, for a player who is known to "come through in the clutch."

One salesman may find himself inarticulate in the presence of an important prospect. His skills desert him. Another salesman under the same circumstances may "sell over his head." The challenge of the situation brings out abilities he does not ordinarily possess.

Many women are charming and gracious when talking with one person or a small informal group, but become tongue-tied, awkward, and dull at a formal dinner, or a big social occasion. On the other hand, I know a little lady who comes into her own only under the stimulus of a big occasion. If you had dinner with her alone you would find her very ordinary. Her features are not particularly attractive. Her personality is somewhat on the drab side. But all this changes when she attends an important party. The stimulus of the occasion awakens and brings to life something within her. Her eyes acquire a new sparkle. Her conversation is witty and charming. Even her facial features seem to undergo a change and you find yourself thinking of her as a beautiful woman.

There are students who do extremely well in day-to-day class work, but find their minds a blank when taking an examination. There are other students who are ordinary in class work, but do extremely well on important examinations.

The Secret of the Money Player

The difference between all these persons is not some inherent quality that one has and the other hasn't. It is largely a matter of how they *learned to react* to crisis situations.

A "crisis" is a situation which can either make you or break you. If you react properly to the situation, a "crisis" can give you strength, power, wisdom you do not ordinarily possess. If you react improperly, a crisis can rob you of the skill, control, and ability that you ordinarily have to call upon.

The so-called "money player" in sports, in business, or in social activities—the person who comes through in the clutch—who performs better under the stimulus of challenge, is invariably the person who has learned either consciously or unconsciously to react well to crisis situations.

In order to perform well in a crisis we need to (1) learn certain skills under conditions where we will not be overmotivated; we need to practice without pressure. (2) We need to learn to react to crisis with an aggressive, rather than a defensive attitude; to respond to the challenge in the situation, rather than to the menace; to keep our positive goal in mind. (3) We need to learn to evaluate so-called "crisis" situations in their true perspective; to not make mountains out of molehills, or react as if every small challenge were a matter of life or death.

(1) Practice Without Pressure

Although we may learn fast, we do not learn well under "crisis" conditions. Throw a man who can't swim into water over his head, and the crisis itself may give him the power to swim to safety. He learns fast, and manages to swim *somehow*. But he will never learn to become a championship swimmer. The crude inept stroke that he used to rescue himself becomes "fixed" and it is difficult for him to learn better ways of swimming. Because of his ineptness he may perish in a real crisis where he is required to swim a long distance.

Dr. Edward C. Tolman, psychologist and expert on animal behavior at the University of California, says that both animals and men form "brain maps" or "cognitive maps" of the environment while they are learning. If the motivation is not too intense, if there is not too much of a crisis present in the learning situation, these maps are broad and general. If the animal is over-motivated, the cognitive map is narrow and restricted. He learns just one way of solving his problem. In the future, if this one way happens to be blocked, the animal becomes frustrated, and fails to discern alternative routes or detours. He develops a "one response," cut and dried, preconceived, and tends to lose the ability to react spontaneously to a new situation. He cannot improvise. He can only follow a set plan.

Pressure Retards Learning

Dr. Tolman found that if rats were permitted to *learn* and *practice* under *non-crisis* conditions, they later performed well in a crisis. For example, if rats were permitted to roam about at will and explore a maze when well fed and with plenty to drink, they did not *appear* to learn anything. Later, however, if the same rats were placed in the maze while hungry, they showed they had learned a great deal, by quickly and efficiently going to the goal. Hunger faced these trained rats with a crisis to which they reacted well.

Other rats which were forced to learn the maze under the crisis of hunger and thirst, did not do so well. They were over-motivated and their brain maps became narrow. The one "correct" route to the goal became fixated. If this route were blocked the rats became frustrated and had great difficulty learning a new one.

The more intense the crisis situation under which you learn, the less you learn. Prof. Jerome S. Bruner of Harvard University trained two groups of rats to solve a maze to get food. One group which had not eaten for 12 hours learned the maze in six trials. A second group, which had eaten nothing for 36 hours, required more than 20 tries.

Fire Drills Teach Crisis Conduct
in Non-Crisis Situation

People react in the same way. Persons who have to learn how to get out of a burning building will normally require two or three times as long to learn the proper escape route, as they would if no fire were present. Some of them do not learn at all. Over-motivation interferes with reasoning processes. The automatic reaction mechanism is jammed by too much conscious effort—trying too hard. Something akin to "purpose tremor" develops and the ability to think clearly is lost. The ones who do manage somehow to get out of the building, have learned a narrow fixated response. Put them in a different building, or change the circumstances slightly—and they react as badly the second time around as the first.

But, you can take these same people, let them practice a "dry run" fire drill when there is no fire. Because there is no menace there is no excessive negative feedback to interfere with clear thinking or correct doing. They practice filing out of the building calmly, efficiently, and correctly. After they have practiced this a number of times, they can be counted upon to act the same way when an actual fire breaks out. Their muscles, nerves and brain have memorized a broad, general, flexible "map." The attitude of calmness and clear thinking will "carry over" from practice drill to actual fire. Moreover, they will have learned something about how to get out of any building, or cope with any changed circumstances. They are not committed to a rigid response, but will be able to improvise—to react spontaneously to whatever conditions may be present.

The moral is obvious for either mice or men: Practice without pressure and you will learn more efficiently and be able to perform better in a crisis situation.

Shadow-boxing for Stability

Gentleman Jim Corbett made the word "shadow-boxing" popular. When asked how he developed the perfect control and timing for his left jab which he used to cut John L. Sullivan, the Boston Strong-boy, to ribbons, Corbett replied that he had practiced throwing his left at his own image in the mirror more than 10,000 times in preparation for the bout.

Gene Tunney did the same thing. Years before he actually fought Jack Dempsey in the ring, he had fought an imaginary Dempsey more than a hundred times in the privacy of his own room. He secured all the films of old Dempsey fights. He watched them until he knew every one of Dempsey's moves. Then he shadow-boxed. He would imagine that Dempsey was standing before him. When the imaginary Dempsey would make a certain move, he would practice his counter-move.

Sir Harry Lauder, the famous Scottish actor and comedian, once admitted that he had practiced a certain routine 10,000 times in private before ever giving the performance publicly. Lauder was, in effect, "shadow-boxing" with an imaginary audience.

Billy Graham preached sermons to cypress stumps in a Florida swamp before developing his compelling platform personality with live audiences. Most good public speakers have done the same thing in one way or another. The most common form of shadow-boxing for public speakers is to deliver their speech to their own image in the mirror. One man I know lines up six or eight empty chairs, imagines people sitting in them, and practices his speech on the imaginary audience.

Easy Practice Brings Better Scores

When Ben Hogan was playing tournament golf regularly, he kept a golf club in his bedroom, and daily practiced in private, swinging the club correctly and without pressure at an imaginary golf ball. When Hogan was on the links, he would go through the correct motions in his imagination before making a shot, then depend upon "muscle memory" to execute the shot correctly.

Some athletes practice in private with as little pressure as possible. They, or their coaches, refuse to permit the press to witness practice sessions, and even refuse to give out any information concerning their practice for publicity purposes, in order to protect themselves from pressure. Everything is arranged to make training and practice as relaxed and pressure-free as is humanly possible. The result is that they go into the crisis of actual competition, without appearing to have any nerves at all. They become "human icicles," immune to pressure, not worrying about how they will perform, but depending upon "muscle memory" to execute the various motions which they have learned.

The technique of "shadow-boxing," or "practice without pressure" is so simple, and the results so striking, that some people are inclined to associate it with some sort of magic.

I remember a dowager, for example, who for years had been jittery, felt ill at ease in social situations. After practicing "shadow-boxing" she wrote me: ". . . I must have practiced making a 'grand entrance' in my own empty living room a hundred times or more. I walked down the room, shaking hands with innumerable imaginary guests. I smiled, and had something friendly to say to each one, actually saying the words out loud. Then I moved about among the 'guests,' chatting here and there. I practiced walking, sitting, talking, gracefully and self-confidently.

"I cannot tell you how happy I was—and I might say somewhat surprised—at the wonderful time I had at the G—— T—— Ball. I felt relaxed and confident. Several situations came up which I had not anticipated, nor practiced—but I found myself 'ad-libbing' them admirably.

My husband is sure that you worked some sort of mumbo-jumbo on me. . . ."

Shadow-boxing "Turns On" Self-expression

The word "express" literally means to "push out," to exert, to show forth. The word "inhibit" means to choke off, restrict. Self-expression is a pushing out, a showing forth, of the powers, talents and abilities of the self. It means turning on your own light and letting it shine. Self-expression is a "yes" response. Inhibition is a "no" response. It chokes off self-expression, turns off or dims your light.

In shadow-boxing you practice self-expression with no inhibiting factors present. You learn the correct moves. You form a "mental map" which is retained in memory. A broad, general, flexible map. Then, when you face a crisis, where an actual menace or inhibiting factor is present, you have learned to act calmly and correctly. There is a "carry-over" in your muscles, nerves and brain from practice to the actual situation. Moreover, because your learning has been relaxed and pressure-free you will be able to rise to the occasion, extemporize, improvise, act spontaneously. At the same time your shadow boxing is building a mental image of yourself acting correctly and successfully. The memory of this successful self-image also enables you to perform better.

Dry-Shooting Is the Secret of Good Marksmanship

A novice on the pistol range will quite often find that he can hold the hand gun perfectly still and motionless, as long as he is not trying to shoot. When he aims an empty gun at a target, his hand is steady. When the same gun is loaded and he attempts to make a score—"purpose tremor" sets in. The gun barrel uncontrollably moves up and down, back and forth, in much the same way that your hand tremors when you attempt to thread a needle (see Chapter 11).

Almost to a man, all good pistol coaches recommend lots of "dry run" target shooting, to overcome this condition. The marksman calmly and deliberately aims, cocks and snaps the hand gun at a target on the wall. Calmly and deliberately he pays attention to just how he is holding the gun, whether it is canted or not, whether he is squeezing or jerking the trigger. He learns good habits calmly. There is no purpose tremor because there is no over-carefulness, no over-anxiety for results. After thousands of such "dry runs," the novice will find that he can hold the loaded gun, and actually shoot it while maintaining the same mental attitude, and going through the same calm, deliberate physical motions.

A friend of mine learned to shoot quail in much the same manner. A good shot on the skeet range, the roar of a quail as it took off and his anxiety for results, or over-motivation, caused him to miss almost every time. On his next hunt, and after learning about shadow-boxing, he carried an empty shotgun the first day. There was no need to get excited, because he couldn't shoot anyway. No need for over-motivation when you're carrying an empty gun! He "shot" some twenty quail that day with the empty gun. By the time he had made his first six shots all anxiety and jitteriness had left him. His companions thought he had lost a few of his buttons. But he redeemed himself the next day when he killed his first 8 birds, and got a total of 15 quail out of 17 shots!

Shadow-boxing Helps You Hit the Ball

Not long ago I visited a friend of mine one Sunday in a suburb of New York. His 10-year-old son had visions of becoming a big-league baseball star. His fielding was adequate, but he couldn't hit. Each time his father threw the ball across the plate, the boy froze up—and missed it a foot. I decided to try something. "You're so anxious to hit the ball, and so afraid you won't, that you can't even see it clearly," I said. All that tension and anxiety was interfering with his eyesight and his reflexes—his arm muscles weren't executing the orders from his brain.

"For the next ten pitches," I said, "don't even try to hit the ball. Don't try at all. Keep your bat on your shoulder. But watch the ball *very* carefully. Keep your eyes on it from the time it leaves your Daddy's hand until it goes by you. Stand easy and loose, and just watch the ball go by."

After ten trials of this, I advised him, "Now for a while, watch the ball go by and keep the bat on your shoulder, but think to yourself you are going to bring the bat around so it will really hit the ball—solidly and dead-center." After this, I told him to keep on "feeling the same way" and to keep watching the ball carefully, and to "let" the bat come around and meet the ball, making no attempt to hit it hard. The boy hit the ball. After a few easy hits like this, he was knocking the ball a country mile, and I had a friend for life.

The Salesman Who Practiced "Not Selling"

You can use the same technique to "hit the ball" in selling, teaching, or running a business. A young salesman complained to me that he froze-up when calling upon prospects. His one big trouble was his inability to properly reply to the prospect's objection. "When a prospect raises an objection—or criticises my product—I can't think of a thing to say at the time," he said. "Later, I can think of all kinds of good ways to handle the objection."

I told him about shadow-boxing and about the kid who learned to bat by letting the ball go by with the bat on his shoulder. I pointed out that to hit a baseball, or to think on your feet, requires good reflexes. Your automatic Success Mechanism must respond appropriately and automatically. Too much tension, too much motivation, too much anxiety for results, jams the mechanism. "You think of the proper answers later because you're relaxed and the pressure is off. Right now your trouble is you're not responding quickly and spontaneously to the objections your prospects throw at you—in other words, you're not hitting the ball that the prospect throws."

I told him first of all to practice a number of imaginary interviews—actually walking in, introducing himself to a prospect, making his sales pitch—and then imagining every possible objection, no matter how screwballish, and answering it out loud. Next, he was to practice "with his bat on his shoulder" on an actual live client. He was to go in with an "empty gun" as far as intents and purposes were concerned. The purpose of the sales interview would not be to sell—he had to resign himself to being satisfied with no order. The purpose of the call would be strictly practice—"bat on the shoulder," "empty gun" practice.

In his own words, this shadow-boxing "worked like a miracle."

As a young medical student I used to shadow-box surgical operations on cadavers. This no-pressure practice taught me much more than technique. It taught a future surgeon calmness, deliberateness, clear thinking, because he had practiced all these things in a situation that was not do-or-die, life-or-death.

How to Make Your "Nerves" Work for You

The word "crisis" comes from a Greek word which means, literally, "decisiveness," or "point of decision."

A crisis is a fork in the road. One fork holds a promise of a better condition—the other of a worse condition. In medicine, the "crisis" is a turning point, where the patient either gets worse and dies, or gets better and lives.

Thus every crisis situation is two-pronged. The pitcher who goes in in the 9th inning with the score tied and three men on base can become a hero and gain in prestige, or he can become a villain who loses the game.

Hugh Casey, who was one of the most successful, and the calmest relief pitchers of all time, was once asked what he thought of when he was sent in a game in the middle of a crisis situation.

"I always think about what *I am going to do,* and *what I want to happen,*" he said, "instead of what the batter is going to do, or what may happen to me." He said he concentrated on what he wanted to happen, felt that he could make it happen, and that it usually did.

This same attitude is another important key to reacting well in any crisis situation. If we can maintain an aggressive attitude, react aggressively instead of negatively to threats and crises, the very situation itself can act as a stimulus to release untapped powers.

Several years ago newspapers carried the story about a "giant" of a Negro, who did what two wrecking trucks and a score of men could not do. He raised the crushed metal cab of a truck up off its pinned driver. He ripped out with his bare hands the brake pedal which had the driver's foot trapped. And he beat out the flames in the floor of the cab with his bare hands. Later, when this "giant" was found and identified, he turned out not to be a giant at all. Charles Dennis Jones was six feet two inches tall and weighed 220. His explanation for his extraordinary feat: *"I hate fire."* Fourteen months before, his 8-year-old daughter had burned to death in a fire which had leveled his residence. ("A Man Don't Know What He Can Do," *Reader's Digest,* October, 1952.)

I know a tall, rather frail man who single-handedly somehow managed to carry an upright piano out of his house, down three steps, up over a four inch curb, and out to the center of his lawn, when his house was on fire. It had required six strong men to place the piano in the house. One rather frail man, under the stimulus of excitement and crisis, took it out by himself.

(2) Crisis Brings Power

Neurologist J. A. Hadfield has made an extensive study in the extraordinary powers—physical, mental, emotional, and spiritual—which come to the aid of ordinary men and women in times of crisis.

"How wonderful is the way in which, with quite ordinary folk, power leaps to our aid in any time of emergency," he says. "We lead timid lives, shrinking from difficult tasks till perhaps we are forced into them or ourselves determine on them, and immediately we seem to unlock the unseen forces. When we have to face danger, then courage comes; when trial puts a long-continued strain upon us, we find ourselves possessed by the power to endure; or when disaster ultimately brings the fall which we so long dreaded, we feel underneath us the strength as of the everlasting arms. Common experience teaches that, when great demands are made upon us, *if only we fearlessly accept the challenge and confidently expend our strength,* every danger or difficulty brings its own strength —'As thy days so shall thy strength be.' "*

The secret lies in the attitude of "fearlessly accepting the challenge," and "confidently expending our strength."

This means maintaining an aggressive, a goal-directed attitude, rather than a defensive, evasive, negative one: "No matter what happens, I can handle it, or I can see it through," rather than, "I hope nothing happens."

Keep Your Goal in Mind

The essence of this aggressive attitude is remaining goal-oriented. You keep your own positive goal in mind. You intend to "go through" the crisis experience to achieve your goal. You keep your original positive goal, and do not get sidetracked into secondary ones—the desire to run away, to hide, to avoid—by the crisis situation. Or, in the language of William James, your attitude is one of "fight" instead of one of fear or flight.

If you can do this, the crisis situation itself acts as a

* J. A. Hadfield, *The Psychology of Power* (New York: The Macmillan Co., 1919).

stimulus which *releases additional power* to help you accomplish your goal.

Lecky has said that the purpose of emotion is "reinforcement," or additional strength, rather than to serve as a sign of weakness. He believed that there was only one basic emotion—"excitement"—and that excitement manifests itself as fear, anger, courage, etc., depending upon our own inner goals at the time—whether we are inwardly organized to conquer a problem, run away from it, or destroy it. "The real problem is not to control emotion, but to control the choice of which tendency shall receive emotional reinforcement." (Prescott Lecky, *Self Consistency, A Theory of Personality*, New York, Island Press.)

If your intention, or your attitude-goal, is to go forward, if it is to make the most of the crisis situation, and win out in spite of it, then the excitement of the occasion will *re-inforce* this tendency—it will give you more courage, more strength to go forward. If you lose sight of your original goal, and your attitude-goal becomes one of running away from the crisis, of seeking to somehow get past it by evading it—this running-away tendency will also be re-inforced, and you will experience fear and anxiety.

Don't Mistake Excitement for Fear

Many people have made the mistake of habitually interpreting the feeling of excitement as fear and anxiety, and therefore interpreting it as a proof of inadequacy.

Any normal person who is intelligent enough to understand the situation becomes "excited" or "nervous" just before a crisis situation. Until you direct it toward a goal, this excitement is neither fear, anxiety, courage, confidence, or anything else other than a stepped-up, re-inforced supply of emotional steam in your boiler. It is *not* a sign of weakness. It is a sign of additional strength to be used *in any way you choose*. Jack Dempsey used to get so nervous before a fight, he couldn't shave himself. His excitement was such that he couldn't sit or stand still. He did not, however, interpret this excitement as fear. He did not *decide* that he should run away because of it. He went forward, and used the excitement to put extra dynamite into his blows.

Experienced actors know that this feeling of excitement just before a performance is a good token. Many of them deliberately "work themselves up" emotionally just before going on stage. The good soldier is usually the man who "feels excited" just before battle.

Many people place their bets at racetracks on the basis of which horse appears to be the most "nervous" just before going to the post. Trainers also know that a horse which becomes nervous or "spirited" just before a race will perform better than usual. The term "spirited" is a good one. The excitement that you feel just before a crisis situation is an infusion of "spirit" and should be so interpreted by you.

Not long ago I met a man on a plane whom I had not seen for several years. In the course of conversation, I asked if he still made as many public speeches as he had in the past. Yes, he said, as a matter of fact he had changed jobs so that he would be able to speak more and now made at least one public speech every day. Knowing his love for public speaking, I commented that it was good he had this type of work. "Yes," he said, "in one way it is good. But in another way it is not so good. I don't make as many good speeches as I used to. I speak so often that it has become old-hat to me, and I no longer feel that little tingly feeling in the pit of my stomach, which tells me that I am going to do well."

Some people become so excited during an important written examination that they are unable to think clearly, or even hold a pencil steadily in their hands. Other people become so aroused under the same circumstances that they perform "over their heads"—their minds work better and clearer than usual. Memory is sharpened. It is not the excitement per se which makes the difference, but *how it is used.*

(3) "What Is the Worst That Can Possibly Happen?"

Many people have a tendency to magnify out of all proportion the potential "penalty" or "failure" which the crisis situation holds. We use our imaginations against ourselves and make mountains out of molehills. Or else we do not use our imaginations at all to "see" what the situation *really* holds, but habitually and unthinkingly react *as if* every simple opportunity or threat were a life-or-death matter.

If you face a *real crisis* you need a lot of excitement. The excitement can be used to good advantage in the crisis situation. However, if you over-estimate the danger or difficulty, if you react to information that is faulty, distorted, or unrealistic, you are likely to call up much more excitement than the occasion calls for. Because the real threat is much less than you have estimated, all this excitement cannot be used appropriately. It cannot be "gotten rid of" through creative action. Therefore it remains inside you, bottled up, as "the jitters." A big excess of emotional excitement can harm rather than help performance, simply because it is inappropriate.

Philosopher and mathematician Bertrand Russell tells of a technique which he used on himself to good advantage in toning down excessive excitement: "When some misfortune threatens, consider seriously and deliberately what is the very worst that could possibly happen. Having looked this possible misfortune in the face, give yourself sound reasons for thinking that after all it would be no such terrible disaster. Such reasons always exist, since at the worst nothing that happens to oneself has any cosmic importance. When you have looked for some time steadily at the worst possibility and have said to yourself with real conviction, 'Well, after all, that would not matter so very much,' you will find that your worry diminishes to a quite extraordinary extent. It may be necessary to repeat the process a few times, but in the end, if you have shirked nothing in facing the worst possible issue, you will find that your worry disappears altogether and is replaced by a kind of exhilaration." (Bertrand Russell, *The Conquest of Happiness,* New York, Liveright Publishing Corporation.)

How Carlyle Found Courage

Carlyle has testified how the same method changed his outlook from an "everlasting no" to an "everlasting yea." He was in a period of deep spiritual despair—"My lodestars were blotted out; in that canopy of grim fire shone no star. . . . The universe was one huge, dead, immeasurable steam engine, rolling on, in its dead indifference, to grind me limb from limb." Then, in the midst of this spiritual bankruptcy, came a new way of life. "And I asked myself, 'What art thou afraid of? Wherefore, like a coward, dost thou forever pip and whimper, and go cowering and trembling. Despicable biped! What is the sum-total of the worst that lies before thee? Death? Well, Death: and say the pangs of Tophet too and all that the Devil and Man may, will or can do against thee! Hast thou not a heart; canst thou not suffer whatso it be: and, as a Child of Freedom, though outcast, trample Tophet itself under thy feet, while it consumes thee? Let it come, then: I will meet and defy it!'

"And as I so thought, there rushed like a stream of fire over my whole soul; and I shook base Fear away from me forever. I was strong, of unknown strength; a spirit, almost a god. Ever from that time, the temper of my misery was changed: not Fear or whining Sorrow was it, but Indignation and grim fire-eyed Defiance." (Th. Carlyle, *Sartor Resartus.*)

Russell and Carlyle are telling us how we can maintain an aggressive, goal-directed, self-determining attitude even in the presence of very real and serious threats and dangers.

Mountain-Climbing Over Molehills

Most of us, however, allow ourselves to be thrown "off course" by very minor or even imaginary threats, which we insist upon interpreting as life-or-death, or do-or-die situations.

Someone has said that the greatest cause of ulcers is mountain-climbing over molehills!

A salesman calling upon an important prospect may act as if it were a matter of life or death.

A debutante facing her first ball may act as if she were going on trial for her life.

Many people going to be interviewed about a job act as if they were "scared to death," and so on.

Perhaps this "life-or-death" feeling that many people experience in any sort of crisis situation, is a heritage from our dim and distant past, when "failure" to primitive man usually was synonymous with "death."

Regardless of its origin, however, experience of numerous patients has shown that it can be cured by calmly and rationally analyzing the situation. Ask yourself, "What is the worst that can possibly happen if I fail?", rather than responding automatically, blindly and irrationally.

What Have You Got to Lose?

Close scrutiny will show that most of these everyday so-called "crisis situations" are not life-or-death matters at all, but *opportunities* to either advance, or stay where you are. For example, what is the worst that can happen to the salesman? He will either get an order and come out better off than he was—or he will not get the order and be no worse off than before he made the call. The applicant will either get the job, or not get it. If he fails to get it, he will be in the same position as before he asked. About the worst that can happen to the debutante is that she will remain as she was before the ball, relatively unknown, and create no great stir in social circles.

Few people realize just how potent such a simple change of attitude can be. One salesman I know doubled his income after he was able to change his attitude from a scary, panicky, "Everything depends upon this" outlook, to the attitude, "I have everything to gain and nothing to lose."

Walter Pidgeon, the actor, has told how his first public performance was a complete flop. He was literally "scared to death." However, between acts, he reasoned with himself that he had already failed, therefore he had nothing to lose; that if he gave up acting altogether he would be a complete failure as an actor, and therefore he really had nothing to worry about by going back on. He went out in the second act relaxed and confident, and made a big hit.

Remember, above all, that the key to any crisis situation is YOU. Practice and learn the simple techniques of this chapter, and you, like hundreds of others before you, can learn to make crisis work *for* you by making crisis a creative opportunity.

CHAPTER FOURTEEN

How to Get
"That Winning Feeling"

YOUR automatic creative mechanism is teleological. That is, it operates in terms of goals and end results. Once you give it a definite goal to achieve you can depend upon its automatic guidance-system to take you to that goal much better than "you" ever could by conscious thought. *"You"* supply the goal by thinking in terms of end results. Your automatic mechanism then supplies the "means whereby." If your muscles need to perform some motion to bring about the end result, your automatic mechanism will guide them much more accurately and delicately than you could by "taking thought." If you need ideas, your automatic mechanism will supply them.

Think in Terms of Possibilities

But to accomplish this—"You" must supply the goal. And to supply a goal capable of activating your creative mechanism, you must think of the end result *in terms of a present possibility*. The *possibility* of the goal must be seen so clearly that it becomes "real" to your brain and nervous system. So real, in fact, that the same feelings are evoked as would be present if the goal were already achieved.

This is not so difficult nor so mystical as it may first appear. You and I do it every day of our lives. What, for example, is worry about possible unfavorable future results, accompanied by feelings of anxiety, inadequacy, or perhaps humiliation? For all practical purposes we experience the very same emotions in advance, that would be appropriate if we had already failed. We picture failure to ourselves, not vaguely, or in general terms—but vividly and in great detail. We repeat the failure images over and over again to ourselves. We go back in memory and dredge up memory images of past failures.

Remember what has been emphasized earlier: our brain and nervous system cannot tell the difference between a "real" experience, and one which is *vividly imagined*. Our automatic creative mechanism always acts and reacts appropriately to the environment, circumstance or situation. The only information concerning the environment, circumstance or situation available to it is what *you believe to be true* concerning them.

Your Nervous System Can't Tell "Real Failure" from Imagined Failure

Thus, if we dwell upon failure, and continually picture failure to ourselves in such vivid detail that it becomes "real" to our nervous system, we will experience the feelings that go with failure.

On the other hand, if we keep our positive goal in mind, and picture it to ourselves so vividly as to make it "real," and think of it in terms of an accomplished fact, we will also experience "winning feelings": self-confidence, courage, and faith that the outcome will be desirable.

We cannot consciously peek into our creative mechanism and see whether it is geared for success or failure. But we can determine its present "set" by our feelings. When it is "set for success" we experience that "winning feeling."

Setting Your Machinery for Success

And if there is one simple secret to the operation of your unconscious creative mechanism, it is this: call up, capture, evoke the *feeling of success*. When you feel successful and self-confident, you will act successfully. When the feeling is strong, you can literally do no wrong.

The "winning feeling" itself does not *cause* you to operate successfully, but it is more in the nature of a sign or symptom that we are geared for success. It is more like a thermometer, which does not cause the heat in the room but measures it. However, we can use this thermometer in a very practical way. Remember: When you experience that winning feeling, your internal machinery *is* set for success.

Too much effort to consciously bring about spontaneity is likely to destroy spontaneous action. It is much easier and more effective to simply define your goal or end result. Picture it to yourself clearly and vividly. Then simply capture the *feeling* you would experience if the desirable goal were already an accomplished fact. Then you are acting spontaneously and creatively. Then you are using the powers of your subconscious mind. Then your internal machinery is geared for success: To guide you in making the correct muscular motions and adjustments; to supply you with creative ideas, and to do whatever else is necessary in order to make the goal an accomplished fact.

How That Winning Feeling Won a Golf Tournament

Dr. Cary Middlecoff, writing in the April, 1956 issue of *Esquire* magazine, said that "the Winning Feeling" is the real secret of championship golf. "Four days before I hit my first drive in the Masters last year, I had a feeling I was sure to win that tournament," he said. "I felt that every move I made in getting to the top of my backswing put my muscles in perfect position to hit the ball exactly as I wanted to. And in putting, too, that marvelous feeling came to me. I knew I hadn't changed my grip any, and my feet were in the usual position. But there was *something about the way I felt that gave me a line to the cup just as clearly as if it had been tattooed on my brain. With that feeling all I had to do was swing the clubs and let nature take its course.*"

Middlecoff goes on to say that the winning feeling is "everybody's secret of good golf"; that when you have it the ball even bounces right for you, and that it seems to control that elusive element called "luck."

Don Larsen, the only man in history to pitch a perfect game in the World Series, said that the night before, he "had the crazy feeling" that he would pitch perfectly the next day.

Several years ago sports pages all over the country headlined the sensational play of Johnny Menger, bantam-sized half-back from Georgia Tech, in a post-season bowl game. "I had the feeling when I got up that morning I was going to have a good day," said Menger.

"This May Be Tough, But It Can Be Licked."

There is truly magic in this "winning feeling." It can seemingly cancel out obstacles and impossibilities. It can use errors and mistakes to accomplish success. J. C. Penney tells how he heard his father say on his death-bed, "I know Jim will make it." From that time onward, Penney felt that he would succeed—somehow, although he had no tangible assets, no money, no education. The chain of J. C. Penney stores was built upon many impossible circumstances and discouraging moments. Whenever Penney would get discouraged, however, he would remember the prediction of his father, and he would "feel" that somehow he could whip the problem facing him.

After making a fortune, he lost it all at an age when

most men have long since been retired. He found himself penniless, past his prime, and with little tangible evidence to furnish reason for hope. But again he remembered the words of his father, and soon recaptured the winning feeling, which had now become habitual with him. He rebuilt his fortune, and in a few years was operating more stores than ever.

Henry J. Kaiser has said, "When a tough, challenging job is to be done, I look for a person who possesses an enthusiasm and optimism for life, who makes a zestful confident attack on his daily problems, one who shows courage and imagination, who pins down his buoyant spirit with careful planning and hard work, but says, 'This may be tough, but it can be licked.' "

How That Winning Feeling
Made Les Giblin Succcessful

Les Giblin, founder of the famous Les Giblin Human Relations Clinics, and author of the book, *How to Have Power and Confidence in Dealing with People,* read the first draft of this chapter, then told me how imagination coupled with that winning feeling had worked like magic in his own career.

Les had been a successful salesman and sales manager for years. He had done some public relations work, and had gained some degree of reputation as an expert in the field of human relations. He liked his work but he wanted to broaden his field. His big interest was people, and after years of study, both theoretical and practical, he thought he had some answers to the problems people often have with other people. He wanted to lecture on human relations. However, his one big obstacle was lack of experience in public speaking.

"One night," Les told me, "I was lying in bed thinking of my one big desire. The only experience I had had as a public speaker was addressing small groups of my own salesmen in sales meetings, and a little experience I had had in the Army when I served part-time as an instructor. The very thought of getting up before a big audience scared the wits out of me. I just couldn't imagine myself doing it successfully. Yet, I could talk to my own salesmen with the greatest of ease. I had been able to talk to groups of soldiers without any trouble. Lying there in bed, I recaptured in memory the feeling of success and confidence I had had in talking to these small groups. I remembered all the little incidental details that had accompanied my feeling of poise. Then, in my imagination I pictured myself standing before a huge audience and making a talk on human relations—and at the same time having the same feeling of poise and self-confidence I had had with smaller groups. I pictured to myself in detail just how I would stand. I could feel the pressure of my feet on the floor, I could see the expressions on the people's faces, and I could hear the applause. I saw myself making a talk successfully—going over with a bang.

"Something seemed to click in my mind. I felt elated. Right at that moment I felt that I could do it. I had welded the feeling of confidence and success from the past to the picture in my imagination of my career in the future. My feeling of success was so real that I knew right then I could do it. I got what you call 'that winning feeling' and it has never deserted me. Although there seemed to be no door open to me at the time, and the dream seemed impossible, in less than three years time I saw my dream come true—almost in exact detail as I had imagined it and felt it. Because of the fact that I was relatively unknown and because of my lack of experience, no major booking agency wanted me. This didn't deter me. I booked myself, and still do. I have more opportunities for speaking engagements than I can fill."

Today Les Giblin is known as an authority on human relations. It is not unusual for him to earn several thousand dollars for a single night's work. Over two hundred of the largest corporations in America have paid him thousands of dollars to conduct human relations clinics for their employees. His book, *How to Have Confidence and Power,* has become a classic in the field. And it all started with a picture in his imagination and "that winning feeling."

How Science Explains That Winning Feeling

The science of cybernetics throws new light on just how the winning feeling operates. We have previously shown how electronic servo-mechanisms make use of stored data, comparable to human memory, to "remember" successful actions and repeat them.

Skill learning is largely a matter of trial-and-error practice until a number of "hits," or successful actions have registered in memory.

Cybernetic scientists have built what they call an "electronic mouse" which can learn its way through a maze. The first time through the mouse makes numerous errors. It constantly bumps into walls and obstructions. But each time it bumps into an obstruction, it turns 90 degrees and tries again. If it runs into another wall, it makes another turn, and goes forward again. Eventually, after many, many errors, stops and turns, the mouse gets through the open space in the maze. The electronic mouse, however, "remembers" the turns which were successful, and the next time through, these successful motions are reproduced, or "played back" and the mouse goes through the open space quickly and efficiently.

The object of practice is to make repeated trials, constantly correct errors, until a "hit" is scored. When a successful pattern of action is performed, the entire action pattern from beginning to end is not only stored in what we call conscious memory, but in our very nerves and tissues. Folk language can be very intuitive and descriptive. When we say, "I had a feeling in my bones that I could do it," we are not far from wrong. When Dr. Cary Middlecoff says, "There was something about the way I felt that gave me a line to the cup just as clearly as if it had been *tattooed on my brain,*" he is, perhaps unknowingly, very aptly describing the latest scientific concept of just what happens in the human mind when we learn, remember, or imagine.

How Your Brain Records Success and Failure

Such experts in the field of brain physiology as Dr. John C. Eccles and Sir Charles Sherrington tell us that the human cortex is composed of some ten billion neurons, each with numerous axons (feelers or "extension wires") which form synapses (electrical connections) between the neurons. When we think, remember or imagine, these neurons discharge an electrical current which can be measured. When we learn something, or experience something, a pattern of neurons forming a "chain" (or tattooing of a pattern?) is set up in brain tissue. This "pattern" is not in the nature of a physical "groove" or "track" but more in the nature of an "electrical track"— the arrangement and electrical connections between various neurons being somewhat similar to a magnetic pattern recorded on tape. The same neuron may thus be a part of any number of separate and distinct patterns, making the human brain's capacity to learn and remember almost limitless.

These patterns, or "engrams," are stored away in brain tissue for future use, and are reactivated, or "replayed" whenever we remember a past experience.

Dr. Eccles says, "The profusion of interconnections among the cells of the gray matter is beyond all imagination; it is ultimately so comprehensive that the whole cortex can be thought of as one great unit of integrated activity. If we now persist in regarding the brain as a machine, then we must say that it is by far the most complicated machine in existence. We are tempted to say that it is infinitely more complicated than the most complex man-made machines, the electrical computers." ("The Physiology of Imagination," *Scientific American,* September, 1958.)

In short, science confirms that there *is* a "tattooing," or action pattern of engrams in your brain for every successful action you have ever performed in the past. And, if you can somehow furnish the spark to bring that action pattern into life, or "replay" it, it will execute itself, and all you'll have to do is "swing the clubs" and "let nature take its course."

When you reactivate successful action patterns out of the past, you also reactivate the feeling tone, or "winning feeling" which accompanied them. By the same token, if you can recapture "that winning feeling," you also evoke all the "winning actions" that accompanied it.

Build Success Patterns Into Your Gray Matter

President Eliot of Harvard once made a speech on what he called "The Habit of Success." Many failures in elementary schools, he said, were due to the fact that students were not given, at the very beginning, a sufficient amount of work at which they *could succeed,* and thus never had an opportunity to develop the "Atmosphere of Success," or what we call "the winning feeling." The student, he said, who had never *experienced* success early in his school life, had no chance to develop the "habit of success"—the habitual feeling of faith and confidence in undertaking new work. He urged that teachers arrange work in the early grades so as to insure that the student *experienced success.* The work should be well within the ability of the student, yet interesting enough to arouse enthusiasm and motivation. These small successes, said Dr. Eliot, would give the student the "feel of success," which would be a valuable ally in all future undertakings.

We can acquire the "habit of success"; we can build into our gray matter patterns and feelings of success at any time and at any age by following Dr. Eliot's advice to teachers. If we are habitually frustrated by failure, we are very apt to acquire habitual "feelings of failure" which color all new undertakings. But by arranging things so that we can succeed in little things, we can build an atmosphere of success which will carry over into larger undertakings. We can gradually undertake more difficult tasks, and after succeeding in them, be in a position to undertake something even more challenging. Success is literally built upon success and there is much truth in the saying, "Nothing succeeds like success."

Gradualness Is the Secret

Weight-lifters start with weights they *can* lift and *gradually* increase the weights over a period of time. Good fight managers start a new boxer off with easy opponents and *gradually* pit him against more experienced fighters. We can apply the same general principles in almost any field of endeavor. The principle is merely to start with an "opponent" over which you *can* succeed, and gradually take on more and more difficult tasks.

Pavlov, on his death-bed, was asked to give one last bit of advice to his students on how to succeed. His answer was, "Passion and gradualness."

Even in those areas where we have already developed a high degree of skill, it sometimes helps to "drop back," lower our sights a bit, and practice with a feeling of ease. This is especially true when one reaches a "sticking point" in progress, where effort for additional progress is unavailing. Continually straining to go beyond the "sticking point" is likely to develop undesirable "feeling habits" of strain, difficulty, effort. Under such conditions weight-lifters reduce the amount of weight on the bar, and practice "easy lifting" for awhile. A boxer, who shows signs of going stale, is pitted against a number of easier opponents. Albert Tangora, for many years the World Champion Speed Typist, used to practice "typing slow"—at half normal speed—whenever he reached a plateau, where further increase in speed seemed impossible. I know a prominent salesman who uses the same principle to get himself out of a sales slump. He stops trying to make big sales; stops trying to sell "tough customers"; and concentrates on making small sales to customers he has come to know as "push-overs."

How to Play Back Your Own Built-in Success Patterns

Everyone has at some time or another been successful in the past. It does not have to have been a big success. It might have been something as unimportant as standing up to the school bully and beating him; winning a race in grammar school; winning the sack race at the office picnic; winning out over a teen-age rival for the affections of a girl friend. Or it might be the memory of a successful sale; your most successful business deal; or winning first prize for the best cake at the county fair. *What* you succeeded in is not so important as the feeling of success which attended it. All that is needed is some experience where you succeeded in doing what you wanted to, in achieving what you set out to achieve, and something that brought you some feeling of satisfaction.

Go back in memory and relive those successful experiences. In your imagination revive the entire picture in as much detail as you can. In your mind's eye "see" not only speech, business deal, golf tournament, or whatever, that accompanied your success. What sounds were there? What about your environment? What else was happening around you at the time? What objects were present? What time of year was it? Were you cold or hot? And so forth. The more detailed you can make it, the better. If you can remember in sufficient detail just what happened when you were successful at some time in the past, you will find yourself feeling just as you felt then. Try to particularly remember your feelings at the time. If you can remember your feelings from the past, they will be reactivated in the present. You will find yourself feeling self-confident, because self-confidence is built upon memories of past successes.

Now, after arousing this "general feeling of success," give your thoughts to the important sale, conference, speech, business deal, golf tournament, or whatever that you wish to succeed in *now*. Use your creative imagination to picture to yourself just how you would act and just how you would feel if you had *already succeeded*.

Positive and Constructive Worry

Mentally, begin to play with the idea of complete and inevitable success. Don't force yourself. Don't attempt to coerce your mind. Don't try to use effort or will power to bring about the desired conviction. Just do what you do when you worry, only "worry" about a positive goal and a desirable outcome, rather than about a negative goal and an undesirable outcome.

Don't begin by trying to force yourself to have absolute faith in the desired success. This is too big a bite for you to mentally digest—at first. Use "gradualness." Begin to think about the desired end result as you do when you worry about the future. When you worry you do not attempt to convince yourself that the outcome will be undesirable. Instead, you begin gradually. You usually begin with a "suppose." "Just suppose such and such a thing happens," you say mentally to yourself. You repeat this idea over and over to yourself. You "play with it." Next comes the idea of "possibility." "Well, after all," you say, "Such a thing *is* possible." It *could* happen. Next comes mental imagery. You begin to picture to yourself all the various negative possibilities. You play these imaginative pictures over and over to yourself—adding small details and refinements. As the pictures become more and more "real" to you, appropriate feelings begin to manifest themselves, just as if the imagined outcome had already happened. And this is the way that fear and anxiety develop.

How to Cultivate Faith and Courage

Faith and courage are developed in exactly the same way. Only your goals are different. If you are going to spend time in worry, why not worry constructively? Begin by outlining and defining to yourself the most desirable possible outcome. Begin with your "suppose." "Suppose the best possible outcome did actually come about?" Next, remind yourself that, after all, this could happen. Not that it *will* happen, at this stage, but only that it *could*. Remind yourself, that after all such a good and desirable outcome *is possible*.

You can mentally accept and digest these gradual doses of optimism and faith. After having thought of the desired end result as a definite "possibility"—begin to imagine what the desirable outcome would be like. Go over these mental pictures and delineate details and refinements. Play them over and over to yourself. As your mental images become more detailed, as they are repeated over and over again—you will find that once more *appropriate feelings* are beginning to manifest themselves, just as if the favorable outcome had already happened. This time the appropriate feelings will be those of faith, self-confidence, courage—or all wrapped up into one package, "That Winning Feeling."

Don't Take Counsel of Your Fears

General George Patton, the hell-for-leather, "Old Blood and Guts" general of World War II fame, was once asked if he ever experienced fear before a battle. Yes, he said, he often experienced fear just before an important engagement and sometimes during a battle, but, he added, "I never take counsel of my fears."

If you do experience negative failure feelings—fear and anxiety—before an important undertaking, as everyone does from time to time, it should not be taken as a "sure sign" that you will fail. It all depends upon how you react to them, and what attitude you take toward them. If you listen to them, obey them, and "take counsel" of them, you will probably perform badly. But this need not be true.

First of all, it is important to understand that failure feelings—fear, anxiety, lack of self-confidence—do not spring from some heavenly oracle. They are not written in the stars. They are not holy gospel. Nor are they intimations of a set and decided "fate" which means that failure is decreed and decided. They originate from your own mind. They are indicative only of *attitudes of mind within you*—not of external facts which are rigged against you. They mean only that you are underestimating your own abilities, overestimating and exaggerating the nature of the difficulty before you, and that you are reactivating memories of past failures rather than memories of past successes. That is *all* that they mean and *all* that they signify. They do not pertain to or represent the truth concerning future events, but only your own mental attitude about the future event.

Knowing this, you are free to accept or reject these negative failure feelings; to obey them and take counsel of them, or to ignore their advice and go ahead. Moreover, you are in a position to use them for your own benefit.

Accept Negative Feelings as a Challenge

If we react to negative feelings aggressively and positively, they become challenges which will automatically arouse more power and more ability within us. The idea of difficulty, threat, menace, arouses additional strength within us if we react to it aggressively rather than passively. In the last chapter we saw that a certain amount of "excitement"—if interpreted correctly and employed correctly—helps, rather than hinders performance.

It all depends upon the individual and his attitudes, whether negative feelings are used as assets or liabilities. One striking example of this is the experience of Dr. J. B. Rhine, head of Duke University's Parapsychology Laboratory. Ordinarily, says Dr. Rhine, negative suggestions, distractions, expressions of disbelief on the part of onlookers, will have a decided adverse effect upon a subject's scoring when he is trying to "guess" the order of cards in a special deck, or is being tested in any other way for telepathic ability. Praise, encouragement, "pulling for" the subject, nearly always causes him to score better. Discouragement and negative suggestions can almost always be counted upon to send the test scoring down immediately and dramatically. However, occasionally, a subject will take such negative suggestions as "challenges," and perform even better. For example, a subject by the name of Pearce consistently scored well above pure chance (five correct "calls" out of a deck of twenty-five cards). Dr. Rhine decided to try challenging Pearce to do even better. He was challenged before each trial with a wager that he would not get the next card right. "It was evident during the run that Pearce was being stirred up to a high pitch of intensity. The bet was simply a convenient way of leading him on to throw himself into the test with enthusiasm," said Dr. Rhine. Pearce called all twenty-five cards correctly!

Lillian, a nine-year-old, did better than average when nothing was at stake and she had nothing to worry about if she failed. She was then placed in a minor "pressure situation" by being offered fifty cents, if she called all cards in the deck correctly. As she went through the test her lips moved constantly as if talking to herself. She called all twenty-five cards correctly. When she was asked what she had been saying to herself, she revealed her aggressive, positive attitude to the threat by saying, "I was wishing all the time that I could get twenty-five."

React Aggressively to Your Own Negative "Advice"

Everyone has known individuals who can be discouraged and defeated by the advice from others that "you can't do it." On the other hand there are people who rise to the occasion and become more determined than ever to succeed when given the same advice. An associate of Henry J. Kaiser's says, "If you don't want Henry to do a thing, you had better not make the mistake of telling him it can't be done, or that he can't do it—for he will then do it or bust."

It is not only possible, but entirely practicable, to react in the same aggressive, positive manner to the "negative advice" of our own feelings as we can and should when the negative advice comes from others.

Overcome Evil With Good

Feelings cannot be directly controlled by will power. They cannot be voluntarily made to order, or turned on and off like a faucet. If they cannot be commanded, however, they can be wooed. If they cannot be controlled by a direct act of will, they can be controlled indirectly.

A "bad" feeling is not dispelled by conscious effort or "will power." It can be dispelled, however, by another feeling. If we cannot drive out a negative feeling by making a frontal assault upon it, we can accomplish the same result by substituting a positive feeling. Remember that feeling follows imagery. Feeling coincides with, and is appropriate to, what our nervous system accepts as "real" or the "truth about environment." Whenever we find ourselves experiencing undesirable feeling-tones, we should not concentrate upon the undesirable feeling, even to the extent of driving it out. Instead, we should immediately concentrate upon positive imagery—upon filling the mind with wholesome, positive, desirable images, imaginations, and memories. If we do this, the negative feelings take care of themselves. They simply evaporate. We develop new feeling-tones appropriate to the new imagery.

If, on the other hand, we concentrate only upon "driving out," or attacking worry thoughts, we necessarily must concentrate upon negatives. And even if we are successful in driving out one worry thought, a new one, or even several new ones, are likely to rush in—since the general mental atmosphere is still negative. Jesus warned us about sweeping the mind clean of one demon, only to have seven new ones move in, if we left the house empty. He also advised us not to resist evil, but to overcome evil with good.

The Substitution Method of Curing Worry

Dr. Matthew Chappell, a modern psychologist, recommends exactly the same thing in his book *How to Control Worry* (Matthew N. Chappell, *How to Control Worry*, Macmillan Co., New York). We are worriers because we practice worrying until we become adept at it, says Dr. Chappell. We habitually indulge in negative imagery out of the past, and in anticipating the future. This worry creates tension. The worrier then makes an "effort" to stop worrying, and is caught in a vicious cycle. Effort increases tension. Tension provides a "worrying atmosphere." The only cure for worry, he says, is to *make a habit* out of immediately substituting pleasant, wholesome, mental images, for unpleasant "worry images." Each time the subject finds himself worrying, he is to use this as a "signal" to immediately fill the mind with pleasant mental pictures out of the past or in anticipating pleasant future experiences. In time worry will defeat itself because it becomes a stimulus for practicing anti-worrying. The worrier's job, says Dr. Chappell, is not to overcome some particular source of worry, but to change mental habits. As long as the mind is "set" or geared in a passive, defeatist, "I hope nothing happens" sort of attitude, there will always be something to worry about.

Psychologist David Seabury says that the best piece of advice his father ever gave him was to practice positive mental imagery—immediately and "on cue," so to speak, whenever he became aware of negative feelings. Negative feelings literally defeated themselves by becoming a sort of "bell" which set off a conditioned reflex to arouse positive states of mind.

When I was a medical student I remember being called upon by the professor to orally answer questions on the subject of pathology. Somehow, I was filled with fear and anxiety when I stood up to face the other students, and I couldn't answer the questions properly. Yet, on other occasions, when I looked into the microscope at a slide and answered the typewritten questions before me, I was a different person. I was relaxed, confident, and sure of myself because I knew my subject. I had that "winning feeling" and did very well.

As the semester progressed I took stock of myself and when I stood up to answer questions I pretended I didn't see an audience but was looking through a microscope. I was relaxed, and substituted that "winning feeling" for the negative feeling when quizzed orally. At the end of the semester I did very well in both oral and written examinations.

The negative feeling had finally become a sort of "bell" which created a conditioned reflex to arouse that "winning feeling."

Today, I lecture and speak with ease at any gathering in any part of the world, because I am relaxed and know what I am talking about when I do speak. More than that, I bring others into the conversation and make them feel relaxed too.

Throughout twenty-five years of practice as a plastic surgeon I have operated on soldiers mutilated on the battlefield, children born with disfigurements, men, women, and children injured in accidents at home, on the highway and in industry. These unfortunate people felt that they could never have that "winning feeling." Yet, by rehabilitating them and making them look normal they substituted for their negative feelings one of hope in the future.

In giving them another chance at capturing that "winning feeling," I myself became skillful in the art of having that same feeling. In helping them improve *their* self-image I improved my own. All of us must do the same with our inner scars, our negative feelings, if we want to get more living out of life.

The Choice Is Up to You

Within you is a vast mental storehouse of past experiences and feelings—both failures and successes. Like inactive recordings on tape, these experiences and feelings are recorded on the neural engrams of your gray matter. There are recordings of stories with happy endings, and recordings of stories with unhappy endings. One is as true as the other. One is as real as the other. The choice is up to you, as to which you select for playback.

Another interesting scientific finding about these engrams is that they can be changed or modified, somewhat as a tape recording may be changed by "dubbing in" additional material, or by replacing an old recording with a new by recording over it.

Drs. Eccles and Sherrington tell us that the engrams in the human brain tend to change slightly each time they are "played back." They take on some of the tone and temper of our present mood, thinking and attitudes toward them. Also, each individual neuron may become a part of perhaps one hundred separate and distinct patterns—much as an individual tree in an orchard may form a part of a square, a rectangle, a triangle, or any number of larger squares, etc. The neuron in the original engram, of which it was a part, takes on some of the characteristics of subsequent engrams of which it becomes a part, and in so doing, changes somewhat the original engram. This is not only very interesting, but encouraging. It gives us reason to believe that adverse and unhappy childhood experiences, "traumas," etc. are not as permanent and as fatal as some earlier psychologists would have had us believe. We now know that not only does the past influence the present, but that the present clearly influences the past. In other words, we are not doomed or damned by the past. Because we did have unhappy childhood experiences and traumas which left engrams behind, does not mean that we are at the mercy of these engrams, or that our patterns of behavior are "set," predetermined and unchangeable. Our *present thinking,* our *present mental habits,* our attitudes toward past experiences, and our attitudes toward the future—all have an influence upon old recorded engrams. The old can be changed, modified, replaced, by our present thinking.

Old Recordings Can Be Changed

Another interesting finding is that the more a given engram is activated, or "replayed," the more potent it becomes. Eccles and Sherrington tell us that the permanence of engrams is derived from synaptic efficacy (the efficiency and ease of connections between the individual neurons that make up the chain) and further, that synaptic efficiency improves with use and diminishes with disuse. Here again, we have good scientific ground for forgetting and ignoring those unhappy experiences from the past and concentrating upon the happy and pleasant. By so doing we strengthen those engrams having to do with success and happiness and weaken those having to do with failure and unhappiness.

These concepts have developed not from wild speculation, a weird mumbo-jumbo about mentally constructed straw men such as the "Id," "Super-Ego" and the like, but from sound scientific research into brain physiology. They are based on observable facts and phenomena, not fanciful theories. They go a long way toward restoring the dignity of man as a responsible child of God, able to cope with his past and plan his future, as opposed to the image of man as helpless victim of his past experiences.

The new concept does carry a responsibility, however. No longer can you derive sickly comfort from blaming your parents, society, your early experiences, or the injustices of "others" for your present troubles. These things may and should help you understand how you got where you are. Blaming them, or even yourself for the past mistakes, however, will not solve your problem, or improve your present or your future. There is no merit in blaming yourself. The past explains how you got here. But where you go from here is your responsibility. The choice is yours. Like a broken phonograph, you can keep on playing the same old "broken record" of the past; reliving past injustices; pitying yourself for past mistakes; all of which reactivates failure patterns and failure feelings which color your present and your future.

Or, if you choose, you can put on a new record, and reactivate success patterns and "that winning feeling" which help you do better in the present and promise a more enjoyable future.

When your phonograph is playing music you don't like, you do not try to force it to do better. You do not use effort or will power. You do not bang the phonograph around. You do not try to change the music itself. You merely change the record being played and the music takes care of itself. Use the same technique on the "music" that comes out of your own internal machine. Don't pit your will directly against the "music." As long as the same mental imagery (the cause) occupies your attention, no amount of effort will change the music (the result). Instead, try putting a new record on. Change your mental imagery, and the feelings will take care of themselves.

CHAPTER FIFTEEN

More Years of Life
And More Life in Your Years

DOES every human being have a built-in fountain of youth?

Can the Success Mechanism keep you young?

Does the Failure Mechanism accelerate the "aging process?"

Frankly, medical science does not have any final answer to these questions. But it is not only possible, but I believe practical, to draw certain conclusions and implications from what is already known. In this chapter I would like to tell you some of the things that I believe and which have been of practical value to me.

William James once said that everyone, scientists included, develops his own "over-beliefs" concerning known facts, which the facts themselves do not justify. As a practical measure, these "over-beliefs" are not only permissible, but necessary. Our assumption of a future goal, which sometimes we cannot see, is what dictates our present actions, and our "practical conduct." Columbus had to assume that a great land mass lay to the westward before he could discover it. Otherwise he would not have sailed at all—or having sailed, would not have known whether to set his course to the south, east, north or west.

Scientific research is possible only because of faith in assumptions. Research experiments are not helter-skelter or aimless, but directed and goal oriented. The scientist must first set up a hypothetical truth, a hypothesis not based upon fact but upon implications, before he can know which experiments to make or where to look for facts which may prove or disprove his hypothetical truth.

In this last chapter I want to share with you some of my own over-beliefs, hypotheses, and philosophy, not as an M.D., but as a man. As Dr. Hans Selye has said, there are certain "truths" which cannot be used by medicine, but can be used by the patient.

Life Force—The Secret of Healing and the Secret of Youth

I believe that the physical body, including the physical brain and nervous system, is a machine, composed of numerous smaller mechanisms, all purposeful, or goal directed. I do not believe, however, that MAN is a machine. I believe that the essence of MAN is *that which* animates this machine; that which inhabits the machine, directs and controls it, and uses it as a vehicle. Man himself is not the machine, any more than electricity is the wire over which it flows, or the motor which it turns. I believe that the essence of MAN is what Dr. J. B. Rhine calls "extra-physical"—his life, or vitality; his consciousness; his intelligence and sense of identity; that which he calls "I."

For many years individual scientists—pyschologists, physiologists, biologists—have suspected that there was some sort of universal "energy" or vitality which "ran" the human machine, and that the amount of this energy available and the way it was utilized, explained why some individuals were more resistant to disease than others; why some individuals aged faster than others; and why some hardy individuals lived longer than others. It was also fairly obvious that the source of this basic energy—whatever it might be—was something other than the "surface energy" we obtain from the food we eat. Caloric energy does not explain why one individual can snap back quickly from a serious operation, or withstand long continued stress situations, or outlive another. We speak of such persons as having a "strong constitution."

Some years ago Dr. J. A. Hadfield wrote, "It is true that we do store up a certain amount of energy derived physiologically, from the nutriment of food and air . . . but several of the greatest psychologists, and, in particular, those clinical psychologists who have to deal with the actual diseases of men, have tended towards the view that the source of power is to be regarded as some impulse that works through us, and is not of our own making. What Janet calls 'mental energy' is a force which ebbs in the neurasthenic and flows in the healthy man; Jung speaks of *libido* or *urge* as a force which surges through our lives, now as an impulse towards nutrition, now as the sexual instinct; there is also the *élan vital* of Bergson. These views suggest that we are not merely receptacles but *channels* of energy. Life and power is not so much contained in us, it *courses through us*. Man's might is not to be measured by the stagnant water in the well, but by the limitless supply from the clouds of heaven. . . . Whether we are to look upon this impulse as cosmic energy, as a life force, or what may be its relation to the Divine immanence in Nature, it is for other investigators to say." (J. A. Hadfield, *The Psychology of Power*, New York, The Macmillan Co.)

Science Discovers the Life Force

Today, this "life force" has been established as a scientific fact by Dr. Hans Selye of the University of Montreal. Since 1936 Dr. Selye has studied the problems of stress. Clinically, and in numerous laboratory experiments and studies, Dr. Selye has proved the existence of a basic life force which he calls "adaptation energy." Throughout life, from the cradle to the grave, we are daily called upon to "adapt" to stress situations. Even the process of living itself constitutes stress—or continual adaptation. Dr. Selye has found that the human body contains various defense mechanisms (local adaptation syndromes or L.A.S.) which defend against specific stress, and a general defense mechanism (general adaptation syndrome or G.A.S.) which defends against nonspecific stress. "Stress" includes anything which requires adaptation or adjustment—such as extremes of heat or cold, invasion by disease germs, emotional tension, the "wear and tear of living" or the so-called "aging process."

"The term *adaptation energy,*" says Dr. Selye, "has been coined for that which is consumed during continued adaptive work, to indicate that it is something different from the caloric energy we receive from food, but this is only a name, and we still have no precise concept of what this energy might be. Further research along these lines would seem to hold great promise, since here we appear to touch upon the fundamentals of aging." (Hans Selye, *The Stress of Life,* New York, McGraw-Hill Book Co., 1956.)

Dr. Selye has written twelve books and hundreds of articles explaining his clinical studies and his "stress concept" of health and disease. It would be a disservice to him for me to try to prove his case here. Suffice it to say that his findings are recognized by medical experts the world over. And if you wish to learn more of the work which led to his findings, I suggest that you read Dr. Selye's book written for laymen, *The Stress of Life.*

To me, the really important thing that Dr. Selye has proved is that the body itself is equipped to maintain itself in health; to cure itself of disease, and to remain youthful by successfully coping with those factors which bring about what we call "old age." Not only has he proved that the body is capable of curing itself, but that in the final analysis that is the only sort of "cure" there is. Drugs, surgery, and various therapies work largely by either stimulating the body's own defense mechanism when it is deficient, or toning it down when it is excessive.

The adaptation energy itself is what finally overcomes the disease, heals the wound or burn, or wins out over other "stressors."

Is This the Secret of Youth?

This *élan vital,* life force, or adaptation energy—call it whatever you will—manifests itself in many ways. The energy which heals a wound *is the same* energy which keeps all our other body organs functioning. When this energy is at an optimum all our organs function better, we "feel good," wounds heal faster, we are more "resistant" to disease, we recover from any sort of stress faster, we feel and act "younger," and in fact biologically we are younger. It is thus possible to correlate the various manifestations of this life force, and to assume that *whatever works to make more of this life force available to us;* whatever opens to us a greater influx of "life stuff"; whatever helps us utilize it better—literally helps us "all over."

We may conclude that whatever nonspecific therapy aids wounds to heal faster, might also make us feel younger. Whatever nonspecific therapy helps us overcome aches and pains, might, for example, improve eyesight. And this is precisely the direction which medical research is now taking and which appears most promising.

Science's Search for the Elixir of Youth

By far the most interesting and the most promising field of medical research today is the search for a "nonspecific" therapy which will help man "all over"; immunize him from or help him overcome *any* disease, in contrast to "specific" or localized therapies for *this* disease or *that* disease. Notable progress has already been made in this field. ACTH and cortisone are examples of nonspecific therapies. They benefit, not just one or two pathologic conditions but a whole host of diseases by operating through the body's own *general* defense mechanism.

Bogomolets gained world-wide renown in the late 1940's with his "Youth serum," made from spleen and bone marrow, which was widely hailed by magazine writers (but not by Bogomolets himself) as a "cure-all" for all diseases. Currently Dr. Paul Niehans of Switzerland is famous for his "cellular therapy" (CT) for all diseases, including the degenerative diseases commonly associated with "old age." Niehans has used CT on Pope Pius XII, Chancellor Konrad Adenauer of West Germany, and many other famous people. Some 500 doctors in Europe now use CT in treating every manner of disease. The treatment itself is rather simple. Embryonic animal tissue is obtained fresh from a slaughter house. These "new" and "young" cells are then made into a tissue extract and injected into the patient. If the liver is malfunctioning, embryonic animal liver cells are used; if the kidneys are ailing, kidney tissue is used, etc. Although no one knows just why, there can be no doubt that some rather startling cures have been obtained. The theory is that these "young" cells somehow bring new life to the ailing human organ.

Is RES the Key to "Aging" and Resistance to Disease?

My own "over-belief" about CT is that it brings improvement and new vitality for quite another reason. The studies of Prof. Henry R. Simms, of the College of Physicians and Surgeons, Columbia University; Dr. John H. Heller of the New England Institute for Medical Research at Ridgefield, Conn.; Dr. Sanford O. Byers of the Mount Zion Hospital in San Francisco, and other researchers working independently, strongly suggest that the real key to both longevity *and* resistance to disease is to be found in the functioning of the cells which make up the body's "connective tissue," known as the reticuloendothelial system, or RES. RES is present in every part of the body, in the skin, the organs, the bones. Dr. Selye describes connective tissue as the "cement" which holds the body cells together and connects the various cells of the body with each other. RES also performs a number of other important functions. It acts as a protective lining or shield. It envelopes, immobolizes and destroys foreign invaders.

Writing in the *New York Times,* William L. Laurence said, "This knowledge of the protective role of the RES has opened up a new line of research that could lead to one of the most revolutionary developments in medicine. The aim is to provide artificial stimulation to the activity of the RES cells by chemical and immunological methods. Instead of combating disease individually, the chemical stimulation of the body's own natural resistance system would thus provide a biological defense against disease in general, infectious as well as non-infectious, including the degenerative diseases that strike the greatly increasing older age groups. . . . Such an approach would, indeed, serve as a check against the aging process itself, keeping the individual at a younger age level by checking the rate of loss of his general resistance."

RES Controls Growth and Anti-Growth Factors

Dr. Kurt Stern of the Chicago Medical School has found that RES cells also have a control effect on the growth and anti-growth mechanisms within the body.

RES at present looks like the best bet as the body's own built-in fountain of youth. When RES is functioning properly, more "life stuff," or adaptation energy seems to be made available. RES is activated by threats, injuries, etc. It has been found to be much more active, for example, during infection, when the body *needs* additional defense. As Dr. Selye has pointed out, the body's general defense mechanism is sometimes "shocked" into increased activity by general stress (infection, electric shock, insulin shock, a harrowing experience, etc.)

My own over-belief is that this is the mechanism through which Dr. Niehans' "cellular therapy" works; not because "new" liver cells activate the liver to grow young, but because the introduction into the system of a foreign protein "shocks" the RES into activity. It has long been known that the body reacts rather violently, and quite often death results, from the injection of foreign proteins. Dr. Niehans' "young cells" do not seem to have this effect, possibly because they *are* young and possibly because the extract is attenuated. I believe, however, that any mild innocuous foreign protein would stimulate the RES into activity, just as the injection of innocuous small pox germs will stimulate the body to produce antibodies against virulent smallpox.

Perhaps the claims of Dr. Aslan in Bucharest, that injections of a form of novocaine—H3—which appears to make old people feel younger, may be due to some chemical in the disintegration of H3 in the body which stimulates the RES.

Nonspecific Therapy for Wound Healing Made Patients Feel Younger

Salves, unguents, antibiotics, etc. are used as *specific* therapy on wounds. Back in 1948 I began experimenting with a *nonspecific* therapy in the form of a serum which I hoped might accelerate the healing of surgical wounds. The results of these experiments were published in *The Journal of Immunology,* Vol. 60, No. 3, November, 1948 if you are interested in the technical details. ("Studies in Cellular Growth. Effect of Antigranulation-Tissue-Serum on Wound Healing in Mice," by Maxwell Maltz.)

The hypothesis which led up to these experiments was as follows:

If you cut your finger, two different mechanisms within the body go to work to heal the wound. Acting through the RES, one mechanism, called the "granulation factor," stimulates the growth of entirely new cells to form new tissue, which we call scar tissue. The cells so created are biologically "young." Another mechanism, also operating through RES, acts as a control or "anti-granulation" factor. It is an anti-growth mechanism and inhibits the production of new cells. Otherwise the scar tissue would continue to grow until your finger became perhaps as long as your leg.

These two mechanisms *work together*—simultaneously, to achieve just the right amount of new growth. One acts as a sort of negative feedback or governor on the other. If there is, at the moment, an excess of the "growth factor," this excess stimulates the "anti-growth" factor. On the other hand, a slight excess of the anti-growth factor should act as negative feedback to activate the growth factor—very much like the thermostat in your home maintains the right temperature. An excess of cold turns on the furnace to bring more heat, and an excess of heat turns off the furnace to lower the temperature.

This back-and-forth, nip-and-tuck sort of control is active *while healing is going on,* but discontinues when the healing job has been completed. Some over-all control then gives anti-growth the upper hand and the formation of scar tissue stops altogether. Thus, there should be more anti-granulation "stuff" present in the final stages of healing—in the scab which has already completed its growth.

Anti-Growth Serum Made Wounds Heal Faster

My anti-granulation tissue serum was made from the scrapings of newly formed but full grown granulation tissue of a healing wound, which, after being suspended in solution, was injected into rabbits, to stimulate them to react against this granulation tissue. Theoretically, this serum containing an abundance of anti-granulation factor should stimulate the granulation factor in a fresh wound and make for a faster growth of scar tissue—making use of the same principle that you could use to turn on your furnace, that is, by lowering the temperature around the thermostat. That is precisely what did happen.

In general, these experiments showed that wounds inflicted on laboratory mice required an average of about eight days to heal completely when no serum was given; and required about five days in another group of mice which received an injection of Anti-Granulation-Tissue-Serum (AGTS). The serum, injected into the mouse at the point furthest from the wound, accelerated healing by about 40%. As might have been expected, "overdoses" of AGTS had the opposite effect and retarded the healing time.

These results were encouraging and led to further refinement of the serum for human use. At the time I began using this serum on human patients, I had no other hope than that it might accelerate the healing of surgical wounds.

There are millions of women in the middle age group who have held down jobs for twenty years or more who suddenly meet the competition of younger people despite their experience and competence. Many of them have come for surgical help to remove the signs of age from their eyelids and face to make them look younger and hold onto their jobs for another ten years. It means economic, psychological and social survival. Naturally in this age group some do not heal as well as others and these slow healers received my AGTS serum.

What I had not anticipated, however, was the number of patients who received the serum and returned several months later to report that they felt younger, had more pep and energy, and that some of their aches and pains had disappeared. In some of these patients the change in physical appearance was quite striking. There was a sparkle in the eye that had not been there a few months before; the texture of the skin appeared smoother; they stood straighter, and walked with a more confident step.

As a doctor, I draw no conclusions from this. Medical "facts" must be substantiated by more than a patient's subjective feelings, or the casual observation of his doctor. To prove anything, numerous experiments would have to be made under control conditions and scientific observation. As a layman, however, I do believe that these experiences tend to confirm my belief that *any factor* (emotional, mental, spiritual, pharmaceutical) which stimulates the Life Force within us has a beneficial effect, not only locally—but generally.

And as a layman I also believe that perhaps I have come closer to a possible break-through in the quest for longer life through the use of AGTS. Granulation tissue is new-born connective tissue—new-born RES—biologically, a rebirth of life in a local area. AGTS produced from such a biological entity should stimulate the RES in a more natural way than any chemical substance.

How Your Thoughts, Attitudes and Emotions Act as Nonspecific Therapy

I began to look for other factors, or common denominators, which might explain why the surgical wounds of some patients heal faster than others. The serum "worked better" for some people than for others. This in itself was food for thought, because the results obtained in mice were practically uniform. Ordinarily, mice do not worry or become frustrated. Frustration and emotional stress can be induced in mice, however, by immobilizing them so that they cannot have freedom of movement. Immobilization frustrates any animal. Laboratory experiments have shown that under the emotional stress of frustration, very minor wounds may heal faster, but any real injury is made worse, and healing sometimes made impossible. It has also been established that the adrenal glands react very much the same way to emotional stress, and to the stress of physical tissue damage.

How the Failure Mechanism Injures You

Thus it might be said that frustration, and emotional stress (those factors we have previously described as the "failure mechanism") literally "add insult to injury" whenever the physical body suffers damage. If the physical damage is very slight, some emotional stress may stimulate the defense mechanism into activity, but if there is any real or actual physical injury, emotional stress "adds to" and makes it worse. This knowledge gives us reason to pause and think. If "aging" is brought about by a "using up" of our adaptation energy, as most experts in the field seem to think, then our indulging ourselves in the negative components of the "Failure Mechanism" can literally make us old before our time. Philosophers have long told us, and now medical researchers confirm, that resentment and hatred hurt us more than the person we direct them against.

What Is the Secret of "Rapid-Healers?"

Among my human patients who did not receive the serum were some individuals who responded to surgery just as well as the average patient did who received it. Differences in age, diet, pulse rate, blood pressure, etc., simply did not explain why. There was, however, one easily recognizable characteristic which all the "rapid-healers" had in common.

They were optimistic, cheerful "positive thinkers" who not only expected to "get well" in a hurry, but invariably had some compelling *reason* or *need* to get well quick. They had "something to look forward to" and not only "something to live for" but "something to get well for."

"I've got to get back on the job," "I've got to get out of here so I can accomplish my goal," were common expressions.

In short, they epitomized those characteristics and attitudes which I have previously described as the "Success Mechanism."

I am not alone in these observations. Dr. Clarence William Lieb says, "Experience has taught me to regard pessimism as a major symptom of early fossilization. It usually arrives with the first minor symptom of physical decline." (William Clarence Lieb, *Outwitting Your Years*, Englewood Cliffs, N.J., Prentice-Hall, Inc.) Dr. Lieb adds, "Tests have been made of the effect of personality disturbances on convalescence: one hospital showed that the average duration of hospitalization was increased by forty per cent from this cause."

It is interesting to note that the figure 40 per cent is almost identical with the results of my own experiments with AGTS. Could it be that induced optimism, confidence, faith, cheerfulness, emotional stasis might work quite as well as AGTS in accelerating healing and in keeping us younger? Is our Success Mechanism a sort of built-in youth serum which we can use for more life, more energy?

Thoughts Bring Organic as Well as Functional Changes

We do know this much: Mental attitudes *can* influence the body's healing mechanisms. Placebos, or "sugar pills" (capsules containing inert ingredients) have long been a medical mystery. They contain no medicine of any kind which could bring about a cure. Yet, when placebos are given to a control group in order to test the effectiveness of a new drug, the group receiving the phony pills nearly always shows *some* improvement, and quite often as much as the group receiving the medicine. Students receiving placebos actually showed more immunization against colds than the group receiving a new cold medicine.

In 1946 the *New York Journal of Medicine* carried an account of a round-table discussion of placebos by members of the Department of Pharmacology and Medicine of Cornell University Medical College. Improvement reported by patients included cure of insomnia, better appetite. "It makes me stronger. My bowels are better. I can walk farther without pain in my chest." Evidence was presented to show that placebos had worked in some cases, "just as effectively as vaccines against chronic rheumatoid arthritis."

During World War II the Royal Canadian Navy tested a new drug for seasickness. Group 1 received the new drug. Group 2 received sugar pills, and only 13 per cent suffered from seasickness, while 30 per cent of Group 3, which received nothing, got sick.

Many doctors now believe that a similar type of "suggestive treatment" is the best form of therapy for warts. The warts are painted with methalene blue, red ink, or any other color, and a colored light is used to "treat" them. The *Journal of the American Medical Association* has said, "The facts of the suggestive therapy of warts seem to make a strong case in favor of the reality of such a process."

"Suggestion" Explains Nothing

Patients receiving placebos, or suggestive wart therapy, *must not be told* that the treatment is a phony, if it is to be effective. They *believe* they are receiving legitimate medicine which will "bring about a cure." To write off placebos as "merely due to suggestion" explains nothing. More reasonable is the conclusion that in taking the "medicine" some sort of expectation of improvement is aroused, a goal-image of health is set up in the mind, and the creative mechanism works through the body's own healing mechanism to accomplish the goal.

Do We Sometimes Think Ourselves into Old Age?

We may do something very similar, but in reverse, when we unconsciously "expect to get old" at a certain age.

At the 1951 International Gerontological Congress at St. Louis, Dr. Raphael Ginzberg, of Cherokee, Iowa, stated that the traditional idea, that a person is supposed to grow old and useless around seventy, is responsible in large measure for persons' growing "old" at that age, and that in a more enlightened future we might regard seventy as middle age.

It is a matter of common observation that some people between the ages of 40 and 50 begin to both look and act "old," while others continue to act and look "young." A recent study found that the "oldsters" at 45 thought of themselves as "middle-aged," past their prime, over the hill, while the "youngsters" at 45 still conceived of themselves as being this side of middle-aged.

At least two ways suggest themselves as to how we may think ourselves into old age. In expecting to grow "old" at a given age we may unconsciously set up a negative goal image for our creative mechanism to accomplish. Or, in expecting "old age" and fearing its onset, we may unwittingly do those very things necessary to bring it about. We begin to taper off on both physical and mental activity. Cutting out practically all vigorous physical activity, we tend to lose some of the flexibility of our joints. Lack of exercise causes our capillaries to constrict and virtually disappear, and the supply of life-giving blood through our tissues is drastically curtailed. Vigorous exercise is necessary to dilate the capillaries which feed all body tissues and remove waste products. Dr. Selye has cultivated animal cell cultures within a living animal's body by implanting a hollow tube. For some unknown reason biologically new and "young" cells form inside this tube. Untended, however, they die within a month. However, if the fluid in the tube is washed daily, and waste products removed, the cells live indefinitely. They remain eternally "young" and neither "age" nor "die." Dr. Selye suggests that this may be the mechanism of aging, and that if so, "old age" can be postponed by slowing down the rate of waste production, or by helping the system to get rid of waste. In the human body the capillaries are the channels through which waste is removed. It has definitely been established that lack of exercise and inactivity literally "dries up" the capillaries.

Activity Means Life

When we decide to curtail mental and social activities, we stultify ourselves. We become "set" in our ways, bored, and give up our "great expectations."

I have no doubt but that you could take a healthy man of 30 and within five years make an "old man" of him if you could somehow convince him that he was now "old," that all physical activity was dangerous and that mental activity was futile. If you could induce him to sit in a rocking chair all day, give up all his dreams for the future, give up all interest in new ideas, and regard himself as "washed up," "worthless," unimportant and non-productive, I am sure that you could experimentally create an old man.

Dr. John Schindler, in his famous book, *How to Live 365 Days a Year* (Prentice-Hall, Inc., Englewood Cliffs, N.J.), pointed out what he believed to be six basic needs that every human being has:

1. The Need for Love
2. The Need for Security
3. The Need for Creative Expression
4. The Need for Recognition
5. The Need for New Experiences
6. The Need for Self-Esteem

To these six, I would add another basic need . . . the need for *more life*—the need to look forward to tomorrow and to the future with gladness and anticipation.

Look Forward and Live

This brings me to another of my over-beliefs.

I believe that life itself is adaptive; that life is not just an end in itself, but a means to an end. Life is one of the "means" we are privileged to use in various ways to achieve important goals. We can see this principle operating in all forms of life, from the amoeba to man. The polar bear, for example, *needs* a thick fur coat in order to survive in a cold environment. He needs protective coloration to stalk game and hide from enemies. The life force acts as a "means" to these ends, and provides the polar bear with his white fur coat. These adaptations of life to deal with problems in the environment are almost infinite, and there is no point in continuing to enumerate them. I merely want to point out a principle in order to draw a conclusion.

If life adapts itself in so many varied forms to act as a means toward an end, is it not reasonable to assume that if we place ourselves in the sort of goal-situation where *more life* is needed, that we will receive more life?

If we think of man as a goal-striver, we can think of adaptation energy or Life Force as the propelling fuel or energy which drives him forward toward his goal. A stored automobile needs no gasoline in the tank. And a goal-striver with no goal doesn't really need much Life Force.

I believe that we establish this need by looking forward to the future with joy and anticipation, when we expect to enjoy tomorrow, and above all, when we have something important (to us) to do and somewhere to go.

Create a Need for More Life

Creativity is certainly one of the characteristics of the Life Force. And the essence of creativity is a looking forward towards a goal. Creative people need more Life Force. And actuary tables seem to confirm that they get it. As a group, creative workers—research scientists, inventors, painters, writers, philosophers not only live longer, but remain productive longer than non-creative workers. (Michelangelo did some of his best painting when past 80; Goethe wrote *Faust* when past 80; Edison was still inventing at 90; Picasso, past 85, dominates the art world today; Wright at 90 was still considered the most creative architect; Shaw was still writing plays at 90; Grandma Moses began painting at 79, etc., etc.)

This is why I tell my patients to "develop a nostalgia for the future," instead of for the past, if they want to remain productive and vital. Develop an enthusiasm for life, create a need for more life, and you will receive more life.

Have you ever wondered why so many actors and actresses manage to look far younger than their years, and present a youthful appearance at age 50 and beyond? Could it not be that these people have a *need* to look young, that they are interested in maintaining their appearance, and simply do not give up the goal of staying young, as most of us do when we reach the middle years?

"We age, not by years, but by events and our emotional reactions to them," says Dr. Arnold A. Hutschnecker. "The physiologist Rubner observed that peasant women who work as cheap labor in the fields in some parts of the world are given to early withering of the face, but they suffer no loss of physical strength and endurance. Here is an example of specialization in aging. We can reason that these women have relinquished their competitive role as women. They have resigned themselves to the life of the working bee, which needs no beauty of face but only physical competence." (Arnold A. Hutschnecker, *The Will to Live*, Revised Edition, Englewood Cliffs, N.J., Prentice-Hall, Inc.)

Hutschnecker also comments on how widowhood ages some women, but not others. If the widow feels that her life has come to an end and she has nothing to live for, her attitude gives "outward evidence—in her gradual withering, her graying hair. . . . Another woman, actually older, begins to blossom. She may enter into the competition for a new husband, or she may embark on a career in business, or she may do no more than busy herself with an interest for which perhaps she has not had the leisure until now." (Ibid.)

Faith, courage, interest, optimism, looking forward, bring us new life and more life. Futility, pessimism, frustration, living in the past, are not only characteristic of "old age"; they contribute to it.

Retire from a Job, But Never Retire from Life

Many men go down hill rapidly after retirement. They feel that their active productive life is completed and their job is done. They have nothing to look forward to; become bored, inactive—and often suffer a loss of self-esteem because they feel left out of things; not important anymore. They develop a self-image of a useless, worthless, "worn out" hanger-on. And a great many die within a year or so after retirement.

It is not retiring from a job that kills these men, it is retiring from life. It is the feeling of uselessness, of being washed up; the dampening of self-esteem, courage and self-confidence, which our present attitudes of society help to encourage. We need to know that these are outmoded and unscientific concepts. Some fifty years ago psychologists thought that man's mental powers reached their peak at the age of 25 and then began a gradual decline. The latest findings show that a man reaches his peak mentally somewhere around the age of 35 and *maintains the same*

level until well past 70. Such nonsense as "you can't teach
an old dog new tricks" still persists despite the fact that
numerous researches have shown that learning ability is
about as good at 70 as it is at 17.

Outmoded and Disproved Medical Concepts

Physiologists used to believe that any type of physical
activity was harmful to the man over forty. We doctors
are to blame as much as anyone for warning patients over
40 to "take it easy" and give up golf and other forms of
exercise. Twenty years ago one famous writer even suggested that any man over forty should never stand when
he could sit, never sit when he could lie down—in order
to "conserve" his strength and energy. Physiologists and
M.D.'s, including the nation's leading heart specialists,
now tell us that activity, even strenuous activity, is not
only permissible, but required for good health at any age.
You are never too old to exercise. You may be too sick.
Or if you have been comparatively inactive for a long
while, the suddenness of strenuous exertion may have a
powerful stress effect, may be damaging and even fatal.

So, if you are not used to strenuous exertion, let me
warn you to "take it easy" and "take it gradually." Dr.
T. K. Cureton, who has pioneered in the physical recon-
ditioning of men from 45 to 80 suggests at least two years
as a reasonable time for *gradually* acquiring the ability to
indulge in really strenuous activity.

If you are past forty, forget the weight you lifted when
you were in college, or how fast you could run. Begin by
daily walking around the block. Gradually increase the
distance to a mile; then two, and perhaps after six months
—five miles. Then alternate between jogging and walking. First jog half a mile a day; later a full mile. Still later
you can add pushups, deep-knee bends, and perhaps
training with moderate weights. Using such a program as
this, Dr. Cureton has taken decrepit, "feeble" men of 50,
60 and even 70 and had them running five miles a day at

the end of two or two-and-a half years. They not only feel better, but medical tests show an improvement in heart function and other vital organs.

Why I Believe in Miracles

While confessing my over-beliefs, I might as well make a clean breast of it and say that I believe in miracles. Medical science does not pretend to know *why* the various mechanisms within the body perform as they do. We know a little bit about the *how* and something about *what* happens. We can describe *what* happens and *how* the mechanisms function when the body heals a cut. But description is not explanation, no matter in what technical terms it may be couched. I still do not understand *why* or even the ultimate *how* when a cut finger heals itself.

I do not understand the power of the Life Force which operates the mechanisms of healing, nor do I understand how that force is applied or just what "makes it work." I do not understand the intelligence which created the mechanisms, nor just how some directing intelligence operates them.

Dr. Alexis Carrel, in writing of his personal observations of instantaneous healings at Lourdes, said that the only explanation he could make as a medical doctor was that the body's own natural healing processes, which normally operate over a period of time to bring about healing, were somehow "speeded up" under the influence of intense faith.

If "miracles," as Dr. Carrel says, are accomplished by the acceleration of, or the intensifying of, natural healing processes and powers within the body, then I witness a "small miracle" every time I see a surgical wound heal itself by growing new tissue. Whether it requires two minutes, or two months, makes no difference insofar as I can see. I still witness some power at work which I do not understand.

Medical Science, Faith, Life,
All Come from the Same Source

Dubois, the famous French surgeon, had a large sign in his operating room; "The Surgeon dresses the wound, God heals it."

The same might be said of any type of medication, from antibiotics to cough drops. Yet, I cannot understand how a rational person can forego medical help because he believes it inconsistent with his faith. I believe that medical skill, and medical discoveries, are made possible by the same Intelligence, the same Life Force, which operates through the media of faith healing. And for this reason I can see no possible conflict between medical science and religion. Medical healing and faith healing both derive from the same source, and should work together.

No father who saw a mad dog attacking his child, would stand idly by and say, "I must do nothing because I must prove my faith." He would not refuse the assistance of a neighbor who brought a club or a gun. Yet, if you reduce the size of the mad dog trillions of times and call it a bacterium or a virus, the same father may refuse the help of his doctor-neighbor who brings a tool in the form of a capsule, a scalpel, or a syringe.

Don't Place Limitations on Life

Which brings me to my parting thought. In the Bible we are told that when the prophet was in the desert and hungry, God lowered a sheet from the heavens containing food. Only to the prophet it didn't look much like good food. It was "unclean" and contained all sorts of "crawling things." Whereupon God rebuked him, admonishing him not to call "unclean" that which God had offered.

Some doctors and scientists today turn up their noses at whatever smacks of faith or religion. Some religionists have the same attitude, suspicion and revulsion concerning anything "scientific."

Everyone's real goal, as I said in the beginning, is for more life—more living. Whatever your definition of happiness may be, you will *experience* happiness only as you experience more life. More living means among other things more accomplishment, the attainment of worthwhile goals, more love experienced and given, more health and enjoyment, more happiness for both yourself and others.

I believe that there is ONE LIFE, one ultimate source, but that this ONE LIFE has many channels of expression and manifests itself in many forms. If we are to "Get More Living out of Life," we should not limit the channels through which Life may come to us. We must accept it, whether it comes in the form of science, religion, psychology, or what not.

Another important channel is other people. Let us not refuse the help, happiness and joy that others may bring us, or that we can give to them. Let us not be too proud to accept help from others, or too callous to give it. Let us not say "unclean" just because the form of the gift may not coincide with our prejudices or our ideas of self-importance.

The Best Self-Image of All

Finally, let us not limit our acceptance of Life by our own feelings of unworthiness. God has offered us forgiveness and the peace of mind and happiness that come from self-acceptance. It is an insult to our Creator to turn our backs upon these gifts or to say that his creation—man—is so "unclean" that he is not worthy, or important or capable. The most adequate and realistic self-image of all is to conceive of yourself as "made in the image of God." "You cannot believe yourself the image of God, deeply and sincerely, with full conviction, and not receive a new source of strength and power," says Dr. Frank G. Slaughter.

The ideas and exercises in this book have helped many of my patients "Get More Living out of Life." It is my hope, and my belief, that they will do the same for you.

Index.

THE 500,000 COPY NATIONAL BEST SELLER
AT $3.95. BILLY GRAHAM CALLS IT THE MOST
IMPORTANT BOOK HE HAS EVER WRITTEN!

Billy Graham

WORLD AFLAME

75146/75¢

If your bookseller does not have this title, you may order
it by sending retail price, plus 15¢ for mailing and handling
to: MAIL SERVICE DEPARTMENT, Simon & Schuster
of Canada, Ltd., 225 Yonge Street North, Richmond Hill,
Ont., Canada. Not responsible for orders containing cash.
Please send check or money order.

PUBLISHED BY
POCKET BOOKS

Heloise

ALL AROUND THE HOUSE

❀ All new, alphabetically arranged, bigger and better than ever!

❀ Here's Heloise, the homemaker's favorite helper, with hundreds of new hints and how-to's for everything, *all around the house.*

❀ Save money, save time, save energy- call for hints from Heloise!

75186/75¢